THE BOOK OF ANNE

THE BOOK OF ANNE

*One woman discovers
6,000,000 parentless children in the
United States of America*

A Memoir

Thank you
Jean – please
share. Love Anne

H. A. Thurston

Library of Congress Control Number: 2007908924
ISBN: Hardcover   978-1-4363-0253-1
      Softcover   978-1-4363-0252-4

1. grand parenting 2. kin care 3. parentless children 4. Social Security 5. title

This book was printed in the United States of America.

Disclaimer

The time, places and people in this memoir are as the author remembers.
The names of some places and people have been changed to preserve their
true identity for reason the author chose.

To order additional copies of this book, contact:
Xlibris Corporation
1-888-795-4274
www.Xlibris.com
Orders@Xlibris.com
45279

Thank you so much

Joyce Maynard, best selling author, for insisting I write.

Ed, my husband, for championing me.

Laura, Rachael and Patrick for remembering times, places and things.

Rachael for the book jacket.

Patrick for suggesting another voice; my alter-ego.

Nancy, our daughter, for answering my Bible questions.

Tobye Weitzke for fun filled editing afternoons.

Ellie Oberlin, for adding her editing magic.

Michelle Cortright, my across-the-fields neighbor for her mentoring.

Kathy Anderson, Ken Stanley, Dr. Peter Pecora, Norvilla Bennet, Senators Carl Levin and Debbie Stabenaw, Congressman Bart Stupak and the Boyne District Library staff for researching answers.

Greg Haigh, Gian Duterte and the staff of Xlibris.

In Memory of

Mary Anne Cassidy-Johnson 1951-1991
Patrick Charles Cassidy Jr. 1950-1985
parents of
Laura, Rachael and Patrick Cassidy III

The Wedding Garter

Smiles of happiness; Laura, Patrick and Rachael—2004

Preface

Laughter to the heart is like sunshine to the day—both reflect on the world about us, bringing the beautiful and the precious into view.

Sadly, when the sunshine disappears or laughter ends the world is plunged into a grayness, which permeates the very soul with discouragement, inadequacy and the pain of loneliness and uselessness.

But let one ray escape the cloud cover, one upward curl of the lips or an outreaching hand sneak into life it is then anything becomes possible. The soul of man soars into that place where all is believable; wherein love dwells.

H. A. Thurston

PART I

Once Upon a Time in Our Day

Prologue

There is no choice. It has to be me who butts in right here, before Anne can say a word. Ever since she began thinking about writing her book I've been concerned she'd leave out happenings which are really important. Knowing her, probably better than any one else, it's exactly what she'll do; it's her way. We've been together forever, at least it feels so. Neither of us is good with dates, so we can't say our acquaintanceship began on March 1, 1923, although it might have. A better guess would be sometime after that, maybe as late as '25 or '26.

It's a known fact she won't screw up the courage to tell about the conversation that she and her dad had when she was eighteen. She'll blow her whole story if the part about Tracy is omitted. The strange thing is she doesn't see where it has anything to do with her life now. It may just be Anne can't bring herself to share that time with others.

We've been close all the way, although we aren't that much alike. We disagree frequently; but eventually she usually see things my way. When is never important, just knowing it will happen is enough for me. It is how the two of us are. Some would call me gifted in my perception of the future. Actually it is more about my being extremely practical rather than a person endowed with mystic powers. When you come down to it both of us work off the same moral code. Some things just make sense if you give them enough thought. Anne doesn't always do that.

This thing with her dad must be inserted here, at the very beginning of her writing. It is very important. Knowing it will help you understand her story in a manner she, herself, didn't for a long time. The day will come when Anne will realize its importance. You'll hear from me a few more times during Anne's story. But only when there'll be those times things which must be said that Anne is blind to, or not yet privy to.

Her story really should begin like this.

It's hard to say why Anne's father asked her the question he did. Even though she was his fishing partner on his annual sojourns into the lake scattered back-woods of Canada as early as 1933 at age ten, it doesn't make any sense. When he brought the subject up she was only eighteen, a senior in Sylvania High School. Out of the blue he turned to her with his question.

Tracy had moved away years before, but somehow time had settled him and his family back into the outlying area of Sylvania in time for Anne and her brother David to find themselves literally following in their father's footsteps by attending Sylvania High School.

His class was small, just four members; on the other hand Anne's, the Class of '41, was much larger. The building wasn't the same three-storied red brick structure on Main Street. The growth of the town, although it remained a small town, had pushed a newer high school out into its western perimeter. It sprawled there in the contemporary manner of the thirties.

Tracy was a farm boy from Berkey, a cross-roads farm community, a mere spot on the Ohio map across the state border from Michigan, not far from Sylvania. When Anne was in grade school she had been driven by the old homestead as it stood in the middle of acres of corn stubble. The air of the November day brought the sweet smell of fresh manure into the car and the rustle of the occasional overlooked dry corn husks found her cold ears. The house itself returned Anne's stare of curiosity in a noncommittal manner. It had nothing to say to her and she could think of nothing to tell it. They were absolute strangers despite Tracy's stories and the points of interest he indicated as they stopped for a few minutes before the old two-storied, wood sided home. The land hurried off in all directions perfectly flat under a darkening sky. Nothing about the farm shared the happy memories Anne's father spoke of.

There was no doubt in Anne's mind but what her father loved her. Besides sharing his favorite fishing lures he taught her the specs of designing a home, which would satisfy FHA loan requirements. She also had his permission to use his oil paints and canvasses whenever she wanted. Yet, none of this explained why he asked the question he did; why he suddenly brought up the subject of heaven. Anne wasn't certain she was hearing right.

"I can't decide whether I believe there is a heaven or not, what do you think?" was how he opened the conversation that day in her senior year.

At a loss for words a silence fell between them as Anne looked at her father. She knew him as a reader, perfectionist and also of the tenderness that was him; but not this part. She hoped he wasn't expecting her to come up with any enlightening observation on the subject. The question just hung there between the two.

They both knew there was no way the subject could be discussed with Anne's mother. Helen Steece Eisele had been nourished, spoon fed on the Bible by a mother whose ancestors moved down the Ohio River from Appalachia. After a generational pause on the river's bank in Ironton they penetrated further north to Columbus becoming staunch Baptists.

Without a question Helen believed in the existence of a heaven. Somehow Anne's father had reached a point in his thinking where he needed to bounce his question off someone. He wanted to have a discussion on the subject. Normally this would be with his Helen, but he knew she would never understand his asking. Because of this he had turned to Anne, his fishing partner. Anne stood there without words. Her mind whirled in every direction in an effort to say something to her dad that would help him. But, she honestly wasn't at all certain where she stood on the issue. It occurred to her that by the time she was as old as her father she hoped she would have it figured out.

It was then Tracy gave her his smile along with a twinkle in his eyes and let his daughter off the hook.

"I don't need an answer today. But down the road if you ever come up with one let me know. I will probably still be trying to figure it out."

A lot has transpired since that day. Anne went off to college, fell in love, married her lieutenant, graduated, raised four children and has a granddaughter, Laura and grandson, Lewis. She's fifty-eight; her father died four years ago after an eighteen year battle with Parkinson's. He never brought his question about heaven up again so she doesn't known whether he ever found his answer.

Helen is eighty-four and in Toledo Hospital worn out from fighting the flu. She and Anne have talked on the phone and Helen is coming along great. Rather than going down to see her right now Anne has decided to wait to make the trip next week to be with her when she is discharged. That way she'll stay with her in the apartment while she regains her strength.

Standing in her kitchen, Anne is ironing, enjoying the warm sunshine streaming through the room's bay window. It's late spring. The old barn and its silo still stand on its lump of ground despite winters of heavy snows and hard winds. It amazes her that the structure with its missing doors and occasional slits in the old hemlock vertical siding is able to remain so square and unscathed by time. Originally home to a dairy herd its use changed when the pastures were terraced and planted to cherry trees. The barn still holds the rare three footed cherry ladders and slatted wooden lugs to carry the harvested fruit to the cannery. The farm is Ed's love, second only to the one he shares with Anne, his wife of thirty-five years.

The phone's ring wedges into Anne's thoughts and she thinks, I wonder if Mom has changed her mind?

To her surprise she hears her sister-in-law, Linda's voice, "Anne, Mother just died of a massive heart attack. I can't locate Dave. What should I do?"

Anne can't assimilate the words and wonders, How can my vivacious mother be dead?

It is obvious Linda is at the hospital. Her words are fractured thoughts that Anne can't keep up with. It is as if Linda is speaking in five or six languages. When she asks Anne what dress to take to the undertaker's to present Helen in Anne knows she can't get to Toledo too fast. Her mother's unexpected death is more than Linda can handle.

"Ed and I will leave within an hour, Linda. Ask the hospital to help you locate David. They know what has to be done, let them handle things. Get a cup of coffee. Find a place where you can sit and wait for Dave." Anne knows her brother will have answers for all his wife's questions.

She puts the telephone down, unaware of the sunny day and even the room in which she stands. She turns to go upstairs to pack and then abruptly comes to a stop. Standing five feet in front of her is her father. He stands in the shadows at the foot of the stairs; a brilliant figure in white. He is a handsome young man, younger than the father she had known; younger than the day he married. Her father's expression will remain with Anne always; it is of such joy and love. With outstretched hands he looks right at Anne, but beyond. He is welcoming his Helen.

What both of us hear her say aloud, as if to him is, "Well, Dad, I guess you found your answer."

As the family works together to vacate Helen's apartment four days later, Anne will see Tracy again in a pre-wedding photo lovingly packed among her mother's memorabilia. The box, an old suit box from the days a man's suit included a vest and two pair of trousers as well as a jacket, will be tucked way in the back of her mother's guest bedroom closet. Within it will be priceless letters, pictures and invitations from her mother's courtship.

Anne will feel her world suddenly focused; she'll know she will be OK. Also, somewhere deep inside herself she'll realize what she experienced will not be shared with others, just her Ed, and me of course. How could anyone understand such a thing without being part of it? She knows others have reported similar happenings, but she has never quite been able to accept such stories. They were just too way out, too strange. And so she keeps her father's answer buried within herself.

Anne is destined to keep other secrets, but they will be ones given to her to guard because of the harm they might cause if known.

Anne never had any intent that this whole scenario about her father should be told. It is certain she would not have told you. She often forgets what happens in her life happens in mine also. She just never gives it a thought. But that is Anne. In my thinking there are two ways to look at this whole scenario, but that is me, the alter-ego talking. You can believe it is a Divine revelation or merely a product of shock. Either way, people should be told such things. If it is shock, a reaction of the brain, medical research has yet to lasso it.

These happenings are way too wonderful to selfishly hide away; they affect our whole life in such amazing ways. In the end Anne will discover how right it is to share her experience.

July 4th, 1994

A Bear, Tubing and Mary

Good advice is worth considering

I stand on the river bank's edge. The warm sand is firm beneath my feet as I let my toes wiggle down into it a bit. I am fascinated by the swiftly moving water in front of me. Instead of the quiet I should expect, I am bombarded with noise. For such a remote spot I wonder how so much sound can surround me. Part of it is that I'm not alone. In fact, ninety percent of what I hear is coming from my husband, Ed, and our three grandchildren. They are behind me, up by the two-track with the van. Together the four all but shut off what would normally be the voice of the river as it swirls rapidly past my toes.

What's before me insists I listen more carefully. I tune out the family's conversation. Their excitement over today's adventure makes them unaware of my lack of participation in unloading the van. So, I'm alone in this moment and I do hear the music of the water. I've been here before; maybe not this exact spot but nearby. The Pigeon River country is a favorite get-away for Ed and me. Less than forty miles from our home, it could be a thousand. There is nothing here that speaks of what mankind is doing to God's world in other places.

The river is crystal clear. Sun spots flicker between its shadows highlighting the gold of the sand bottom. If I stand here long enough a trout will swim by slowly, intent on his own agenda. On the river's surface aspen leaves and bits of twigs are floating down stream in their search for adventure. Fifteen feet wide at the best, it isn't deep, except for occasional holes where the water's force has cut away beneath submerged rocks or tree trunks. I watch its rapid, intentional movement, working itself around obstacles in a nonchalant manner, refusing to

19

be deterred by anything. Its banks are low and the land is flat in a undetectable downhill direction, allowing the water to move along without tumbling over rocks or down ledges. Although surrounded by hills the Pigeon finds a course of least resistance by moving between them.

It has a distance to travel before reaching the mouth of Mullet Lake, forty-some miles to the north of me. Its twists and turns add to the distance. Once it meets the lake it can rest, slow down and join waters from other sources to frolic in waves, massaging beaches, rocks and colorful pebbles. Summer folk plumb its depths for fish and rile its surface with paddles, oars and motors. In the winter ice and snow hide it from the sun and sooth it into a long quiet isolation. Take the summer visitors out of the scenario and the process has been underway for eons; ever since the great glaciers scoured out the lakes, swamps and hills of northern Michigan.

I feel euphoric in my trance. Is this the Peace beyond all understanding; this thing I have going with the river? Are we in conversation, just the two of us, on this hot August afternoon out here in the middle of nowhere? Does it know my secret? Is this river aware of my feeling of others standing beside me? Or am I the only one who feels their presence.? I don't turn toward them. I've done that before and found nothing. I don't have to let my eyes look into theirs. Their presence doesn't have anything to do with sight.

It is just something inside me, someplace I can't put my finger on, that tells me Mary and Pat are with me. I even believe they are smiling. This is no surprise at all. I often feel them near by. I never tell this to anyone, except Ed. He understands. Others would suggest I visit a psychiatrist. Everyone knows both our beautiful, vivacious daughter and her handsome young husband are dead. Pat left seven years ago, just days before his thirty-fifth birthday and Mary followed him six years later in 1991. A year has moved by since then, almost to the day. Mary's funeral was on August 20th, a month and three days before her fortieth birthday. Today is August 16th, 1992 and hot like it was then.

I expected them here today. After all, if it weren't for Mary I wouldn't be standing beside the Pigeon River. She had thought this day would be wonderful for her children. I asked her about bringing them here before I even asked Ed what he thought about taking our three grandchildren over to go tubing. I am standing wiggling my toes in this sand by this river because I said to myself, What would Mary do?

Just a week ago the grandchildren had found me in the kitchen. I knew immediately something was up. It was written all over their faces.

With the priority of being the oldest Laura spoke first, trying her best not to let her anxiety show. "Gram could we go tubing?"

Our dreamer, Rachael quickly reinforced her sister by adding, "We're all good swimmers."

Pat never took his brown eyes off my face as if he knew I could never deny him a thing.

To say I was caught off guard would be right on target. Like any wise parent I hedged.

"Wow, what an idea. You know, this is one I'm going to have to run by Grandpa. What if I let you know tomorrow?"

My ploy worked. All three were satisfied. It made perfect sense that a decision as momentous as a tubing venture should be decided by their grandfather. They ran off, excitedly exploring their idea. I automatically returned to my job of snapping the ends off the green beans I had brought in from the garden earlier; my mind considering the best way to lay this bomb on Ed. I couldn't let the idea alone. All afternoon it floundered in and out of my brain. It was almost supper time when I heard myself saying, I wonder what their mother would say to such a proposition? I knew immediately what Mary would do. There I stood, stirring the gravy, laughing. Of course, Mary would think it a wonderful idea and without hesitation start the necessary plans.

Mary had been Miss Spontaneity herself. How well I remember. The ten years we traveled together to our country's major cities to set up our small booth in the National Needlework tradeshows were successful because she was the front person. Her wonderful smile and charm sold the products I designed. We were a team. This was back in the 70's and early 80's before the economic crunch of 1983. I thank the Lord every day for those years I had with her. They were the lifetime I won't have now.

Oh, her husband, Pat's death in '85 brought us together again but even that was destined to end. Four years later I knew before she did that her cancer, which came on the scene the year after Pat died, was winning. It was there when Ed and I viewed the X-rays taken after she fell in the grocery store and broke her hip. Mary never saw what appeared to be small black polka dots all over her skeleton. I couldn't share the visible proof of the cancer's hideous advancement. It became Ed's and my secret. As long as she believed she was winning the battle I wasn't going to take away her hope for her tomorrows. The X-rays went home with me in their over-sized manila envelope and I hid them on the top shelf of the front hall coat closet under a tennis racket of Ed's that no one used because of its antiquity. Thinking back I wonder if I wasn't hiding them from myself as much as from Mary.

Two years more went by. Ed and I completed building an addition to our back deck. We were spread out on our lounge chairs in the mid-morning August sunshine when Mary phoned. I couldn't believe my ears when I heard her say, "Mom? OK if I stop by for a while later this morning? I want to see what you've done with the deck. It's the annual reunion luncheon of my high school and college friends at One Water Street"

After assuring Mary we'd be home I turned to Ed to say, "Hon, you aren't going o believe this, but Mary is going to be here in less than an hour. She's driving over from Gaylord.

Ed was as surprised as I. Mary had given up driving months before.

She was absolutely radiant when she walked out on the deck. Although wearing leg braces and clumpy sneakers she looked lovely in a soft summer dress and perfect makeup. She was one of those women who always looked gorgeous, no matter what or where. Time evaporated like an early morning mist. As suddenly as she had arrived she was standing to leave. With hugs and kisses she said, "I wish I could just stay here. I think I could sit under this maple forever. I love what you have done with the deck, Dad. I can't believe you actually built it around the tree instead of cutting it down."

Her last words, flung over her shoulder eased her leaving. "I'll try to stop by on my way back to Gaylord."

She didn't make it back.

A call came from Gaylord in the late afternoon to tell us she had been just too tired to stop by. We understood. Her get-together at the restaurant had been fun. Everyone had shown up. Neither Mary, Ed nor I could have known that the close knit group of friends who lunched with her that noon would be pallbearers at her funeral in less than three weeks.

Two days later an urgent call came from Larry, Mary's second husband of about two years. Could I come over as fast as possible? Mary needed me. She was in terrible pain and wanted to go to the hospital, but couldn't get in the car.

Though I didn't understand what it was I could do to help, I told Larry we'd be on our way immediately.

A little over a half hour later Ed drove into Larry and Mary's drive and we ran to the house to find them waiting for us. Mary was sitting on the edge of the hospital bed they had set up for her in their living room early in the spring. It was placed so she could look out across the back yard, through its trees and onto the ninth green of the bordering golf course. She enjoyed watching the ever changing saga of golfers as they teed off, added scores, parked their carts, agonized over club selections, stood and talked, smoked or trotted off to use the nearby relief station.

I saw tear streaks on Mary's cheeks as I reached out to give her a hug and ask what I could do. Before my arms could even arrange themselves in the proper curves she yelled at me. "Don't, Mother. Don't touch me. I can't stand to have anything touch me."

I immediately became a statue twelve inches away from my daughter.

Larry walked to my side and explained, "I have tried to help her walk to the car, Mom, but she screams if I so much as touch her. The pain is unbearable. There is nothing either of us can come up with that will get her out of the house and into the car. She won't let me call an ambulance as she is certain they would go right ahead and pick her up. It was her idea to have you come over.

Mary looked at me and pleaded, "Mother, help me, please."

I looked through the dining room at Ed standing helplessly in the kitchen. He wore the same look as Larry. My mind was blank, yet it kept acknowledging the fact Mary believed I could help. She was so certain that she had Larry call me and then sat on the edge of her bed and waited for me to come thirty-five miles to her aid.

I glanced back through the dining room again to look at Ed and saw the answer. Of course, right in front of us and so simple. I quickly walked to the nearest dining room chair and set it down within Mary's grasp. Then I moved a second one a long reach from the first. Ed and Larry saw immediately where I was going and in a matter of seconds extended a line of six chairs well into the kitchen. Before the men were finished Mary was on her way, pulling herself from her bed in the living room, then chair to chair, through the dining room headed for the kitchen.

My husband and son-in-law began moving the first chair to the end of the line, keeping the row of furniture snaking its way through the kitchen and then with a right turn into the utility room to the back door which opened into the garage. As Ed finished the last chair Larry hurried into the garage, positioning the car so that Mary could step down into it by reaching for its opened door. As she pulled the door shut she called out, "I love you, Mother." I heard Larry start the car and they were on their way.

As a family we weren't overly demonstrative at that time and her words were new to my ears, although I had always known a deep love held all of us together. I have never forgotten those four words and the lesson I learned that afternoon. The only other thing Mary said before she died ten days later was when we arrived at the hospital the next day.

She asked, "Laura, Rachael, Pat?"

I answered, "They are down the hall with Lynn, Julie and Corrine."

Her face held no expression, no tear ran down a cheek. Her eye lids slowly closed and my daughter whom I loved with every inch of my being left. Somehow I knew she was content. She had left us ordered and organized. It was as if the story of her life had been written, folded and inserted into an envelope, the flap sealed and all laid to rest on the pillow beside her head.

Mary lay in a coma. The next days were endless as we stood by waiting until her young, aerobic heart wore itself out. Her brother David arrived and never left his sister's side as long as she lingered. Their brother Tom had died the year before as cancer won its battle with him. Dave had learned the hardest way possible what it was to loose someone you love deeply.

Why I have traveled back in my mind to Mary's last days troubles me. I thought I had finished with that. It is a fruitless journey, seemingly serving no purpose. Then I remembered the children's request and I understood. It wasn't about Mary's death, but about knowing what Mary would do if the kids had asked her rather than me. I immediately accepted the fact I wanted very badly to take the kids tubing. Heck, if Mary could do it I darn well better pull it off too. All that was left was to sell the idea to Ed.

I should have known; Ed's response was, "What a great idea. I've noticed a place near the Pigeon River State Forest campground that rents tubes. You planning to take a picnic?

So here we all are today, beside the Pigeon. The picnic is in the van, ready to eat after we make our way down the river and return.

I turn toward the sandy two-track fifteen feet behind me and realize I am the only one who has rushed down to the water's edge. The other four have been busy with five gigantic, shiny-black inner tubes. Four have been lashed to the roof of the Aerostar with rope Ed borrowed from the old fellow who rented the tubes. The other one is protruding from the open top half of the tailgate like a bloated monster.

Ed and I are thrilled to be back in Pigeon River country. We've been here often; all seasons. There was the winter trip on our cross country skis when I all but knocked myself out as I negotiated a turn on a hill and watched my skis decide to go their separate ways around a sturdy maple tree. The scientific fact is that trees are much harder as they stand frozen than when the sap is running. I literally used my head to figure this one out.

I smile at the memory of the camping trip back in '73. We brought Mary and her then, boy friend, Patrick with us. Of course, Ed and I really checked the poor guy out pretty thoroughly on that trip as we figured there must have been something more than just friendship behind Mary's decision to bring such a city slicker into Michigan's wilderness. The young pre-law student was a good looking, personable fellow of Irish decent whose parents had named him Patrick Charles Cassidy, II. We later learned his father was a big, six foot four Detroit policeman; captain of the department's Tug-O-War team. Pat's interest in law was a direct result of the days he accompanied his dad into the courtroom with prisoners.

Because of his sheltered city life I had taken along food I normally would never consider for the two night campout in the remote State Forest campground; even the butt end of a small ham. I was going to really seduce this guy for Mary with a ham and egg breakfast.

It all backfired the first night when a large, six hundred pound black bear meandered into our campground. The animal could only have been larger if he had been a sow expecting triplets momentarily. Even Jack, our fearless big black lab had the sense to remain mute as the intruder knocked over an oil drum full of wet ashes and garbage five feet from the pup tent he was in with our twenty-three year old son, Tom and Pat. Somehow Ed had all of us, including the dog, silently inside the van before the beast brought its head and shoulders out of the drum where he had rolled it. With his nose in the air he followed the scent of a delicious southern, honey-smoked ham to the large Styrofoam cooler on our picnic table. Again I had broken a standard rule of camping by not closing all food inside the car. I couldn't believe I had been so careless.

Five of us watched behind closed windows through the half light of the pre-dawn as our visitor stood at the table and dispatched the ham. Strangely, when he ambled off he left the bone. Even more strange, our lab would have nothing to do with it.

The tortured sound of claws ripping open the foam container still echoes in my ears. It is almost the sound of the tubes as they are dragged off the van's roof today. I instantly leave my memories of Mary and Pat behind in answer to Ed's command.

"Ok, everyone, into your swim suits and let's get the show on the road. You coming, Anne?" His days as a captain in the Army Air Corps penetrate his demeanor yet.

We choose sides. Pat and Ed change into their swim trunks on the river side of the Aerostar while the two girls and I get into our swimsuits on the lee side.

Ed says, "Don't roll your tube. You don't want it to get in the river without you. You may not see it again."

It's not easy to get the unwieldy, monsters down into the water.

"Keep a good hold on your tube. Don't let it get away from you. This river is moving right along," Ed calls outs out again. His words of warning heighten the sense of adventure we all feel.

Not one of us steps into the fast water without an unconscious intake of breath. It is icy. On such a hot August afternoon the contrast with the heat we feel on our shoulders and the frigid water aren't in sync. My immediate reaction is to jump back on the bank's warm sand.

Laura catches my action and calls out, "Come on, Gram. It isn't that bad once you get used to it,"

I look down at her feet in the clear water and see the redness of them.

Oh, Yeh, I think. You're only eleven and I'm seventy. Looking out in the water where Ed is standing I chastise myself. Come on Anne, your husband will be seventy-three in two months, who are you to complain? Look at him, he's having a ball.

Ed is oblivious to the cold water as he stands waist deep. An athlete all his life his strong legs and arms along with his big shoulders are what is needed to help Laura and Rachael onto their tubes while steadying them in the current. Then to keep them from taking off down the river he pulls them within reach of an overhanging deadfall where they can get a firm hold. Turning to help Pat the two soon discover that there is no way our grandson can stay on top of his own tube. At seven his legs and arms simply are not long enough to stretch across and over the diameter of the rubber circle. I know the day will come when he will stand taller than his six foot two grandfather. His Uncle Paul is six five and his grandfather, six four.

"Come on big guy," Ed says, "your grandmother can shove your tube up on shore and you can share my ride."

I find myself in the water reaching for the extra tube with no time to consider what I am doing. I then push it up on the shore.

"Do you think I should lock it in the car, Hon?" I call to Ed.

"No. There won't be anyone else this far back in here today. It'll be OK."

This accomplished I pull my tube out into the river to the girls and with their help manage a not too graceful flop onto it. I dearly love all kinds of outdoor activity but will never be the athlete my husband is. Growing up tall and spindly I have never been able to do as well as I think I should. Even now with a generous padding everywhere, I still come up short in my opinion.

By this time Ed and Pat are by our sides. As soon as Ed arranges himself across his tube, feet sticking straight out well over its edges he reaches for his grandson and hoists him onto his lap.

"Everyone all set?" Let's get on our way."

Once our grip on the dead tree is loosened the river takes over. If I thought it was noisy before it certainly is now. From his perch on his grandfather's middle Pat becomes the reconnaissance officer of our small platoon, shouting out warnings and directions. The girls yell and scream as only young females can. To be honest, I can hear myself shrieking too as the cold water quickly finds a way to soak me from head to foot. There're obstacles on all sides and even beneath us.

Eventually the laws of science take over. The lighter voyagers move into the lead until Ed and Pat are well in the rear. He admonishes us to keep in sight. We all shout our promises. To prevent Rachael from leaving us all behind I grab her hand and the two of us swirl down the river side by side, arms stretched to their limits. Laura trails behind about half way between her grandfather and us.

Beneath us, the river has its way.

The problem with tubing is that as boats, the large, black inner tubes are almost four feet across, solid with air but bottomless in their centers. Oh, there's no danger of falling through the middle as the boater maintains his lounging position by hanging legs and arms over the tube's edges. The real danger is the liquid ice, melted snow flowing from the forest and swamp. Back in the deep shade of the trees snow can lay unmolested by the sun well into the summer. I can envision the white, compacted crystallized fluff hidden against the southern banks of the river's edge and under the dense cedar and giant hemlocks beyond.

I wonder if the animals don't roll about in the patches for the sheer joy of ridding themselves of pesky flies and mosquitoes. The image of our big black visitor from years ago, on his back, muscular legs stretched aloft, wiggling his big haunch and shoulders in the delicious coolness all but makes me forget where I really am, in the cold Pigeon River.

The river is so clear the sandy and nature littered bottom seems to rush by before my gaze. It certainly creates the illusions that the water alone is moving. But not so; the big rubber tubes are in competition with the Pigeon. The five of us are merely spectators from our desperate and abnormal perches on the tubes' tops. The tush becomes numb within minutes and therefore not responsive to the dead wood snags that lurk below the gushing torrent of the stream. The Pigeon River is no theme park.

It is problematical whether the joyous, screaming, careening and swirling tubers will emerge with or without their swim suits in tact. We move into longish stretches of straight water, uncluttered with excessive debris and I feel my grip on Rachael's wrist relax. It is glorious out here in this no-man's land on such a perfect summer day. The sky overhead is the bluest of blues. A few early afternoon puffs of white clouds huddle on the western horizon. I occasionally glimpse them in breaks in the shoreline foliage. The sun's heat on my body is luxurious. Too bad it can't reach my behind. That portion of me is suffering from hypothermia.

I am lulled into a lethargic state of shear bliss. I have no idea how far we've come and could care less. Suddenly the river changes course and we are carried abruptly around a bend. Rachael and I are jerked out of our reveries as we see where the river is intent on taking us. Our yells startle a Jay and its call slides in over ours. My grip on Rachael's wrist tightens. Both of us watch the water ahead disappear into a pair of corrugated metal pipes which support a sandy two track road that crosses the river one hundred yards ahead. No more than ten feet wide at the point the river is squeezing itself through the cylinders. Rachael and I both realize that unless we let go of each other it is obvious serious damage will result to us both.

I hear Ed behind me calling out a warning of the approaching hazard but it is too late for us. I can picture the other three racing in our wake. Pat, too small to trust about slipping through the center of a tube, is safely in Ed's grasp. Laura, whose eleventh birthday was last month is on her own. Her long legs and arms of the Cassidy Clan securely hold her in place despite her necessary movements to miss rocks, fallen trees and other obstacles. I am certain she will find a way to stop herself before the road.

With no time to think of an alternative course of action, laughing wildly, Rachael and I disengage, yell our goodbyes to each other and disappear into the five foot wide pipes. She vanishes into the left tube while I sail into the right. In a matter of seconds we are pushed through the long, dark tunnels. As I plunge back out into the bright afternoon sun I see Rachael, the lighter, has gained on me. Twenty yards ahead she is entering a way too wild section of the river.

As I watch, my granddaughter snags into a tangle of overhanging willow and alder. The tube flips and she is caught upside down in the icy water. All I see is the shiny wet rubber held cockeyed against the protruding brush. Rachael is out of sight under the rushing river. Terror is my companion as I struggle to reach Rachael's side. The enormous, fat tubes are in my way while my fingers, numb with the chill of the rushing water, try desperately to separate my upside down granddaughter from the clutch of the grasping branches. That she's caught beneath the river's surface is a nightmare.

At the same time I know I must somehow keep the tubes from leaving the scene without us. They have no handles on their slippery surfaces to offer a hold. We have to have them to work our way against the current and back through the metal pipes. It will take our combined strength to manage. There is no way we can leave the tubes and climb out onto the shore. Such an escape is simply not an option because the stream's banks are inaccessible with a wild mat of undergrowth. No fisherman has stood along this stretch of the Pigeon to cast for the illusive Brookie. My mind records all this data in long, elastic seconds as I struggle.

Rachael fights the current with me. I learn what an exceptional child she is. Not once does she panic. Her hands work with mine to untangle her long blond hair with its mass of curls and her slim legs which are entwined in the relentless grasp of the submerged and overhanging brush. My feet search for the river bottom and find nothing. I can't stand. We're over a deep hole hollowed out by the water as it curves into the swamp. The whole episode appears to be far more frightening for me than Rachael. Although badly scared Rachael at nine doesn't realize her grandmother at seventy might not have the strength to help her. She trusts me. I have to do this alone.

Ed, Pat and Laura have all wisely stopped before coming through the pipes. The large aluminum cylinders are blocking Rachael and me from their view. Even if Ed could see us there is no way he can get to us in time. He has Pat on his tube. Shaken, I know I should have been more alert and perceived the danger.

Rachael's face emerges and she gulps air. A few strands of hair in the alder testify to our struggle.

She smiles and says, "Hi, Gram."

We did it. The sun still shines from the blue sky above and the jay calls from a nearby cedar as Rachael and I force our way up the river, making it back through the pipes. Scratched, cut and bloody we emerge. Wet from head to foot; we are as cold as blocks of ice. Ed, Laura and Pat stare at us. They have no idea what we have done.

"What happened, Snork? You were gone so long I was about to get the kids on shore and come for you,"

Laura, the one who sees herself responsible for her brother and sister asks, "Gram, you and Rachael are all bloody. What did you do?"

Rachael tells our story and underneath her words I hear the fear she didn't allow to surface when she was submerged in the water, so tangled in the brush. I hope the incident will not permanently make her afraid of water. Pat is enthralled by Rachael's tale.

Nothing has changed but me. And that happened in the brief moment I thought my granddaughter was drowning. I suddenly understand I'm not just the children's grandmother anymore, but their mother as well. Ed and I alone are the sole responsible persons for their safety, health and growth. Those who will back us are to be just that, our backups. We are now Mom and Dad although the three will always call us Gram and Gramps. It is us who will be their parents as long as God grants us tenure on His earth. I silently promise myself I will retire from my position as director of the consignment shop at the McCune Community Arts Center in Petoskey next week. I had taken the job when Ed had retired. It was done so we could have three days a week to call our own. At the time togetherness was proving to be smothering. I laugh to myself knowing that togetherness has arrived in a different form.

I look at Ed and wonder, did he already know this? Has he been ahead of me about our future? I'll never ask him. I really don't need to. The answer is in his eyes as he looks toward me. We're partners all the way.

His love will always give me the freedom to do whatever I feel needs to be done—even to go tubing. Today he's proud of his wife of forty nine-years and that I have safely brought Rachael back from what might have been a tragic tubing accident. Now as this crazy, fun day winds down and we sit on the grassy riverbank, drying ourselves, eating peanut butter and jelly sandwiches a glance from Ed's eyes promises me the years ahead will remain ours even though we'll not be alone very often.

When Anne has no idea what so ever action is called for next with her new family, she'll find it helpful to stop in her tracks and say to herself, "What would Mary do about this?" This short question is all that will be required. It'll work no matter how desperately or frequently she needs help to choose the best thing to do with or for her grandchildren. Usually the question will be a silent one. But she'll blurt it right out loud when no one is close enough to hear or answer.

To me the question's value will often lay in the fact it makes her think. It causes her to take the time to juggle possibilities. Sometimes she'll really feel as if Mary is standing beside her or with her children and there's an exchange of ideas. An answer will always appear. At times it'll be so obvious she'll all but laugh aloud with relief and disbelief. She'll wonder why she ever questioned her faith about the presence of God in her life. She didn't know it back when her father asked her about the reality of a Heaven that she was being nourished for these years over fifty years away. Now you can understand why I had to tell you about that time when she was eighteen. To me it explains this whole story she is telling.

This habit of seeking Mary's opinion about what her next step with the children should be will lead her into participating in a number of activities not normally chosen by women of her age. The results will be exactly what should be done. Other times they'll be insanely funny or even scary.

Patrick with Laura 1981

The Call, Windows and a Gurney

Morning will come and with it another day

Ed and Anne love the old cherry farm. Their house sits on top of a hill some two hundred feet above Boyne City. Whitetail deer shortcut across the property moving from cedar swamp to cedar swamp. On this night the far forest covered hills lay silent in the blackness. Only an occasional light in the town a mile below indicates others are nearby. Anne and Ed like the seclusion, its peace and promise of continuity; that morning will come and with it another day.

It is two in the morning and the phone rings. Instantly awake, I reach for it. Normally difficult to wake up once I'm asleep, it's strange I answer the call rather than Ed. Even in the few seconds my hand needs to find the phone in the dark bedroom I wonder about it. He sleeps on oblivious to its ring.

"Hello."

"Anne, this is Jeff. Is Ed there?"

"Yes, right here. Do you want to speak to him?"

"No, that isn't necessary, I guess. I just want to be sure you aren't alone. This is hard to say, Anne, but Pat is dead. He just died in his sleep. Julie and Lynn are here at Mary's with the kids. She has gone in the ambulance with Pat to the hospital. We thought you would want to go up to be with her. Would you like me to come get you and Ed?"

The lamp on Ed's side of the bed switches on. Just a forty watt bulb, it shows our faces even though the corners of the room remain dark enough to make them not quite there.

Ed, after one look at me asks, "What's wrong Snork? Tell me."

"Just a second, Jeff. I have to tell Ed."

Turning to my husband I answer, "Pat's dead." I can find no other words to share what has happened. I feel nothing; no panic, no horror, no anger, nothing. Without knowing what I am doing I drag the phone across myself and into Ed's reaching hand. Then I turn away to crawl back under the covers, pulling them over my head to take up with sleep, where I'd so recently been; as if there had been no call, no interruption. It feels right to curl my body into the warmth of the sheets and blanket, blocking the dim light from the bedside lamps. In our forty-two years of marriage I have grown used to expecting Ed to take charge when something rears its head up unexpectedly. His whole being is given to taking care of me, no matter what. Having served in the Army Air Corps as an officer he found the manner and the means to carry out self-imposed duty. A big man for his generation, Ed stands six foot two and keeps his body at a tight and athletic one hundred and eighty pounds. He is handsome enough that the fact he is prematurely bald doesn't detract from his looks. To me he is one in millions and I will never think otherwise.

Ed, up on his elbow next to me, the phone to his ear, his strong body against mine feels good. It's an awkward position for him, but long ago the decision was made that the alarm clock should be on his bedside table and the phone on mine. It was the sort of set-up married couples make. Because I'm such a sound sleeper Ed thought the alarm should be easy for him to reach to turn off in the mornings. Since the phone is not known to ring during the night, our kids now grown and long gone, it should be on my table. It made sense to both of us.

Ed speaks, "This is Ed, Jeff. Anne says Pat is dead. How has this happened?"

"He died in his sleep, just a little while ago. He woke Mary up and indicated he couldn't breath. She tried artificial respiration and failed. She called the hospital and medics came, but it was too late, Pat was already gone. Both of them have been taken up to emergency. She wants her mother to come up to be with her. And she'd like you to be with the girls. Both Lynn and my Julie are here at the house now and will stay with you."

"We'll be right over, Jeff. And thanks for calling." Ed hangs up the phone. Looking down he pulls the covers back from my face, gently saying, "Snorkie, Mary needs us. Let's go."

Neither of us have anything to say. My brain feels frozen, incapable of making sense of Jeff's words. It is much easier to follow Ed's lead and crawl back into the clothes I'd removed three hours earlier. Somewhere inside myself I watch the two of us dress. I can't believe how methodically we work, even buttoning buttons, not able to hurry. In sync as Ed ties his shoes I pull on mine. Together we turn off lamps, head into the hall and out the door to the car in the dark driveway. It's so silent we listen to our footsteps crossing the stepping stones, the only sound in the deep night.

As Ed turns down the gravel lane to Wildwood Harbor Road a pair of headlights suddenly appear turning toward us out of the darkness at its far end. As we meet, Ed slows his car to a halt, recognizing the other vehicle as a Boyne City Police car. I don't understand why suddenly the police should be headed up to the house. But Ed knows. His Barber Shopper Chorus friend, Auggie, winds down his window and asks, "Can I drive you over to Mary's, Ed?"

Ed replies, "Thanks, Auggie, but I'm OK."

"You're sure?"

"Yes."

Accepting Ed's refusal Auggie looks across Ed to where I sit. His eyes on mine he simply says the only words he can find, "I'm so sorry, Anne."

I nod in gratitude having no idea how many times I'll hear those same heart felt words from family, friends and those I know and don't know in the days to come.

Ed turns onto Wildwood Harbor Road, then a right on Clute and on to where Shadow Trails converges from the left and to Mary's drive. Every window in her home is alight, reinforcing the knowledge that something is not as it should be. Once up to the house Lynn and Julie are at the car, opening its doors before either of us can. Their tear stained faces overflow with concern for us, Mary's parents.

"The girls are sound asleep," Julie reassures us. "They slept through the whole thing. I think it's because their rooms are on the lower level."

Lynn is all business, "Mary is expecting you, Anne. She road with Pat in the ambulance. Would you like me to drive you up?"

"No, I'm all right."

I am speaking the truth. I know my mind to be as clear as the star studded night. "I don't mind driving; there won't be many cars on the road this time of the night. I suppose I am to go to the emergency entrance?"

"Yes. Are you sure you don't want company?"

"I'm Ok, Lynn. This is something I can do for Mary. It's so little."

Turning to Ed, I am hit with the need to stay with him. He is looking at me with such sorrow and concern I crawl into his embrace and the shelter of his strong arms. By allowing him to comfort me I give him my love, his comfort.

"Oh, our Mary. Why, Anne, why? The girls have lost their father and the baby will never know him. Why, why?"

I have no answers. Ed's questions are mine. Instinctively I know there will be no answers. Never. No words of explanation exist in man's vocabulary.

"This has happened to others," I tell myself. "But this time it's real, it is ours. Our beloved Patrick is gone. How can this be happening?"

Like another son to Ed and me, the hurt is unbelievably deep. Not yet thirty five and beginning to see his law practice start to grow, the timing seems wrong. As I find myself still in Ed's safe embrace I am reluctant to leave it. Gently pulling back, I feel his lips meeting mine in a kiss; another way to keep in the present, where the world is still ours. Now is all we have, the future no longer exists.

"I have to go, Mary is waiting," I say. "As long as the girls are sleeping why don't you stretch out on the couch? I suspect today is going to be the busiest day of our lives. I love you. We will make it through this with Mary."

"Are you sure I shouldn't go with you?"

"No. I'm OK." I believe my own words.

Climbing in the car I leave Ed and the two young women. They have been close friends of Mary's from grade school all the way through their college years at Central Michigan University. In less than five minutes after Ed drove into Mary's driveway I'm on my way to join my daughter at the hospital in Petoskey, the next town to the north. Large enough to have a big health care facility it is the town where Patrick practiced his law. I feel robot-like. My hands guide the wheel and my feet rest on the pedals. I realize I have turned on the headlights, but have no idea when.

The darkness of the night is solid and true to my prediction there are no other cars in the nine mile trip. The houses I pass reflect the night; not a light glows from a window. No green eyes peer from the roadsides as I subconsciously check for deer. The eerie feeling of being alone, too small in a too large world creeps into me despite the familiar hills and curves of the road.

I wonder aloud, How long before did the silent ambulance whisk our Mary and Patrick down this same highway? And no one in all these homes knew.

Is this all a death means? I continue. Do we just come and go, day after day, all over this earth, so silently, so unnoticed? Why are we even here?

Staring ahead into the night I answer my own question. I'm here because of Ed and he; for me. We are each other's gift from God just as Pat was Mary's. This shouldn't be happening to her. I can't wrap myself around widowhood for our Mary.

My mind flips three hundred miles south to all Pat's family; his mother and father, sleeping as their oldest child dies. His brothers and sisters, all seven completely unaware of what morning will bring. Then as quickly my thoughts are in Wisconsin with Mary's younger sister, Nancy, the youngest of our four and her Paul and two children, Melissa and Christopher. Then my mind zigzags back to Indiana and our oldest, David and his Cathy and their son, Lewis. Then I am in Traverse City with our Tom and his Sue Ellen.

Oh, God—do they all have to know? my mind pleads.

Even the city is empty. The bars pushed their late customers out their doors over an hour ago. The traffic light before the turn-off into the hospital's emergency entrance merely blinks off and on as if to remind the stray night-time driver it is there, still on duty if only in a symbolic manner. The hospital parking lot is a sea of black asphalt absorbing the amber hued night lighting hung above on skinny necked poles. There are hundreds of choices of parking spots, a first time occurrence for me. Normally I'd drive up one lane and on to the next and next before finding an empty spot; but not tonight.

The large red lettered neon 'EMERGENCY' sign hanging over the nearest entrance at the end of a ramp beckons me with a feeling of urgency. Ambulances parked adjacent to it are unattended except one whose motor still runs. Two men in white move in its lighted interior straightening equipment. I shudder. A ripple of muscle activity runs across my shoulders and down the length of my body. I notice my feet don't take part in the involuntary act. I am certain I had never been so acutely aware of a shudder before. This shudder is because I understand Pat had been carried out of the vehicle such a short time before. I know now I am not a robot but a human being in shock.

Did they help Mary out also? I wonder as I turn off the car's ignition, climb out into the dark night and lock the doors. My mind won't leave the idling ambulance alone. Agile as Mary is I can't quite imagine her leaping forth complete with her all but nine month old child-to-be-born-any-time-now leading the way. Everything inside of me from the top of my head to the tip of my quiet toes churns with denial, with unspeakable grief. Yet there is this burble of humor as my imagination creates the image of beautiful, aerobic Mary leaping down to the pavement despite manly offers of assistance. There's not a doubt within me but what I'll find Mary waiting inside, completely in control.

Through the weather vestibule and into the emergency room I can see Pat on a Gurney less than ten feet away. Contrary to TV there is no sheet pulled up over his body. He seems peacefully asleep; his Irish good looks contentedly composed; there is no sign of his struggle to breath. Nothing appears changed. But I know better. It's all changed. Nothing will ever be as it was. A life has left this world. I still don't cry. Although I hear my thoughts, they remain only that. Reality is out of reach.

Mary stands by Pat's side as the hospital Chaplin, David, a good friend from high school holds her hand. As Chaplin, David has walked this path before, but this time has to be more difficult, the two are peers. He is exactly who Mary needs. Hearing the door slide open they turn and quietly welcome me, drawing me into the silence which no words can break. My tears begin to slowly flow down my checks and I find myself included in David's ministration. This large, kind and gentle man brings calmness into the room. It's apparent God is in charge as my whole being relaxes in acceptance as the tears fall. I think of Pat's family so far away and know they should be here rather than me.

How will I ever share this feeling of peace with them? I never will. I won't find the words. They will be locked inside me forever.

If Anne had been able to stand back and observe herself she would have known she wasn't locking her feelings inside. They were there on her face and in her eyes as she talked with those who arrived during the following days. Everyone was aware Anne, like her Ed, had somehow come to terms with their son-in-law's death, although none understood how. And of course no one said a thing to me. They had no idea of my presence. A tragedy is never about one person. It is about all people

A Secret, an Autopsy and Search

Secrets seem to be such dangerous things

Secrets don't bother some people one way or another, but to Anne they seem to be such dangerous things. For her they are scary and carry a demand of never, ever slipping, divulging the wrong thing to someone or as the old saying goes, 'letting the cat out of the bag'. She honestly gets all bent out of shape over them. Of course it can be true they can involve the reputation of another, especially if sharing the secret might do irreparable harm. But how often do any of us have to deal with that kind of information? It is more likely to be the secrets of Christmas, birthdays and celebrations where nothing but happiness is the result and in the end they're not expected to be kept anyway. No, it is those which must be carried to the grave that frighten Anne. She doubts her ability to keep mum. The thing that is so ridiculous about all this is she knows darn well she'll never, ever allow herself to slip. She is far better with secrets than most of us tend to be.

By morning the tragedy is known throughout the area. If a special edition of the Citizen-Journal had hit the street the news would not have been disseminated any faster. The shock waves flow through the family, the law community, Mary's generation, Ed's and mine, the church, the hospitals, and on and on like colorful balloons released into the sky. Within the day the Cassidy clan arrives from the greater Detroit area. Dave, Nancy and Tom, along with their children and spouses pull in from Indiana, Wisconsin and Traverse City to be with Mary. I treasure Paul and Nancy's edge on all of us as their experience as ministers leads them in their words of condolence with all of us. The family is enveloped within many arms, held tightly against the strong chest of men and the soft haven of women.

Voices are anguished, thick and tear choked. I am pulled against wet cheeks, stubble and perfumed makeup. Words are whispered, hands reach for mine. I have absolutely no idea what or how I respond. At times I realize I move beyond just words and actually enter into conversations. Words flow out of me, leaving me completely at a loss as to what might be said.

Periodically my eyes roam the room until they find Ed. I have to know he is here with me; that he is managing. At those times our glances meet he comes to me and puts his arm around my waist and draws me close. In those moments our world comes back into focus for both of us.

Others takes over. I am unaware who is smoothly taking care of all that needs to be done for Mary. And I am amazed at my daughter's calmness and her ability to bring her daughters into the process of saying goodbye to their father. It is almost as if Mary had done this many times before in her short lifetime. I am in awe of her concern for everyone else and her continuous effort to reach out to them. Her calmness sets the stage for us. There are no hysterics, wailing or desperate comments. Her girls reflect their mother's manner. Later three year old Laura will confide to her mother that she has figured out how her father found his way up to be with God. She takes her mother's hand and leads her out to the side yard.

Pointing to the tallest of the many old white pines growing close to the house she says, "See that tall tree, Mommy? I think Daddy climbed up to its very top and God reached down and pulled him up with Him. Do you think that is how He did it?"

Looking up into the spreading bows of the towering pine Mary agrees that though she hadn't thought about it she is quite certain Laura is right. Laura is content.

The funeral is planned for the traditional third day, allowing travel time for those who live some distance away. I appreciate this gift of time that tradition has set before us. I won't remember when all is over whether Ed and I ever returned to our house, alone or with each other. It will seem I never leave Mary's kitchen as folk seek me out with memories of Pat. It is from the ones I meet for the first time as a cup of coffee is placed in their hand that I learn so much about the goodness and outreach of Mary's husband.

I hear things which would never have been told under other circumstances. It amazes me to find out how he mended marriages when divorces had been sought. The entire law community appreciated our son-in-law's ability to listen and help. All this makes it harder and harder for me to accept his death. I find myself questioning the whole event just as Ed did. My mind asks me, Why such a fine young man? Why before he ever had time to know his son? Why this for Mary and her children? Why have the Cassidy's lost their oldest son; their first born? It isn't that I am angry. It is because none of it makes any sense to me.

Deep down inside I know none of it ever will. There will never be an answer. But saying it is just life doesn't solve the problem either. That old cliché must have been uttered by someone who was five sheets to the wind.

The day after Pat's death Nancy singles me out among those in the house. No one quite knows why they are here, but just seem to feel the need to be with others. She finds me by the back door talking with a couple who have carried in a large red basket of fruit. Everything in it looks so beautiful and mouth watering. My expression shows my pleasure with the thoughtful gift. Red is my favorite color and the slatted basket with its reds, yellows, oranges and purples looks like a painting I could frame and hang it over the kitchen table. As the couple departs Nancy motions me into a shadowy corner of the entry hall. It is relatively quiet at the moment as we stand facing each other. My eyes question my daughter about the need to be apart. It is then Nancy confides that at seven months pregnant she hasn't felt her baby move since she had arrived at Mary's house. Having experienced four successful deliveries and healthy children myself Nancy's words seem unreal.

Hasn't Nancy had two fine babies? I think.

The only thing I can come up with is to urge Nancy to see our doctor immediately. She nods her head and tells me even before she shared her problem with me she knew calling the doctor would be the only possible course to take. But in the midst of everything else that was happening she was reluctant. Another problem at this time shouldn't be rearing its ugly head. For some reason she couldn't explain even to herself she hoped I would have an alternative suggestion. I look up the number and Nancy makes the telephone call.

The nurse tells Nancy to come right over. She'll find a time to squeeze her in. Not able to accompany her, I feel torn between Nancy's needs and Mary's. In the end all I can do is stand in the doorway as Paul heads out for the doctor's with her. My numbness reaches the far corners of my body and mind. I feel disengaged from those around me. Their voices are unheard, the fly on the screen door is unseen and Laura's tug on my skirt is unfelt.

Later in the afternoon, after resisting the urging of Lynn to go upstairs and rest I plop myself down on the little chair by the telephone. I have dragged it into the corner in the dining room where I am away from the activity around the kitchen table and back door. I am certain I will get a call that every thing is OK; that Nancy's baby is well and healthy. I sit; I pray.

When the phone does ring someone else who is walking through the hall picks it up before I can. After answering he turns toward me and places the phone in my outstretched hand. "It's for you, Anne."

The voice isn't Nancy's or even Paul's but that of a close friend, Tammia. Together we have been active in the Presbyterian Women of Mackinaw for a number of years, often driving each other to its meetings. Both Tammia and her husband, Frank, were born in Egypt. Her father was a missionary on the Nile. Tammia's amazing life and her knowledge of the Bible have always fascinated me. The few times I've seen Frank, he was every inch the very quiet gentleman his country breeds. A beloved pathologist, I understand why Tammia left her pursuit of a medical career to become his wife.

"Anne, Frank just called from the hospital and the lab report from your son-in-law's autopsy has come back showing the presence of drugs. Knowing you and your family Frank questions the report. He has checked the drugstore records in Petoskey and surrounding areas and has found no notation of the sale of drugs of any kind to Patrick. He is asking that you check the medicine cabinets at Mary's, Pat's dresser drawers and his car to see if you can find any. He suggests you accomplish this without letting anyone, including Mary, know what you are doing. Frank sees no reason in upsetting others at this time. He is disturbed enough that he has to ask you to do this search, but he feels it must be done before he questions the report. Can you manage a search and will you call me back as soon as possible? Frank will wait."

Overwhelmed with my friend's concern and obvious effort to protect me and our family I answer, "Oh, Tammia, how good of you and Frank. I will do my best and call you the minute I finish looking. Please thank Frank."

Not at all certain how to go about being a sleuth, I recognize Frank is right. There is no way anyone else should find out about this. They already are struggling with the tragic situation of Pat's death. There is no choice. I can't even wait until evening; it has to be done immediately. It seems that the possibility of drug use wants to enter my mind and find a corner to lodge in, Is this how the innocent are branded?

At this thought I decide not even Ed will be told. Never in all our thirty seven years of marriage have I kept anything away from my husband. That the drug question on top of Pat's death would be devastating to Ed confirms my thinking. The secret will be mine alone. I feel no guilt, only the weight of responsibility.

Mary is in the kitchen with three of her friends. They surround her like a shield. The thought skims my mind, I wonder if those three were here all night? I can't remember and besides it has nothing to do with this terrible thing I must carry out right under their noses. All four of these women are sharp as tacks. The idea of proceeding with Frank's request looms like the highest of peaks I must climb and with no gear or practice.

As Anne stands thinking she has no idea how little of the three days between Pat's death and his burial she will remember. Year after year there will never be time to think back to them. They will hang in limbo until the years ahead pile up, one upon another until finally a day will arrive when Anne's life will slow to a normal pace. Then the memories will surface in vivid sound and color, never to be put aside; always to be with her.

The lavatory is off the utility room, which opens into the kitchen. The telephone normally hangs on the kitchen wall next to the opening into the dining room. Fortunately the receiver has a long enough cord it can be pulled away for private conversations.

Thinking about my course of action; a way I can check all the points Frank has requested and not let anyone in a house teeming with people know what I am up to is not in my normal range of expertise. I decide to go up to the bedroom to look through Pat's dresser drawers first. I know the four women I'll leave behind in the kitchen are oblivious of my movements. They are deep in conversation as they sit at the small kitchen table.

It is a lovely dark brown cherry wood drop-leaf with a hint of red in its shiny surface. I remember Nancy finding it in Michigan's UP at a garage sale in an all but abandoned mining town not far from Copper Harbor. She brought it down to Mary last year. Paul helped Nancy secure it and its four old chairs to the top of her Tempest with a fifty foot hank of clothes line. The result resembled a clip from the old 'Grapes of Wrath' movie. The table and chair set have been a perfect fit for the small kitchen. It stands by the window overlooking the flower garden. Mary loves it. She always has a vase of flowers setting on it; a reflection of those growing around her back patio. Today there are roses. White and yellow beauties someone has left in memory of Pat.

I catch myself and realize I am daydreaming, putting off that which must be done. I force my mind to leave the flowers and all they represent and think about the task ahead.

Determined, I move at a normal pace which is someplace next to a gallop. I have tried to keep up with Ed's long stride for too many years. Progress is slow as I move through friends and family, stopping to exchange words along the way. I try my best to look as if I have no destination; that time is of no importance. Upon accessing the stairs I start to climb, leaving the women at the kitchen table and those in the living and dining rooms well out of sight.

The big bedroom, which Mary, Pat, Ed and I had just built onto the house the year before is a dream of Mary's. She drew the plans for the addition which include the girl's room on the lower level, next to the nursery awaiting their yet-to-be-born brother. Mary trimmed the little room with a wallpaper border. A small train filled with happily waving animals and balloons seems to chug around the room. The crib is the one both girls used. In fact, Rachael at almost two agreed to relinquish it only because of her excitement over baby brother's arrival.

Mary and I had worked with Ed and Pat on the project. When it came time to put the shingles on the new bedroom's roof it was Mary and I who worked our way from the eaves to the ridge, nailing the overlapping pieces of asphalt in place. Ed at twenty-six had fallen two and a half stories when the wooden extension ladder he was standing on broke. He rode it part way down then fell onto a concrete patio just missing a 8 inch foundation bolt. Pat just couldn't fit the roofing job into his comfort zone, either. Little Laura watched her mother and me from a safe place on the sub flooring of the new second floor, carefully guarded by the two men as they refilled our nail aprons and returned an occasional dropped hammer.

I know my way around the bedroom, the one directly above the nursery, the master bedroom. After all, Mary and I wallpapered and painted its trim. A large room; the windows on three sides look out into the green of the big pines which surround the house. The king sized bed is a jumble of sheets and blankets attesting to the fact Mary has not been back to the room since she left with Pat in the wee hours of the morning. The sight of the unmade bed is almost too much for me as I think about the part it has played in my daughter's and son-in-law's life; the dreams and joys they had woven as they shared it. I have a strong urge to make the bed, yet fight it knowing it can be done after I finish this darn search. I have to report back to Tammia. She and Frank are waiting.

One large bay holds Mary's sewing things and the other has been turned into an at-home office for Pat. The papers on it are in orderly piles. His brief case is at one end, open, but empty. I wonder which client's case he had worked on last evening. Someone will have to gather it together and take it up to his law partner, Roger.

My gosh, I think. I bet no one has called Rog. I'll have to be sure to get that done when I am through here.

On the wall beyond the desk some four feet stands Pat's five drawer bureau. The search begins, drawer by drawer. I feel as if I am someone I have never met. I can't believe what I am doing. Even though Mary is my own daughter I feel I have no right to be pawing through her husband's things. Besides what will I tell her if she walks in the room and catches me in the act. I certainly can not divulge the real reason behind my actions. No other answer is available anywhere in my brain. All I can do is move faster and get out of here.

There is no way Pat could be using drugs, I am certain.

There have been times in my life when I have had the feeling someone is looking over my shoulder or following me as I walk down a street, placing their footsteps carefully in my own. This time I feel the presence of eyes, squinted narrowly, peering out from every crack and crevice in the large room. The light streaming in the windows hurt the eyes; they only squint more. The whole idea is so unreal I force myself not to look around into all the room's nooks and crannies. Instead I search thoroughly, intent on negating their stares and the charges against Pat.

Patrick, the wonderful man, so compassionate with those who sought his aid, so crazy about his girls and Mary; he could never touch anything which would jeopardize all he held so close to himself. The whole idea is beyond belief. That I am doing such a ridiculous search deepens my effort to prove it all wrong. Finally I softly close the last drawer.

Why am I trying to be so quiet? Why didn't I just shove the thing shut? Because no one is to know about all this drug stuff. I hate everything I am doing. But I know I'm lucky to have this chance to help Mary and Pat. So, why not enjoy it? Mary would if the circumstances were different.

Pat's closet reveals nothing other than the usual in his clothing. I prod every pocket.

My bedroom mission is accomplished. There are no drugs. Convinced there will be none where I look next I hurriedly leave the bedroom and its unmade bed.

I avoid moving by the kitchen club by exiting the house through the side door. It is actually the front door but the kitchen entry is more accessible to the drive and everyone uses it instead of the real thing. I stroll across the grass underneath the towering pine and spruce. The day is as it is, day after day. The seasons have changed on schedule and the living things are rejuvenating themselves for another cycle.

Violets are everywhere under foot. Ignoring the grass, they color its green a vivid purple. If by chance anyone glances out of a window they will see Mary's mother stroll over to the garden by the drive, reach down and pick a few daffodils, bring their yellow and white blossoms to her face and stare off into space smelling their fragrance. I endeavor to appear unhurried although well aware of the urgency I remember in Tammia's voice.

I deviously approach Pat's car from the side not visible from the kitchen window or any of the others, no matter what room. To prevent any sound I open the door slowly wondering why I'm being so cautious, as Pat's car door would never squeak, not his beloved Saab. I opt to not climb in the car, but reach under the seats from where I stand, stooped out of sight. I feel for whatever it is the drugs might be in.

While my hands search I think, I have no idea whether drugs come in bottles, boxes or bags. How am I to know if I find some or not?

Locating no boxes, bottles or bags I shelve my question and open the glove compartment. Everything is neatly in place; the operator's manual, the folder holding the insurance and title papers, the flash light, a pen and pencil, a free oil change card but nothing else. There are no drugs, just as I knew there wouldn't be. Nothing of a suspicious nature lurks in the car; under its seats or in the glove compartment. I stop for a moment and consider the trunk and hood. Other than the fact that I have no clue as how to open either I decide doing so would certainly blow my cover. I can just imagine what would happen if some guy came out of the back door and saw me with my head under the Saab's hood. What would I say? That I lost my lipstick? No, I don't think I want to get into that situation, so I call the second search done.

Dreading the third and final location I have been asked to look in I thread my way through the jumble of cars parked not only in the drive but helter-skelter across the lawn. I begin to access the house by way of the kitchen entry. Passing the swing set and sandbox teeming with children; cousins and friends, all oblivious to the solemnity of their parents they are thrilled to have each other to play with. Their immersion into this special day is wholehearted in every corner of the play area. Stopping long enough to say hello and give the two in the swings a couple of good pushes I enter the back door wondering how I'll work my way past those clustered in the small kitchen and on into the lavatory without being asked what I might need. The women are intent on waiting on me hand and foot.

Remembering the flowers in my hand I know how to pull off this next hunt. Once inside I move across to the sink, circumventing those seated at the small drop-leaf table as they oh and ah over the daffodils. I run water into a vase for the flowers and plunge their broken ends into the container, a white hob-nailed milk glass beauty my mother had enjoyed for so many years as she traveled about doing flower arrangement demonstrations. Moving some of the stems a bit to separate the blossoms and turning to set the vase on the table I ask if any of the coffee cups need refilling.

Lynn replies, "Anne, go rest. We are the ones who should be pouring your coffee."

Giving Lynn a hug I tell her I will try, but first I need to use the bathroom. I feel so clever. Turning away I walk through the Pullman-type laundry and into the lavatory. Closing the door I lean back against it and sigh. My snoop job is almost done and no one is even faintly aware what is going on. How can this be me? How can Pat be dead? Why is Mary's little house teeming with everyone and their uncle? Why in the world am I hiding in Mary's lavatory? I don't have any idea what time of the day it is. Heck, I don't even know what day of the month it is or day of the week. I don't even have time to search for the answers. I have to do this crazy drug search.

I look at the mirrored cabinet over the wash basin. It has no knob, but I know how to put my fingers underneath its edge and pull the little door open. I rummage through the medicine cabinet. The usual; some make up, hand cream, Neosporin, Band-Aids, tooth brushes, paste and more. Nothing to report to Frank. Reaching to flush the toilet I run water as if washing my hands, all to give credence to a bathroom visit. Somewhere inside myself I enjoy a rush of success and the hint of a giggle.

"Why do I feel relieved?" I ask myself. Did I think there would be drugs?

Starting back into the main part of the house I head for the telephone to call Tammia. I think, I never had a doubt, yet it would seem the minute the suggestion was made some part of me became frightened about what if it was all true. It is like this whole death thing. I was so certain Pat would stand next to my grave with Mary some day that the suggestion this isn't going to happen seems as impossible as the thought of Patrick using drugs. Tammia and Frank knew this. Frank has been through similar situations before. He understands what he has spared all of us.

I will never tell anyone but my Ed about this whole fiasco. And even then I will wait until long after all this has been laid to rest. I don't want to plant a seed of doubt in anyone's mind about the integrity of Patrick. This is my gift of love to him and his Mary. Heck, to his whole family and ours.

Tammia answers her phone, "Anne?"

"Yes, and I found nothing."

"Just what Frank suspected. He will be so relieved. Thank you Anne, for your help."

"No, Tammie, the thanks are to you and your kind husband. If it had been someone else I don't even want to think what Mary would be going though right now. You are both so wonderful, two of the kindest people I have ever known."

It doesn't surprise me a bit that Anne never tells anyone except Ed about the near calamity. She has far more guts than she gives herself credit for. She really might not have understood what a small town would do with such a juicy tidbit, but she felt the tip of the iceberg in her own mind and it scared her into never saying a word. The search remains Ed's and hers alone. None of the family, not even Mary, will ever know about the whole scare. As time goes by Anne sits back and relives the moment, laughing at the image of herself playing the detective and finding it difficult to accept the fact she had succeeded in pulling the whole thing off. The episode was pretty darn funny. The two of us are frequently at each other over all sorts of big and little ideas. But, that is my job, to keep her on the straight track.

Tammia did report back to Anne that her husband called the Lansing lab and it was discovered materials had been mistakenly switched. The careless worker was dismissed. Frank, the pathologist, could not accept such irresponsible procedure.

Mary with Laura 1981

A Baby, Casket and Full House

Believing in the Lord isn't always easy

In our forties and fifties Anne occasionally observed life with me much as one looks at the exterior of a home and wonders what it might contain. Thinking over the years of her marriage it seemed to Anne that Ed and she had always had nothing but the best. My feelings on the matter echoed hers. Even Ed's unexpected decision to volunteer for service during the Korean War in the early 50's proved beneficial despite the fact it caused them to leave their home outside of Ottawa Hills just beyond Toledo's western boundary. Also Ed's business as a painting contractor was left behind. But the resulting memories, unforgettable friendships and knowledge of another place and people were priceless.

Their contentment with life has been so overwhelming and unbelievable it causes Anne to ask herself, "Why us? Why do bad things always happen to the other person? I think I believe in the Lord, but how do I really know I do? I've never had to call upon Him."

Listening to her when she was in such a questioning mood brought Tracy and his question about the reality of Heaven back to me. The whole scenario has me shaking my head and wondering what it will take to get Anne to put things together in her head. Unlike her father she never seeks an answer from Ed or even me. I'm not sure what Ed would tell her. What he thinks is off limits to me. But my way would be to lay it all out right in front of her.

Later in the afternoon Paul and Nancy return from the doctor. With one look I know the news isn't good. The doctor confirmed the death of the fetus. My insides shrink as the feeling of inadequacy filters through my mind.

46

I want to shout out, "Listen You up There, can't You do something. Does this have to be happening right this very minute? How about some other time? Or better yet, how about canceling the whole idea?"

I try not to let my face broadcast my frantic feelings. I wonder if Nancy or Paul can see my sadness. Certainly my eyes which everyone tells me are so very blue must be disclosing my disappointment as I gather Nancy to me.

The news is shared only with the family. Another layer of sadness descends on us all. I fight a paralyzing numbness as I watch Ed, the most caring of men, receive the news. He is devastated. However he knows Paul and Nancy will get through the loss because they have each other.

What I struggle with is the thought that Nancy must carry her baby until full term. This is not understandable to me but I accept the fact there must be a very justifiable medical reason. Next she tells me on the way back from the doctor's she and Paul decided she will stay after the funeral until Mary's son is born. Paul will return to Sagola, over on the western border of Michigan's Upper Peninsula with their two children while she remains behind. Nancy wants to be with Mary to help her through the days ahead. I am overwhelmed her thoughts are about Mary rather than herself. To me it is the ultimate gift.

We are interrupted when Mary finds us to say, "I've been looking all over for Dad and you. It's time we run in town to talk to the undertaker and choose a casket. Our appointment was set for three."

Jim, the funeral director, has a large building attached to the funeral home and it is there he leads the three of us. The room and its contents are a surprise to me, appearing much like a large furniture display. I had never given a thought to why it stood where it did. The caskets are artfully arranged, one after another in what seems an endless display. I can't help but visualize a wonderful game of hide and seek happening here among the many coffins. There would, of course, have to be the rule that no one dare to climb up into one and quietly close the door. But I suspect there would be one who would do it anyway.

Silently the three of us gaze about as our host says, "Take your time. The prices are on the ends. Call me if you have questions. I'll be in my office in the back." With a smile he leaves us. Experience has taught him of the need for his customers to have time to think and talk with each other.

Wandering off on our own choice of direction Ed and I begin our search for Pat's coffin. We call out to Mary and each other as something seems a possibility. In the end it is an easy choice as the three of us converge on a highly polished oak version It reminds us of Pat's office and the oak furniture he had loved. Why that becomes our criteria I can't explain except that we knew Pat must have preferred oak when he chose his office décor. How does one choose a coffin? Other than being certain its interior dimensions are roomy enough for the body for which it is intended, what other criteria might there be? Probably, if one wants to be honest, it would be the price tag on the end of the casket.

The service is held in St. Matthews Catholic Church. People from Boyne City with its population of 3,500, its larger neighbor, Petoskey as well as Charlevoix, East Jordan and the surrounding area fill the pews beneath the sanctuary's high ceiling. Others from across the country are seated on the oak pews. Light filters in through the colorful long windows on each side. In the tradition of the denomination embraced by Pat and the rest of the Cassidy clan, Mary is followed by her family and her husband's as she walks behind the casket down the long center aisle. Those present are in awe of Mary's resilience, looking beautiful as a mother-to-be can. She bares within her Pat's and her son, who will be born two weeks later. The unfamiliar ceremony further entrenches the total unreality of the day for me. There is no doubt in my mind but what it is Ed who holds me together. He remains always at my side; big, sturdy and completely focused on me. I love him so much. Sometimes I wonder how it is possible to love someone more every day; but I do.

We move back into our own home. Like Mary's, our bed was waiting for us just as we left that night so long, long ago. Because I know it isn't possible so much can fit itself inside three days and nights it has to have happened way back when sometime. We aren't really back home as every day there is a reason to go back to Mary's. Slowly the extended families return to the demands of their own lives until only Nancy remains with Mary.

Our grandson, Patrick Charles Cassidy, III is born on schedule with Nancy, Lynn and Julie with Mary in the delivery room at Charlevoix Hospital. The birth is uneventful as Mary's favorite music plays. Champagne is shared after the event. The rest of the world, if interested, reads about the birth in the next day's issue of the Petoskey News Review.

Within days everything returns to a more normal routine as Nancy goes back to her home. Mary's friends pick up their lives where they dropped them. Their husbands make appointments with various insurance agents to up the amount of life insurance they carry. A sense of mortality has suddenly descended on many young, thirty old males in Charlevoix and Emmett counties.

A twenty four hour schedule of feeding, changing and burping is put in place at Mary's. She sets her pace because she knows she has no back up. Despite the appearance of normalcy I knows it isn't the same and never will be. Patrick is gone. His son, Patrick Charles III, grows sturdier each day, never to know his dad. His father won't sing him to sleep or read him stories. He won't set him in the cab of the old brown truck as he plows the winter snow or admonish him about the dangers of the nearby highway.

Rachael, the two year old will gradually fill her mind with other people and places. Only Laura at four will remember bits and pieces of him. Patrick's handsome face will be left for his son; as will the large brown eyes, lush, wavy dark hair and from some place deep inside, the humor of the Irish. The smile that lit the days of more people than he ever realized will spread across the face of his son, Patrick Charles III, who will simply come to be called Pat. When we look into his face Ed's and my hearts will turn over in memory of the time Mary's husband was like another son to us.

Every day becomes a challenge for Mary. Pat's insurance coverage is small; just $25,000. She decides it is to be invested and saved for the children's college education. She'll manage without it and she sets about doing just that. The Cassidy clan arrives one weekend to complete work on the house addition Mary and Pat had been in the midst of building when he died. Mary refuses any monetary help from her dad and me. Paul, Pat's younger brother, also an attorney, takes care of the will and law partnership. He also gives me a sizable check for Mary with the instructions that she is not to be told who it is from. At sixty two I am guarding other's secrets, something I've never done before. I'm not sure I am up to it all.

It is difficult for her and she struggles, uncomfortable with her fear of accidentally spilling the beans. I understand, for someone like Anne who has always told the truth withholding it seems the same as lying.

Mary is grateful for the generous gifts of friends and family; however she finds it a struggle to live in the world of a single parent. She refuses to leave her three small children to join the work force until they enter school. A budget is adopted with their Social Security income, public assistance and her savings. I help her take the children to county health clinics for their shots and shop for Wick approved products to extend food money. Occasionally I sit with the children so Mary can get off on her own with friends who never withdraw their support and love. I find sewing and gardening with Mary is fun for both of us. Probably best of all are the times she and our grandchildren come over for meals.

The church membership stands beside the little family. She has her brood in Sunday school every Sunday. I teach. Something I have done for years. My pre-school class is indicative of the times. In addition to Patrick, fatherless from birth, the class consist of five other youngsters. Melinda's estranged father has raped her and her sisters by crawling over the roof and into a second story window of their lock secured home. Simon and Joel both live in blended families because of divorce. Katie lives with her birth parents, the only example of what has always been to me the true American family and way of life.

It takes two years before I can drive to Petoskey without having tears roll down my checks. I don't share this with anyone, not even Ed and certainly not Mary. In my car I mourn my son-in-law silently, knowing he had driven the same route to and from work all his professional years, short as they were.

The Cassidy family never ceases to reach out to Mary and the children as the absence of their beloved Patrick becomes part of their lives. The children will be members of the Cassidy Clan forever.

Anne shares with me that at thirty three Mary, an unemployed widow with three children under five has no health insurance. This concerns her and Ed. They find this absolutely unbelievable. It tears at their hearts yet they respect their daughter's need to be independent. With forty two years of extraordinarily happy marriage, neither can comprehend that their exceptionally beautiful and gifted daughter and her children have been plunged overnight into such sadness and want. They begin to realize that much of what is theirs and truly precious has become the intangibles that exist between a married man and woman. There is no way they can be transferred to anyone else, even those loved as deeply as their children.

Ed and Anne decide what they can do for Mary is remain a solid anchor of love and safe harbor for her and the grandchildren. Mary will never doubt their love, hers as long as they live and beyond. Although Mary refuses monetary help from her parents they find other avenues to ease her way. It becomes their solace. When it comes to worrying about the future my way is to look in to the unknown more than Anne. She simply trusts that with the Good Lord's help she'll make the right turns in the road. As for me, conversely, having a road map in my hand, no matter how tattered and torn, is preferred. Somehow, it isn't that hard to lull me into getting things back the way they were, rather than looking into our tomorrows, it's the comfortable way to go. It never dawns on me that there might be more to this whole change than that which is foreseeable.

A Birth, Meeting and Coffee
The number of committee meetings held is questionable

It's a struggle for me to understand the need of 99% of the committee meetings women attend. As for those men hold, the same probably holds true. To spend two hours out of my life with seven other women discussing the merits of dark or powder blue napkins for a benefit luncheon absolutely turns me off. Who will ever know two colors have been so laboriously debated, anyway? But Anne's attitude is far more realistic. She limits herself to how many groups she will join and then devotes two hours of her time to the business on hand. It may involve napkin color or how to disperse money where it is most desperately needed. She views committee meetings as an essential part of the American way of life.

A few days after Pat's death Paul's expected call comes: their unborn infant is to be delivered. It tears me apart to leave Mary, but she will have it no other way. The fact Lynn, Julie and Corrine will be there for her, the new baby and the girls eases my concern. Ed wants me along. He believes Nancy will need me and that Mary will have all the care she might require. I have to admit he is probably right. There will be Nancy and Paul's two little ones to care for when their mother goes into the hospital.

The trip north and west is wonderful. Leaving the turmoil of the last days behind we drive through the semi-wilderness of Michigan's Upper Peninsula. The miles of panoramic views along Lake Michigan calm our souls. Everything is as it has always been. Every hill is in place. The forest reaches beyond our vision. Waves rhythmically splash the rocks of the shore to recede for yet another try. They have done so day and night for eons except for winters when their frozen selves lock them into silence. We are the strangers on this trip. We aren't who we were the last time the drive was made. We alone have changed. Near Escanaba Ed calls my attention to the sinking sun. The gray waters of the enormous lake disguise themselves in a shimmering gauze of pinks, oranges and crimsons. Out at the very edge of our world, the yellow-orange disc slips gently into the lake. I listen for crashing symbols and a drum roll but only silence surrounds the vanishing vision.

As a child it was easy for Anne to envision the sun falling through uncharted depths to emerge as her Dad's Gordon Setter would, sopping wet, to shake itself dry over in the place called China. Everyone told her it was on the other side of the earth. When she shares this childhood belief with me we admit we no longer believe everything other people have to say.

Two days later in Florence, Wisconsin, just across the state border from Michigan I am elected to stay behind to be with the grandchildren, Chris and Melissa, as Ed heads out to the hospital with their mother and father. He calls a few hours later to say all has gone well. Along with Nancy and Paul he held his tiny grandson briefly, a beautiful child in every way. He says the infant is named Edward Anthony. Ed's pleased he has a namesake, although he was only able to know him for those few minutes he cradled him in his arms. The Pastor from the Marquette Presbyterian Church, an old friend, was with Nancy, Paul and Ed during their time with the baby.

We leave the next day, feeling the tug to get back home. There is no reason to stay. Nancy is feeling well and Paul will see that she has a time to rest. A day or two later Nancy calls. She and Paul have decided to bring their tiny son back to Michigan for burial. They realize being in the ministry they might move often and no telling to where. Although surprised I admit that the idea makes a lot of sense.

"Will you call the pastor and ask him to join us for a short committal service at the grave side? And call the undertaker to take care of the burial. Could you have coffee and cookies at the house for a short get-together following the time at the cemetery?"

I respond with a 'yes' to all Nancy's requests wondering how often my daughter has made similar arrangements for others. It is obvious she has thought the whole scenario out.

Our pastor's unbelievable refusal to conduct the graveside service leaves me speechless. I can't believe his words. It is difficult to believe my ears.

"I'm sorry, Anne, but I have a Presbytery committee meeting at the Sault church that day, which I can't miss."

I think, I have heard joke after joke about the Presbyterians not being able to do a thing without first having a committee meeting, but this is as insane as it can get. What committee meeting is so urgent that it can't be skipped?

A call to the east side of the state to a good friend, the pastor at the Alpena Church brings a sincere and troubled refusal. "Oh, Anne, I'm so sorry. I can't believe Nancy has lost a child on top of everything else your family has gone through. But I have a funeral scheduled here in the church that very same time. There is no way I can break away and travel across the state to be with you. Please extend my deep regrets to Paul and Nancy. Have you thought about the Pastor John or Pastor Dottie at the Sault church?"

John and Dottie sound like a wonderful idea. John is pastor at the big red brick church on the canal in the Sault. The water that surges by is from Lake Superior and is used for the city's electric generating plant before it flows into Lake Huron. The canal's size and length exemplify the work and vision of man just as does the graceful five mile long bridge, which connects Michigan's upper and lower peninsulas. The church is historic in its deep red brick and high bell tower. The town is full of history as its business area borders the Sault and Canadian Locks which allow freighters to move from Lake Ontario into Lake Superior, bypassing the treacherous rapids of the natural waterway between the two Great Lakes.

John doesn't hesitate. "Dottie and I will certainly come down and be with Nancy and Paul. I do have a Presbytery meeting scheduled for one o'clock that day, but the members can just wait until I return."

The service, the day and the fellowship with John and Dottie are exactly what Nancy and Paul sought. The tiny Styrofoam coffin is placed into its grave site and the earth gently sifted on its top. Words are spoken and not one of those present can help but think 'what if'. In a matter of a few days our family has brought two of its sons to leave at this place. Neither had known the other, but they'll remain as family forever. It is all beyond belief for me as I stand hand-in-hand with Ed next to the grave listening to the spoken words and feel tears slipping down my cheeks. Unlike Ed, Paul and Nancy, I had not been able to see my grandson, to fit my finger in his little hand and wonder at the miracle of birth. I don't even know if he had hair. I hadn't thought to ask. I have no picture of him to hang in my mental gallery.

The time at the house afterwards is healing. Neither John nor Dottie seem to be in any rush to leave. This is hard for me to understand as I have come to realize the meeting John has left to be with Nancy and Paul must certainly be the same one my pastor could not miss. He must be sitting in one of the meeting rooms up at the Sault church waiting for John's return.

After everyone leaves, Ed and I find ourselves thinking over the day. Turning to my husband who I have shared my life with for so many years I can't resist the urge to say to him, "Once again God must be chuckling over His people."

"Why do you say that?"

"Because our pastor had to sit and wait for John to return. I'm certain John is the chair of the committee that met at the Sault church today."

"You're kidding?"

"No, honey, I speak the truth."

Ed grins. His grin always goes right to Anne's heart. Her eyes glow when it happens. Little Edward Anthony is buried in one of the plots near Pat's. As Clerk of Evangeline Township Anne purchased eight sites for the family when the need arose for Pat's burial. Eight were randomly chosen because of their four children. She thought that some time way down the road others would need burial after she and Ed, of course. Little did she dream a stillborn grandson would be interned so soon after his uncle's burial. None of us, myself included, entertained the thought, despite my tendency to think about a lot of 'what-ifs'.

As the one responsible for the care of the cemetery and the sale of its lots Anne selected a block of sites in the back by the fence and woods beyond. They are just east of the small Potter's Field section where the unknown of the area's past rest. Unrelated to the local population they may have been the lumberjacks who met with fatal accidents in the lumber camps or land seekers who didn't live long enough to marry and have a family. No records remain. The sites Anne chose are in a quiet and seldom visited part of the small burial ground at peace with the world. Someone else probably would have looked for something nearer the front. What Anne purchased is perfect.

She has a feeling of proprietorship about the cemetery. As the township clerk she had been responsible for having the grounds re-surveyed. The records she had received had been kept on index cards. In many instances scratched out names plus poor spelling and handwriting had made it almost impossible for her to know who was where within its boundaries. The survey helped. About the time the work was done one of the older trustees had returned from a trip to the southern part of Michigan with tales of horror. It had been his discovery that cemetery sites were selling there for as much as two hundred dollars. Evangeline Township's sites cost twenty-five.

The trustee then envisioned a scenario of a down-state entrepreneur arriving to buy up all the available lots in the township's cemetery to sell at two hundred or more dollars each. So taken in by their fellow trustee and neighbor of many years the Township Board deliberated long and hard on the problem. The resultant law raised the price of a cemetery site to fifty dollars. In addition only a resident of the township or a blood relative could buy a lot. Anne has never had an enterprising out-of-the-area person request even one site.

Honorary, Angels and Laughter
Time has little to do with healing

For Anne time has been less than friendly. To her daughter, Mary, every day disclosed itself the worst of enemies and yet the most precious thing in her life next to the love she held for her children. When it is considered, the phrase 'Time heals', is just another one of those bits of wisdom we allow to flow out of our mouths when we have no idea of the validity of the two words and all they promise. Time has little to do with healing when all things are considered. In matters of the physical body the expression can be very prophetic, but in matters of the heart and mind time can be the terrible protagonist. It can heap insult on injury, set traps, conjure situations and happenings beyond imagination

I am seated front and center, as the old army saying goes. Seventy-one year old Ed is on my right and six year old Pat, on my left. We are a sandwich and I am the filling. I am the peanut butter and jam that would be nothing but a useless mess if it weren't for the bread that contains it. Mary's casket is directly in front of us, within range of my grasp. All I'd have to do is lean forward from the hips and my fingers will touch the flowers which cover its lid. Every blossom might be from Mary's garden, the one I helped plant and she tended the last five years of her advancing cancer. Each soft color and unique shape the florist has thrust into the blanket reminds me of the days Mary and I, with the help of her children, my grandchildren, planted, watered and weeded. At three Pat knew a pansy from a petunia.

The church is sweltering. The day is a typical late August one that happens near the southern shores of the Great Lakes. The humidity is visible in the air, thick enough to all but form floating clouds overhead. The church is so packed folding chairs have been inserted to accommodate the guests. Dressed in their best I know there isn't one present who isn't wishing they were almost anyplace else. For those young enough a plunge into Lake Charlevoix's icy cold waters stands forth in their minds. It does in mine. I glance sideways past Pat to see Laura and Rachael in the pretty dresses they wore in their mother's marriage to Larry just two years ago. I had to do a bit of fancy letting out for them to fit for today, but no one will guess and they are thrilled. Like Pat, his sisters are intent on the events unfolding before them.

I wonder if they have any memory of their father's funeral a little over six years ago. Certainly Laura must. This time have they had this all figured out? Did the three of them understand their mother was dying these last months, these last weeks? Just a month ago when she threw such a fun filled birthday party for Laura in her backyard, did they all know somewhere in themselves that their laughing, fun mother who loved them so much wouldn't be with them the next time? It was a day complete with games, a piñata and cookout. And the month before it had been a picnic at the beach for Rachael and her friends, all in their swimsuits playing beach ball tag in the lake. Pat's sixth birthday party had been in May two months earlier with his pre-school friends and all the wrappings. Every cake was made and decorated by their mom. Every prize was wrapped and every decoration hung by Mary. I was there to help and as I think back I can remember no hint that any of us were admitting Mary wouldn't win her cancer battle. She was just too alive to be that sick.

I force myself back into the present. It is a trap to think about the past.

The minister drones on but all I hear is the rustling of my family around me. There are two long pews of us; all front and center. Larry, the children's step-father is up on the stage. There he stands with his red hair and beard, guitar at the ready. Mary's farewell service has been changed into a three-ring circus in my view and I am thankful the children are unaware of the failure their step dad is having in his effort to eulogize their mother. In the first happy year of their marriage Mary had bubbled over with the excitement of finding someone to love again and someone who would be the father the children were growing up without.

About three years ago she told me with tears in her eyes that Larry was an alcoholic, coming home after his day in the class room and isolating himself in their bedroom with his bottle. As her cancer had progressed he let her understand if anything happened to her he had no intention of raising her kids. In the end all Larry amounted to was his health insurance. I know this is an awful thing to sit here in church and think about someone. But it's true. I have absolutely no respect for the guy. All this is probably why I don't even want to look up and see him being such a Mr. Goodie-Good today.

I am keeping my sanity by simply tuning it all out. For me a memorial service should not be an old fashioned pulpit-call to those in attendance. Ed's face doesn't give a clue as to what his thoughts are. At least I don't have a necktie and button-down collar to contend with. I reach for his hand and the minute mine touches his he has it in his clasp.

I start counting off funerals. First it was Pat's in the big Catholic church on the other side of town. Then it was Edward Anthony's under the towering hemlock in Evangeline Township Cemetery. Next it was our Tom's in a contemporary Baptist church in Traverse City in July of last year. Like our Mary, her brother died of cancer. There was a period of time back then when Ed and I alternated days between the two. One day we would drive down to Munson Hospital to visit with Tom and the next over to Gaylord to be with Mary.

His was stomach cancer. The day I joined Sue Ellen in the waiting room during the unexpected surgery remains like a paused TV show to me. The earnest young physician, Sue Ellen's blanched face, the tiny cubicle set aside for just such doctor-patient words and the prognosis; six months to live. My gut response was to take care of my quiet, fun loving daughter-in-law to whom our Tom was her whole life. It was terrible as we waited in the cafeteria with our untouched soup. Neither of us shed a tear. We were too numb with the shock of the unexpected. It seemed forever until Tom was taken out of recovery and into a bedroom. After a few minutes I left them alone. Their time to be with each other had become measurable.

As I drove home that evening it hit me that Ed and I were loosing a son we loved so very much. As I let the road lead me it came to me that Ed and I had Tom so many more years than Sue Ellen. It didn't seem fair. We would always have the memories of his childhood, youth and adulthood to flood our minds with all he was while she could only cling to those few short years of their marriage. It struck me as a terrible lack of fairness and brought with it a feeling of longing to do something I never can. I want so much to give my memories to her; to make them hers also. To all our amazement Sue Ellen and Tom stretched his life out for a year; creating and fulfilling a want-to-do list to accomplish before he died.

The day of Tom's funeral his open casket was placed in an area of the sanctuary behind the rows of pews. Not like today's placement of Mary's directly in front of me. It was there his nieces and nephews, who he so adored, converged unnoticed except by me from across the large room. I was far enough away I couldn't hear their words as they huddled around Tom, but their actions told me all. One of the oldest, I don't recall whether it was Lewis, Chris or Laura, reached over and raised the soft white satin blanket which covered their uncle's lower half. They all took a turn to look. At that moment their questions were answered. They knew whether Tom was fully dressed, even if he had on shoes. As for me I still wonder.

My mind won't recall the exact day in 1986 when Mary's daily morning phone call included the words, "Mom, I just heard from the doctor's and I have breast cancer. I didn't want to worry you about it until the biopsy results came through."

I do remember having trouble assimilating the words biopsy and cancer.

But the worst came later when we had to stand by and support her decision not to have chemotherapy or radiation. She had no health insurance. She couldn't afford any treatment. Our daughter convinced herself she could win her battle through sheer will.

About a year ago she again caught me by complete surprise when she asked, "Mom, if it happens I don't win my battle with this cancer will you and Dad raise my children?"

It was the only time in her long struggle to live that either of us looked her cancer in the face. It was all so matter of fact; almost as if it had been rehearsed.

Without hesitation I heard my self respond, "Of course, honey. Your Dad and I would have it no other way."

But she wasn't through. There was another answer she needed.

"But you don't have enough room, Mother. You only have one bedroom."

My answer was waiting. Without a thought it came, "You remember how there are no windows on the north end of our house?"

"Yes."

"Well, because the land drops off fast at that point we can add a two story split-level addition with an upstairs gabled bedroom for Pat and a large bedroom for the girls below his. We would turn our little office on the main floor of our house into a split bath and lavatory. There would be a half flight of stairs for the kids to use to access it and the main house."

Mary saw the new wing immediately in her mind. "Oh, Mom, that would be perfect. How about a big bay on the back of the girls' room to let in plenty of daylight and sunshine?"

And that was the last time the subject was ever mentioned between the two of us.

When I asked Ed about having the children he never hesitated. Anything his Mary might want was his command. He adores his children. As for the three grandchildren I never mentioned anything about 'what-if' their mother should die. I am certain no one else did. With cancer it is the easy path to follow. Life for all intents remains the same day after day and there is no adjustment necessary. Routines, if disturbed are done so almost without notice. Occasionally there is a bump but rarely anything drastic.

For us the one exception is the time Mary fell in the grocery store and broke her pelvis. We were vacationing on the coast of Alabama when her call for our help arrived. We drove straight through, taking turns as the miles flew by the car windows. It was one of the times we stayed right at Mary's with the children.

Sitting here in this hot church I can still bring up the vision of the enormous X-ray Dr. Jim hung on his office wall at the hospital. It was Mary's skeleton completely covered from the very top of her cranium to her feet with tiny black polka-dot areas. That was three years after Pat's death. Mary's breast cancer had silently metastasized. Jim didn't have to tell Ed and me, his expression of pain told us our Mary was not making it.

Once again Anne decided to add another secret to her stash. The x-ray went home with her to be hidden away in the front hall coat closet. Mary was never to see it. It was Anne's gift to her daughter to allow her to cling to the hope of winning her battle. Ed concurred. That what they did was what should have been done remains a moot question. It proved to be a double edged sword as the secret also became a way for Ed and Anne to believe they were actually doing something to help their daughter's life be easier to live. It had been so hard for them to watch her struggle along without any treatments. Although the cancer won in the end, Mary did reach her goal of living until her son was ready to enter the first grade.

As I sit here now and count the days, it will be only a little over a week until the classroom doors swing open and Pat will be in Mr. Ladd's first grade room. And a month from tomorrow would have been my Mary's fortieth birthday. How will we all get through the day?

Normally I sit in the front right of the sanctuary under the huge stained glass window of Jesus in the Garden of Gethsemane. For years it has been my choice of pews. From there I can look up at the choir and find Ed in its back row. I love to watch him as he sings. Music is such a part of him and I am envious. Singing even Happy Birthday is beyond my abilities although the notes ring true somewhere within my head. But God chose to keep me humble and not grant me all the gifts I might wish for. Mine are with brush and pen. The days the sun streams in the window I can hardly keep my eyes off it. Today is one of those times. I know because I have sneaked a look to my right and marveled at the radiant picture of the Christ. There He is and all He represents. It is so difficult to believe in eternal life. But I have come to do so with no reservations although I don't have the faintest idea how God pulls it off. But then he got me here to start with. Not just me but every one in this room; heck, every living soul in our world is His doing.

If I believe all this why I am having a difficult time right now keeping the tears from rolling down my face?

I feel as if I am on the verge of sobbing aloud and I simply can't do that. Ed will crumble also if he hears me break down. Why am I doing this? It isn't like deciding I am hungry and choosing to make myself a sandwich and pour a glass of milk. I haven't suddenly said, 'I'd better cry.' I suppose it is because I was doing all that memory about Mary and Tom the last five years. But why tears? What am I sad about? It can't be because neither of them are here with us anymore.

I understand they are living the ultimate life and in God's time we will all be together in love once again.

So, are my tears for her, for me, for the children, for all of us who loved her so very much or are they just because I am bone tired, hot and wanting to be home, away from all this tradition of saying goodbye? One thing for certain, that old cliché, "Go ahead and have a good cry; get it out of your system." Is a bunch of bee's wax. There are just some things one never gets out of one's system and the death of a child is one huge one.

Anne doesn't yet realize how right she is on this one. As the years go by there will always be those things which trip the faucet and the tears will well up in her eyes. This is especially true on Sunday mornings as she sits beneath the beautiful stained glass window; or when someone mentions Mary or Tom or the grandchildren's father. She will never be able to control the response of tears. She will come to attribute them to her passionate approach to living and cherish them, thankful she is so full of emotion and love for those who walk with her through life, even the strangers she will never call by name. The tears cease to bother her, in fact she will often find herself laughing as they flow as she accepts the fact that happiness is all about loving and you can't love without finding pain.

The century old brick church is packed to the gills. This August heat is unbearable. The windows are open in lieu of air conditioning. I pray the powers to be are about to bring this service to its end. We all need to get out of here. At least it will be cooler up at the house after the burial for those who want to visit with the family. Cold drinks, salads and desserts will be waiting in the big yard with its maple, apple trees and flower gardens, all in their end of summer regalia.

I turn my attention to the minister as he stands to close the service. I feel so good that I thought of asking him to have Mary's close friends, classmates from high school and college, be designated as honorary pallbearers. They are the reunion group Mary had lunch with two weeks ago during the unexplainable surge of wellness she felt just before she lapsed into a ten day coma and death released her. All have been so faithful to Ed and me as well as the children throughout Mary's long struggle with cancer. Each is a very special person. As they stand it seems unbelievable there can be ten such beautiful young women in one place. After all, Boyne City isn't Hollywood. All are dressed in lovely summer gowns and wearing high heeled shoes in their effort to look their best at Mary's farewell. I think of Charlie's Angels and know these are Mary's. They have been seated to our far left.

As Ed stands to leave he leans toward me and comments, "What a gorgeous group of women. And our Mary was as beautiful as any of them."

The attendees are directed to exit the sanctuary row by row. With Ed, I find myself moving toward the front entry with our grandchildren. Everyone gathers on the grass, sidewalk and street below the long flight of eleven steps, descending from the dark oak doors which are fastened open, one to each side of the wide entry. The sun beats on heads and backs. I long for the shade of a tree.

What happens next seems unbelievable. The entourage of casket and pallbearers begins to appear as they approach the narthex doors. The wide church entrance allows a full view of those emerging.

I lean toward Ed and whisper, "I can't believe this. Don't they understand the word 'honorary'? Why in the world are the girls carrying that heavy casket down those darn steep steps? My Lord, if one of them stumbles she'll kill herself. And they've left the flowers on the top. What if the whole mass of them slide down and off the casket? Will they all walk on them? Will they trip?"

Ed answers quietly, "It's Ok, Snorkie. The flowers are fastened on somehow. Look at the girls' faces, Anne. They are all concentrating."

He's right, as usual, I have to admit, glancing from one face to another. Each is obviously holding on with all her strength to the highly polished wooden casket and its blanket of flowers which are miraculously staying in place; each woman looks as if she is part of a very special act. They are proud and pleased to be doing this for their friend. Their love is the greatest tribute I could want for our Mary. I squeeze Ed's hand saying I understand what he sees and how right he is. I owe this wonderful man of mine so much. How can I be so lucky to call him mine?

A voice reaches our ears from directly behind us.

It is Jeff's, Mary's dear friend, as he mumbles, "I can just hear Mary saying, "For Christ's sake, don't drop me now."' His wife, Julie, a beautiful blond, is one of the women carrying the coffin.

Laughter begins somewhere inside of me. It is rushing through every nook and cranny of my being. Suddenly the day becomes Mary's day and she is here with me. Jeff is right, Mary would be telling her friends how to carry her. She would be laughing and making the whole occasion a time of love and joy.

Somehow Jeff's words bring the memory of my grandfather to my side; his bigness and his eyes twinkling with Irish humor and love. It is in this memory of him I can appreciate the true glory of the day. My mind remembers the warmth of his large hand as it held my small one while he walked me through his apple orchard in search of morels. I was three or four, maybe even five; it was so long ago. I don't understand why he should return to me at this moment. Now it is my Ed who stands big, strong and wonderful beside me. It is his love and smile, which smooth my way today. It is his hand that firmly holds mine. I am ready for whatever lies ahead.

No matter how frequently Anne's thoughts return to the day it will be to remember Mary's friends descending the church steps and Jeff's astute remark.
She'll turn to Ed and ask, "Remember Mary's funeral and Jeff?"
Ed will grin and reply, "Who could forget? That was a wonderful day."

A Will, Probate and Paul

Government freebees #101

At the gathering on the farm after the service it is as if everyone is reluctant to see the day close, for as long as they stay Mary is with them. They watch Ed and Anne with Mary's children and marvel at the peace, which seems to surround them. The bonding is already in place. Their father's sudden and totally unexpected death thrust a sense of maturity on Laura and Rachael. They have the resilience to handle this replay. As for Pat, Ed is the only father he has ever known, even though he calls him Grandfather. Somehow he has absorbed his sister's quiet acceptance of his mother's death. I believe Mary prepared her children for this day by surrounding them with her love and attention during their early childhood. Added to this was her dedication to making her Faith part of their lives. When she was unable to take them to Sunday School Mary asked Larry or Anne to do so. Perhaps it is simpler for a child to accept the concept of a life after death than for so many adults.

It is hot in our back yard, although a slight breeze is finding its way to us over the tree covered hills and the lake beyond. The old apple trees are pruned into strange twisted shapes that nature never intended. This practice kept the apples in easy reach of the harvesters who used to work the orchard. Our place once was a large fruit orchard. I've counted over two dozen varieties of apples, even the sweet snow apples of my youth which are seldom seen anymore. They aren't in the fruit markets as they don't have the shelf life required. I suspect they have silently become an endangered species.

Today the escapees from the church service have pulled the folding chairs over under the trees to enjoy their shade. Normally a large expanse of grass as far as the edge of the fields, the yard looks rather strange today with clusters of people here and there. The only tree that has escaped a conclave beneath its branches is the swing tree. The kids have taken it over. Those who can't swing are climbing its gnarled limbs to reach the yet green red delicious apples. I don't see a mother objecting despite the 'best' clothes.

The less hardy guests are inside wandering about. Most are filling plates at the spread my friends from the church have prepared and are busily setting out. Our friends and family search for an unoccupied place to sit or stand and visit with each other. I feel so blessed that they are all here to say their goodbyes. A few visit with the grandchildren, but most shy away from the three. They have long ago lost the ability to converse with a child.

Neither Ed nor I have sat down with the kids and involved them in a discussion about what has happened. Somehow I sense they are at peace with their mother's death. I can find nothing left to say. None of them have asked what is to happen to them. They have figured it all out. Ed and I will fill the gap as we have been doing off and on over the past few years. Whenever Mary had to spend a few days in the hospital we either stayed at her place or they were here with us. The children do not expect anything to change.

That evening after the guests and Larry leave the children's uncle, Paul Cassidy saunters on to the back deck to talk with Ed and me. A superb attorney and concerned man he is six foot five, every inch in charge of whatever situation he finds himself. I have listened to Mary talk about his achievements and what a caregiver he is for his extended family. It turns out it is just such a concern he has on his mind as we sit beneath the maple tree we built our deck around. With our cold iced teas we are peacefully watching the western sky turn color as the sun prepares to set.

Paul quietly asks, "Do you have Mary's will? I would like to take care of it for you." Mary's will had never entered my mind; nor Ed's, for that matter. Glancing at each other we shake our heads. "She never brought the subject up to me," Ed says.

As Paul looks my way all I can do is admit I know nothing about one either. Surprised about our admissions Paul asks to use the phone. He will contact Larry.

We can hear Paul's side of the conversation through the open window. It sounds as if Larry knows of a will.

Paul returns to the deck and says, "Larry will be over with it tomorrow morning before we have to leave for home." Then, leaning forward he asks, "Are you certain you want the responsibility of the children? Our side of the family has no problem with your doing this, but I want you to know Rhonda and I will take them and raise them as our own if you ever decide the children are more than you can manage."

For a moment I felt sheer panic. What if the Cassidys don't think Ed and I are the ones to have the children? I have worried since Mary asked me if Ed and I would be her children's parents that the Cassidys might not be willing. I believe I would just curl up and die if the three were taken almost three hundred miles away. But Paul isn't saying that at all. He is saying it is OK for them to stay with Ed and me. It is only if we want to give them up that they would step in. I feel my breathing return to normal. I look at Paul and his expression doesn't waiver. He is completely unaware of the fright I have allowed myself to suffer.

Ed is answering, "We have talked this over, Paul. There is no other way we want it than to have the children with us. It is what Mary asked and what we promised. We thank you for your generous offer and will keep it in mind if the day should ever arrive we will need assistance. You and Rhonda would be great and we will call."

"That's good. But remember, anytime I can help I will be just a phone call away. One other thing; you will have to attend a probate hearing. I will come up and be with you on that day."

At this moment I feel that once again someone else is in charge. Someone else is holding our hand and leading the way. I feel safe. I feel cared for.

The following day Larry brings over Mary's will. It is in a number ten business envelope.

When I ask him to come in he defers, saying, "Can't, Anne, I have to get right back. If there are any further questions I'll be home this evening."

I find Paul and Ed and hand them the envelope. Upon opening it Paul pulls out five torn—off yellow lined sheets from a legal pad. Written in pencil various things Mary owned are listed and to whom they should be given. No mention is made of any money or the home. Strangest of all, the will is unsigned.

Paul finds the whole thing unbelievable, especially since it is in Larry's handwriting. We learn later that he calls Larry that evening. Larry doesn't budge; he claims the will is what Mary asked him to write for her. At this point Paul suggests to us that he pursue the whole matter and be allowed to settle Mary's estate on behalf of her children. We are both relieved not to have to spend time with the whole thing and agree to Paul's offer.

It takes over two years, but eventually the home sells and the proceeds are placed in a trust for the kids. Deciding not to adopt the children for the simple reason they believe they should keep their father's surname, Anne and Ed go through the probate system. They are appointed conservators and guardians of the three minors. Once again the Lord reaches down to help and places the five in the hands of the Probate Judge of Otsego County. Within his court rooms Ed and Anne learn a side of living in the

United States that most of its citizens remain unaware of. It will never enter their lives. For the two grandparents it is an adventure and an education to observe first hand how the system can work or not work according to who is administrating it.

They also learn that much of the help available remains unknown to the 'would be' recipients unless they are street-wise about government handouts. Since neither of the grandparents have ever had a course entitled 'Government Freebees #101' they'll pay their own way through ignorance. Neither are savvy enough to know what questions to ask. Admittedly Anne gets no help although supposedly it should be forthcoming, There is no advance knowledge on the subject of government assistance. For Anne and Ed it will be live and learn the hard way in the years yet to come; climaxing on Laura's eighteenth birthday and the letter that arrives.

Construction, Drifts and Toes

Shopping seems a waste of time

Shopping is an absolute waste of time to Anne. She'll procrastinate as long as possible, probably because of her Depression days. She's inclined to blame her Scot-Irish blood, but Anne really doesn't enjoy spending money just on a whim. To go off to spend a day with a group of women in a town sixty five miles away to wander through shops, holds as much enticement as jumping into the cold waters of Lake Charlevoix in April. She shops for groceries once a week with the exception of fresh items. As for clothing, only when something shrinks or becomes threadbare. Christmas shopping is done in one fell swoop.

"Life begins at forty" is an expression that has been around for quite some time. What wit coined it is not historically recorded, but it could have been a birthday card company's designer.

For Ed and me it is different. The saying needs to be altered slightly to read, "Life begins again at 68 and 71". No, we weren't 'born again' at these ages. Rather life truly flips back in time to the year we were 33 and 36 and our children were ten, eight, five and three; a span of thirty five years. Here we are in late August of 1991 reaching out to gather to ourselves three young children. We are to become a family of five for the rest of our earthly days. This means shoving our 'golden years' forward to a time when we can once again retire and say, "What are we going to do with all this time we have on our hands?"

What neither Ed nor Anne perceives is that retirement will not fit itself back into their lifetimes. Anyway, their retirement funds will vanish. Patrick at six, Rachael at eight and Laura at ten and their grandparents will discover in each other the way to keep the past and weave it into the future. The children's parents, Mary and Pat, will always be part of this new family. Ed and Anne through remembering, will seek advice in the raising of this second family. For Anne it will always be, What would Mary do about this? This should bother me, as normally she talks things over with me, but the answers she'll seek must be those Mary can give. Mine would never be nearly as on target.

The fun begins right after the burial in the township cemetery. Mary's body was laid next to her young husband's back by the fence and its dense woods beyond. I won't return to the area under the towering hemlock very often. To do so brings me too close to what was and might have been if I allow myself to dwell on such an imaginary world.

When we get back to the house it and the yard are full of family and friends unwinding from the long difficult day. My friends from the church set out the food and tidy things up in the late afternoon. It is after they are gone and only near family collapses on the deck or in the house that I finally realize I am tired. I need to kick my heels off.

The children have been staying with us the last days of Mary's life as she lay in a coma at Munson Hospital. Cared for during the days by Mary's wonderful friends, they were returned at night to be put to bed. Their bedroom is a temporary place in the small 10 x 12 basement area next to the furnace room. Sleeping bags are spread on the carpeted floor, cardboard boxes and brown paper sacks of clothes dot the perimeter. It is chaotic. To my eyes it is a scene from Hell.

The rest of the house is large. Built as our retirement home it has only one bedroom and bath plus a tiny catch-all office room. True to her goal Mary has stayed with her little family until the week before school is to open. It never entered my head to begin the addition. It seemed too preemptive, as if Mary was about to die soon. And of course I couldn't accept such a thought even though somewhere inside myself I must have recognized the reality of it all.

The tiny windowless basement room the children are using is carpeted. Opening directly into the stair well that leads to the main floor and its balcony above it is nothing but a pit in my mind. I can't stand to admit it is all I can offer the children for a place to sleep. And then there are the Cassidy's; Grandmother and all the uncles, aunts and cousins. Will they accept such accommodations or will they change their minds and ask to raise the children.

These thoughts goad me to devote every possible minute on working drawings for the addition Mary and I had created in our discussion the year before.

Two weeks after the funeral I complete the plans for the addition, have them blueprinted and call our builder, Ron. He is back with a bid in a couple of days. Ed talks to the bank. A construction loan is floated. Ground is broken. A goal of having the children out of the basement and in their own rooms is set for before Christmas. Ron, like the whole town, steps forward to do all he can to help us with our new family. I relax about the basement dungeon, its chaotic appearance and absolute lack of the faintest aesthetic value.

All this is going on when I suddenly face the need of having the three children ready for school. It hits me two days after the funeral just a couple of hours after I start to work on plans for the addition. Something jolts my brain into realizing I have a little more than a week to do it. Shopping proves to be fun this time; good for everyone. It is a positive embracing of the future. Lunch boxes, pencils, binders, socks, underwear, hair clips, jackets and all the other gear required are located and purchased. Mary and I had both been oblivious to the advent of school as we passed through her last days. When I see the magic first day of school on the calendar it hit me that Mary had indeed given her children over to her dad and me. Our daughter had never mentioned their return to school or their needs. I glow with the thought that Mary knew her children would be loved and cared for. As I stand in the kitchen looking at the calendar and its picture of a field full of daisies and goldenrod tears of gratitude for such a gift overwhelm me. They fill my eyes, running over my cheeks. I slowly draw a circle around the first day of school.

Mary's birthday, September 23, one month after her funeral, is allowed to slip by. I am uncertain what to do about it, deciding to tackle that question the next year. Halloween becomes a different story. All the stops are let out full blast. I gather together costumes; buy pumpkins for the kids to carve and special they-can't-cut-little-fingers knives. We stuff a scarecrow for the front porch, attend school parades and go trick or treating. Ed is in on it all, even donning a costume with me for the night.

Between Thanksgiving and Christmas the addition becomes habitable and the movers are called. Excitement runs high. Our house sits on top of a Michigan hill about two miles outside of Boyne City. Our land, was once a beautiful cherry and apple orchard that seduced Ed into buying it. Hundreds of trees were wearing bridal finery of white blossoms on a beautiful May day when he first looked out across the orchard. The bluebirds and honey bees were ecstatic. The hillside became my husband's second love. From the top where he built our home the view is tremendous. He swears on clear, below zero winter days he can see straight across Little Traverse Bay, beyond the hills of Harbor Springs, all the way to the North Pole. On the not so clear days we can get hit with a blast of winter weather that will stack snow in huge drifts against any standing object. This habit of wintry blasts is the theory behind snow fencing. Set back from a road or driveway some ten or more feet the wired length of orange sticks will fool the wind into dropping its load of snow before it can dump it where cars need to drive.

On such a day, blustery and cold with a grey sky threatening more snow the moving van arrives in the late afternoon. Looking through the windows all five of us watch as it climbs the curvy, hilly road up to the house. We see it slip in the thick wet December snow. The truck comes to a stop sideways across the narrow road about halfway up to our house.

Ed bundles up and struggles down through the knee deep snow as it clutches his legs with each forward step. He intends to help shovel around the big tires and loosen the snow's hold on the heavy truck. After a period of futile digging he confers with the driver and they decide to call Frank's Wrecker Service. By this time neighbors, Bob and Mark, are on the scene with their shovels. With the wrecker and a concentrated effort by all, the moving-van is jockeyed back onto the road. Everyone stands exhausted; leaning on their shovels as the truck slowly works its way up to the house. Three excited children watch as their earthly possessions are unloaded and carried inside.

Frank will mention the day to Ed and Anne whenever they meet in the years ahead. The entire town relishes whatever opportunity arises which offers a chance for them to help the grandparents and their grandchildren. They view the whole scenario as a burden for Ed and Anne, not the miraculous gift it becomes.

Ed and I decide to move our maple drop-leaf dining room table and chairs into the attic to store them. We bought the set in Chicago on our way back home after World War II. It was part of our going-into-housekeeping blow out. Mary's big round old oak table, which had been Ed's family's when he was growing up, is set in its place. Its old oak chairs are grouped around it ready for meals, studies or games. The table will become the center of family life for the years ahead. The sideboard, also brought off the truck, joins the table in the room as the hutch heads to storage with the dining room set. It was Grandmother T's when Ed was little.

With the beds set up and the dressers in place the children dive into unpacking boxes. It becomes Christmas or birthdays as forgotten toys are rediscovered. Once the last pieces of wadded up newspaper and packing boxes are thrown out a deep peace and contentment settles in. I'm able to forget the basement days as if they never happened. I am quite certain I'm the only one who can close her eyes and see that impossible mess in bright, full color.

It is in February Pat comes to me to tell me his toes hurt. "I've been curling them under, Gram, but that isn't working any more."

Horrified I bend over and take off a shoe and sock to see his red toes. "Oh, my gosh, Pat, I completely forgot to buy you new shoes when we went school shopping. I am so used to wearing my shoes for five or six or more years I forgot your feet are growing. I wonder if Laura and Rachael are having the same problem."

"They are."

After school the kids and I pile into the car and drive to Petoskey's Payless Shoe Store to outfit them in new shoes. It is important to me to do this as rapidly as possible. I don't want anyone to ever know how cruel I've been; how negligent a grandmother. When we discover Pat needs shoes two sizes longer than those he has been wearing I feel even more horrible. Both girls need longer sizes also. Urging the three to choose two pair, one for everyday and one for Sunday School and special times I watch them really delve into the selection process with all their attention. I'm not in on what is 'in', being part of the Buster Brown era. Back then a child's foot was measured by a salesperson who then brought out boxes of the right size to show the mother and her child. Today's self-help procedure seems strange to me. Considering how important a person's feet are all their life, it is downright awful to learn the shoe world has sunk to profit oriented self-service.

But then, this is why I am in this particular store and not in a more upbeat one downtown or on Lake Street. What we buy here fits my pocket book. Neither Ed nor I are eligible for employment any more which leaves us only our Social Security Insurance income along with that of the children's. We aren't anxious to dip into our retirement funds as they are supposed to continue earning interest until the day comes we truly retire.

The way the kids are growing I don't have to be concerned about how long a pair of shoes will last. The shoes will become too short before they can possibly fall apart. In light of our life style change I believe Ed and I will be buying our shoes here also.

Free to pull down one box after another the three children compare information and advice. I feel invisible. They obviously can do this by themselves. No grandmother is required.

Finding something they like they turn to ask, "Gram, feel this one. Do you think it is the right length?" It is never, "Do you like this style or is this what you think I should get?" They seem to know what it is they should consider.

I relearn a lesson. Children are capable of far more than we care to give them credit for. The grandchildren are amazingly mature in their approach to the need for new shoes. They are all business, yet alert to what it is they think is 'cool'. Their selections have to be comfortable and a good buy, but at the same time look exactly right. They are conscious of price and when in doubt turn to ask, "Gram, is this too much? Do you think it's kind of pricy?"

It's a whole new adventure for me. I am having a great time. I wish I had waited to bring Ed along on this shopping trip, I think. He'd be amazed at these three. I am as excited as the kids are over the six boxes of new shoes plus the three pair of slippers.

As a non-shopper Anne fails to consider the legion of similar shopping sprees which lay ahead. They'll go on and on until Pat's feet require size fourteen shoes. These will not be available at any area store, only seventy miles to the south in Traverse City or on line. Either place, the price tag will be staggering. The frivolity of paying professional basketball players millions of dollars comes into focus for both of us. Gosh, just check out their shoe sizes. Those big guys need what they make just to keep their feet encased.

Laura, Patrick and Rachael on Mackinac Island—1991

Ed, Goals and Legalese

There are no excuses for questions not asked

Both Anne and Ed fail to ask the questions they should when they begin to untie the governmental red-tape in which their three orphaned grandchildren are wrapped in on their arrival at their home. There's nothing for me to do but stand back and refrain from shaking my finger under Anne's and Ed's noses because their actions are understandable. They are handicapped by a complete lack of experience in governmental assistance, having always considered themselves able bodied and minded. Hardly needful of outside help, certainly not public welfare they are completely out of the loop as to its availability. Unless one has grown up during the Great Depression years it is next to impossible to understand the lasting affect it has had on the citizens of this country. To survive you learned to do for yourself and your neighbor. This philosophy became Ed's and Anne's.

The day will come when Anne will understand raising the grandchildren was like Pin-the-Tail-on-the-Donkey, the ancient birthday party game. One is blindfolded and then instructed to pin a tail on a picture of a donkey. The part about first being blindfolded and then for good measure spun around just short of becoming so dizzy falling over is a possibility, is where the US government fits in especially well.

In the midst of our suddenly unbelievable schedule Ed and I eke out the time to establish some goals for raising the three grandchildren. This may sound like an office think-tank sort of situation and it isn't at all. It happens spontaneously as the two of us lie together in how-can-all-this-really-be-happening stupor at the end of the second day after the funeral. This is unusual

72

for us, this planning. Neither of us have been planners; we definitely lean toward the spontaneous. There was the time the old cherry orchard two miles northeast of town seduced Ed with its spring bridal finery and bird convention. Two months later, after a number of trips to Battle Creek to confront its owner, Ed bought the orchard and its farm house. The old man had vacillated in his drunken stupor while his wife refused to sell. The last trip to their home had been at eleven o'clock one night in April a year after Ed's first glimpse of the farm. Back home at three a.m. Ed told me he was certain there had been a beating to produce the wife's agreement. Her name was on the contract but she was nowhere to be seen.

The farm has been our home ever since. We lived in the old farmhouse which came complete with a dairy barn, a 'four-holer' outdoor biffy, hand pump on a white cast iron sink in the kitchen and knob and tube wiring until we decided a five bedroom home was too large for the two of us. The house was sold, but not the farm. A smaller retirement home was built up beyond the cherry and apple orchards on the top of the rise behind the old house. We live there now. As for the orchard—well, that is a story to be told another day.

With our own four children parenting was a different matter. It was all new and wonderful. As first time parents it was awesome to just watch parenthood unfold. Like our peers we trusted our abilities to be there when we might be needed and to do what was required. We sorted through our own childhoods to salvage those things our parents had done, which seemed in retrospect good and discarded those things which didn't appear all that wise. Dr. Spock was around, but basically I ignored him.

Today there are great books on parenting. There is even a monthly publication or two given over to the subject, but it takes time to read them and I feel I don't have the time. I suspect they are aiming their self-help ideas at the young, first time moms and dads, not a couple of retirees in their seventies. One daily news column devotes itself to grand parenting, but not on the level of a permanent parenting situation.

Ed's wonderful younger brother, John sends me information about an annual contest that is underway. He thinks if I write our story of having the grandchildren to raise that we'll walk off with the prize. I would love to do it for him, but writing takes hours. There is no such thing as extra hours in this household these days. I file the idea away thinking maybe someday, John, after this episode in my life is finished I'll sit down and write of it. The idea of writing a memoir is stuffed into some corner of my mind, that God conceived computer. I don't do the calculations and fail to realize longevity is not infinity. Death intercedes.

But this time it's different. The three Cassidy children aren't ours. They are just on loan; a gift given to Ed and me in love and trust by our daughter. Lying beside each other we know there is no way we'll deny the trust or disappoint the love. We gaze down an unmapped road and set about making plans for the future.

I turn toward Ed and say, "Honey, this time around I am going to do a few things differently. One of the rules is going to be that there will absolutely be no fighting. What do you think?"

"Sounds great if you think you can pull it off."

"I'm determined. It was the only part of raising the children that I hated. At the time I didn't see it as my fault. Heck, everyone's kids got into it. It was just considered part of growing up. But now I believe that is wrong. If kids are taught alternative routes to choose, peaceful ways to solve problems, then I believe they will be able to do that throughout their lives. Maybe we could have peace in our world."

"Makes sense, Hon. We'll give it a try."

I lie on the bed beside Ed staring at the ceiling thinking about what we have just said. I wonder if I am full of it or if I really can do a better job than the first time around. Not that our own kids aren't the best, but somehow I think I should have made it easier for them. A humble feeling has descended on me; this discovery that I am going to have another go around in raising a family. Why me? How can I be so blessed? My gaze penetrates the ceiling and the roof and on up through the sky to wherever the Source of Life dwells. I send my gratitude on its way.

Turning back to Ed I find him looking at me. "What are you thinking, Snorkie? You are so quiet."

"I am feeling special. Why among all the people we know have you and I been given this opportunity to enjoy a second family?"

"I know. It's hard to believe; one of those things you are always telling me has no answers. I guess the thing we are to do is accept it as a gift. That's all we can do."

Then another idea enters my head.

"I think in this day and age, unlike the situation when our kids were growing up, life has become more and more global. There is a blending that is happening world wide. It began in our country three hundred years ago when people from nations from around the globe traveled to live together in America. We are on our way to becoming one nation world wide, not just here in the United States. It is going to be part of our grandchildren's lives. We need to figure out ways to travel with them so they can feel at home with others wherever they might go."

'Well, you know me, Snork. There is nothing I love more than traveling. I'm all for it. Just let me know when and where and I will make the arrangements; after all that has been my life's work."

I wonder how we'll manage this goal. Ed and I had visited my cousin, Jamie, in Ireland the year before Pat's death. Next we squeezed in a trip to Europe with our wonderful friend, Grace before Mary broke her pelvis. None of us had a surplus of money so we rented a small car and drove from one youth hostel to another across France, Germany, Austria, Switzerland and Italy. It was October and the young folk who would have normally filled the hostels were back in college. We had the facilities almost to ourselves, three oldies. We returned with our bags on overload, filled with enough adventures to fill a book and a lifetime of memories of the people we had met. But travel takes money and that is the one thing I believe we will be short of this time around. I think of that old adage, 'Where there is a will there's a way'. Dad was forever telling me, "If you want something bad enough to work hard for it it'll be yours.

The one thing Ed and I took for granted for our own four children was they would be college educated as our parents had done for us. Well, almost. In my case Ed took over after he married me during WWII and saw that I finished my last two years of college. He would have it no other way and bragged to those we came to know out in Fresno, California where he was stationed, that he had a kid in college. I knew Ed was meant to be mine the first time I looked in his direction my freshman year at Ohio State. I was eighteen. It was less than two years later I watched him slip a wedding ring on my finger in a small white Congregational church in Sylvania, Ohio, the town from which my brother and I graduated from high school, following in our Dad's footsteps of some twenty years before. I was twenty. The war capsulated time for everyone in 1941. It was the catalyst to many an early marriage. Ed will still laughingly declare he put a child through college as soon as he was married.

So, it is a foregone conclusion that the tradition of college educations is to be there for the grandchildren. As appointed conservators of the children's estate Ed and I are permitted to determine how their income will be spent. Of course, the Court System will be looking over our shoulders every step of the way, not 'holding our hands'. To be certain the money will be available for their college education the sixty thousand dollars from Mary's insurance is set aside in secure investments to grow in value and to be split three ways for Laura, Rachael and Pat.

The only reason Ed is permitted to invest the money is because in the legal process of becoming the kids' conservators and guardians he learns insurance rewards are not subject to probate. Please don't ask why. I have no idea but felt the fewer questions asked was by far the best road to follow. Although in retrospect I learn there were some for which Ed and I should have sought answers to.

We both love our country and its form of government but we admit there are times when one has to wonder why we and our fellow men don't have better choices on the ballots. Or have a more direct control over who our leaders choose as cabinet members and advisors; so often placing the welfare of our country in their appointee's hands. Some are great; others are disastrous failures. The nation's history attests to this.

Both of us graduated from college debt free, but our grandchildren will leave college with burdens of thousands of dollars owed. What a tragic way to smother the enthusiasm and drive of young adults. How can they dream the American dream of a better tomorrow? It is the very thing which brought their ancestors across oceans to step onto this country's shores. I wonder where we have gone astray in our educational goals. They certainly are not for the poor. Or even much of the middle class, no matter what the potential may be. I can't help but grieve for my grandchildren, all seven and their peers. They still clutch the dream, determined to be the best they can; but what a price they pay.

Theirs is not the world of opportunity Ed and I held, despite the horrors of WWII. Even the complete disruption of our life and Ed's business by his volunteering to return to the service during the Korean conflict came nowhere near the affect the burden of debt load will have on the generation now posed to enter the work field in the United States. Why aren't more of those in this country who have the money stepping forward to lesson this load? Don't they realize they can't take it with them? Obviously our government has no clue as how to help. It's vision is short range and therefore its priorities. God help us all.

We discover the courts are positioned in all legal aspects to become the parents of orphaned children. The process has been fine honed and is overseen in great detail on an annual basis. The emphasis is on the financial end. This means tracking the Social Security monies due the children as a result of their parent's participation in the system. The legalese is phenomenal. And there is no time for either Ed or me to return to college for a law degree to attempt to understand it all.

And remember there is the element of shock in all this. We have just gone through six years of unbelievable, unthinkable deaths among our children. We are in a phase of our lives in which we'll remain forever; not able to understand it has all transpired and having no possible way to accept it as true. That river of loss flows beneath our daily life as strong as ever. We pray it will not deepen for many years. We both are all too aware of our own mortality. Wanting to grow to be very, very old has nothing to do with ourselves but everything to do with our new family. We need to be here for them.

We are introduced to the legal world of the orphan in September, shortly after the funeral. Labor Day is squeezed in and then comes the time for us to return to Gaylord with the grandchildren. None of us have ever entered the Otsego County building in the heart of the small city about a forty-five mile drive from Boyne City. Like all court houses this one has the same extensive labyrinth of empty halls to echo our foot steps no matter how quietly we try to walk. Talking to each other seems an infraction of some rule, so we lower our voices to whispers.

The official procedure is conducted in what appears to be a mini sized courtroom. To Ed and me it's obvious this is all the same old stuff to the attorneys and the judge as they greet each other, arrange papers and decide whether the windows should remain open. A secretary comes in to place a file of papers on the judge's table. Obviously information on the five of us is inside the manila folder. Someone has reduced our situation into words carefully punctuated and arranged on court forms.

The feeling of not actually being returns to me. I have felt this queer state of suspension before. It recalls my search for the drugs and the drive to the hospital the morning Pat died. I am able to relax only because Pat's brother, Paul is with us; representing his nieces and nephew. Tall Paul, as the kids call him, is awesome; a ready match for the judge, who is a handsome man of a near height standing before us in his long black robe. He looks directly at us, the grandchildren included; each of us in a deliberate examination and then smiles.

I immediately sense we are in excellent hands. I see it in his eyes; an awareness of the responsibilities he is about to shoulder shines within. There is no, 'ho, hum, another day, another dollar, about this man. Later I will learn he is the father of four daughters and I'll wonder how he survives the often pathetic treatment of children by their parents and society. When he returns to his home at night he must all but fall apart at the sight of his own. The judge and I, through my annual contacts bond in purpose. My respect for him will have no bounds.

Before we leave the court room we learn we are to furnish an annual report to the court on the welfare of each of the grandchildren. We are further advised an attorney can do this for us. Remembering Mary's words to me about how Social Security benefits diminish if a third child is born and thrown into the equation I instantly see big bucks going in some attorney's pocket from the money that is to be the children's sole income. Probably the work will be that of his secretary and bear his signature. Something tells me it will take every possible cent I can hang on to in my effort to give the children the life they should have. With utter confidence I decide on the spot that if a lawyer's secretary can prepare the annual report I can handle any paper work thrown my way.

Anne is so naïve. She doesn't have an inkling of what will be involved. At this point in time she has had no reason to suspect the complexity the government can create when dealing with the simplest of things. She should have had some clue, after all Ed had been in the service twice. Just traveling as a dependent with three of their children to Guam during the Korean War to be with him should set off bells and gongs. Admittedly Anne can't be held too accountable for her actions. She is way off in never-never land these days since nothing is as it has been for her first sixty eight years. Thinking about it all it comes to me that the two of us resemble a couple of flounders in strange waters. All we can do is keep swimming in the belief something recognizable will loom out of the dark ahead.

Their impression the money was secure lasted until the stock market took a tumble in 2003. It is then Anne foresees a possible financial struggle ahead. Yet the red flag is tiny and on a distant horizon, barely visible.

On the judge's retirement the courts move the responsibility of the grandchildren to the Charlevoix County Court system. After all, they live in it now. Once again they go through the inspection of their home and themselves. Anne discovers the opposite side of the coin in a judge. There are no smiles or nods of recognition. The judge is simply all business. Throughout the years Ed and Anne are the children's guardians the court system never leaves an 'I' un-dotted in their procedural protocol. It is a world of de-humanized paper work and time-lines.

Rachael and The Major

A Dog, Car and Cat

The constant through it all is a love shared

As Anne thinks back to those weeks after Mary's death none of her thoughts deal with the daily things of life. Those simple, routine doings become the background for far more important memories. This is probably as it should be. Helen, Anne's mother, was right when she rolled up her ironing in a towel and shoved it in the ice box. She was setting the stage for today's life style of no-iron clothing. Born into the wrong generation of womanhood she was wise enough to make her own rules. Anne is doing the same thing. However through it all is the constant love Ed and she share. With it everything stays possible.

After the funeral the first hectic days of shopping, building and moving things gradually slows down. Everything finally become as it was before Mary went into the hospital a little over two months ago. Compared to what went on before and after Mary's death the daily routine seems ordinary. I have no idea I will come to realize it is anything but.

First, there's the matter of the car. Ed and I had decided to become a one car family after his retirement. It was one way we could cut back expenses. When you live in a small town daily car use is cut down to a matter of a couple of miles and small segments of time. We could share, or tag along when one or the other of us decided to take off. It not only negated a second car payment, but the insurance, license tags, tune ups etc. We even anticipated probable savings on gasoline as the two of us would be riding together.

Mary's old Dodge Caravan comes with the kids as does Tippy, their cat. The dog, Mandy, a big fluffy long haired gentle soul who was thought to be mostly collie had become sick in July. It was almost August that I took her to the vet on Mary's request. The diagnosis was, believe it or not, terminal cancer and she was never able to return home. Mary assumed the responsibility of telling her children the sad news of their pet's death. Ed brought Mandy to our back yard where he buried her in a small area set aside for deceased pets.

I remember standing next to Ed and the freshly exposed dark, sandy loam behind my herb garden and wondering what he was thinking. Mine were shouting throughout my whole being; this damn cancer can't even leave the kid's beloved Mandy for them to play with. How low can things get? Why one more thing for Mary to have to share with her three? Nothing seemed fair.

I reached for Ed's hand and held on. His firm clasp as he pulled mine close to his body said it all. We were on the same wave length and our tears weren't for the dead dog, but the children and all that was crowding itself into their young lives.

But the cat, Tippy, and the Dodge make it with the kids. Tippy spent his kitten life with Nancy when she lived in Albion doing her internship ministry. Once it was time to return to Dubuque to seminary she had to find another home for him. Mary was the logical choice. She gladly took the soft furred, grey cat with its white paws and face off to Ohio with her when Pat entered law school at Ohio Northern. The second year at the college their landlady, very elderly and prone to forgetfulness took a sudden reversal on her stand on pets in their apartment. Tippy had to come home to us for that year. As cats do, the young tom took this all in his stride assuming the role of the well traveled gentleman. He became everyone's love. When Mary and Patrick moved back to Michigan, Tippy was returned to them because Nancy's Paul was allergic to cats.

I wonder now what in the world the cat must think about the grandchildren bringing him back to live with us once again. It is the new house he moves into not the old farm house where he had once lived. He investigates the house from top to bottom before he can admit his life is once again to his approval. I'm not supposed to know it but he sleeps on the girls bed when I am not in their room.

The van's age prompts Ed to suggest it be traded in on a newer version. Even at six, the opportunity to invade a car dealership rockets Pat off into space. What a sight the five of us must present as we walk into the Ford dealership's show room in Charlevoix. The salesman knows immediately he has a potential sale. His anticipatory eye had watched our group arrive in the old Dodge and park it in front of the show room. Then three children spew out of its rear door. An older couple had brought their grandchildren to help their grandparents choose a new car. How nice!

Ed never goes shopping in jeans and a sweat shirt. No, it has to be slacks, shirt, tie and if the weather is cool enough, a sports jacket. There is no way for the salesman to know whether this dignified gentleman is in the market for a Lincoln or a Mustang. Farthest from the salesman's expectation is that Ed will ask about the elongated Aerostar parked on the outside sales lot with a bright red balloon tied to its antenna that flaps madly in the wind.

His hand is outstretched as he greets Ed and there's a nod of greeting for me. It tells me more than he intends. This middle aged, slightly overfed, well groomed man despite his open manner long ago decided that women, when accompanying their husbands, have little interest in what he decides to purchase. Oh, maybe the color, but certainly not the engine size.

"I'm Howard. Are there any questions I can answer for you? Any particular model you are interested in?"

Ed clasps the hand firmly and responds, "Yes. An Aerostar, the elongated model. I think I saw one out on the lot as we drove in."

Smooth Howard never blinks as he assimilates Ed's request.

After checking out every model on the floor the children look around for their grandfather. They spot him in earnest conversation with the salesman. At the same time a mechanic drives up in front of the show room to park a dark green Ford Aerostar. It is to be their car for more years and more adventures than any of them can possibly foresee. They rush to look through the windows of the big vehicle. Once given a permissive nod by Ed they crawl in the van. It takes no time for the children to evaluate every button, lever, handle and dial.

None of the kids look back at the old Dodge as we leave the lot to head home.

Tippy dies two years after he moved back in with us, on Memorial Day. The children are devastated. They have lost so much. First their father, then their Mandy dog, their mother and now their beloved Tippy. I have learned the only cure is replacement. Didn't Ed and I gather the three grandchildren to us in lieu of their mother and father? Certainly our Bucky, a black Hovavart work dog has tried his best to fill the empty spot Mandy left behind. Obviously a kitten must be found and soon.

Despite the holiday traffic we head for the pet shop in Traverse City's largest mall some seventy miles south of us. It is a gorgeous day and what better to do than to set off on a kitten buying spree? One thing I'm is certain of is that there will be kittens available. There are always kittens.

The mall's parking lot is jam packed. Ed maneuvers into a spot some distance from the festive entrance. A large gilt carrousel can be seen circling just beyond its expansive windows. At a half run and half walk, the kids precede us through the large mall doors, past the carousel, food service shops, the center aisle venders and on down the walkway in a bee-line for the pet store. They've been here before to look at all the cute puppies, kittens and even snakes. The kids know where they are heading and it is OK as they disappear around a corner. Ed and I know they will stick together and be waiting.

As we walk into the shop's open entry the grandchildren call out the impossible, "They don't have any cats. What can we do now?"

The clerk approaches us, the older couple who have entered and obviously are with the children. The concerned young woman peers at us through fashionable glasses. Reaching out to us she affirms the grandkids' words, "I am so sorry, but we don't have a kitten in the shop today. I am certain we will this coming week and I will be glad to call you."

I can see by the look on the kids' faces that waiting isn't an option. The tears for Tippy are still hanging in there, right behind their eyes. Even Ed is looking at me as if I alone has the answer to this whole impossible situation.

No kittens in the pet shop. I can't believe this. Aloud I thank the young woman, telling her, "It is hard to believe. I thought pet shops always have cats. Thank you for your offer, but I think we will look further. It is important we find our new kitten today." I recognize the timing is really the whole issue.

Ed and the kids are looking at me and someone asks, "Where?"

Out of the blue the answer is on my lips, "We'll buy a Traverse City newspaper and look in the want ads. Someone will have kittens to sell or give away. There are always kittens to be had."

Ed finds a vending machine in the mall lobby and we spread the want ads out on a table in the cafeteria. Not an ad for a kitten can be found. As a temporary bit of salve Ed suggests that we all take time out for a hamburger and then head back home to look in the News Review, the local newspaper. Even this unexpected treat does little to re-inflate the excitement that had led the way into the mall. There are times when even the well-known hamburger and French fries or slice of pizza fail to cheer the saddened child.

Two hours later, back home the want ads are once again checked out; this time in the Petoskey paper. There are kittens available at Walloon Lake just four miles away. This seems so ironic to me after already having driven over one hundred and fifty miles in our search for a kitten. With the family's eyes on him Ed makes the phone call and finds the owner home, not off enjoying a holiday picnic as might well have been the case. Ed is to come right over with his grandchildren.

We hold our breath as Ed drives the four miles around the lake's end to find the homey log cabin set back under pines just as the owner had described. The front door swings opens and a small woman laughs and welcomes us. The three children reach the house at a dead run. There are five, six-week old kittens napping in a large box in the lady's living room. She invites the children to pick up the kittens to decide which one they want to take with them. All are absolutely beautiful in their individual color systems of black and white. None are striped, but the markings are all different and I'm immediately apprehensive the decision will be to take three home. I brace myself to stand firm for just one.

Ed is almost as bad as the kids. He loves anything with four legs. As questions and answers are thrown back and forth the woman learns the children are orphans and we are their grandparents. She looks at the two of us in awe and says what we've heard so many times, "You two will certainly be given a special place in heaven with crowns on your heads."

And the reply I give is the one I repeat every time anyone makes this statement. It is a spontaneous and heartfelt denial of such regard, "Oh, no, our reward if one is to be, is here on earth and being given such a special chance in our lives as to have a second family. So few ever receive such a gift."

Again, a miracle occurs. All three of the children zero in on the smallest kitten whose bright green eyes seem to dare them to choose him. He's shiny black with just a hint of white on his paws and face. The little guy wins everybody's heart on the spot.

Mine all but stops as the owner reaches for the kitten and snuggling it against her murmurs, "This is the one I had planned to keep. He's my favorite."

The children stand in place, unable to believe what they hear. And so it is that the woman smiles and hands the kitty back to the children, "But he is yours. I could never play with him or love him as much as you will. I am happy for him and all of you."

Cradled in Laura's arms Major joins our family.

Tippy's nickname had been 'The Colonel'

Because of this Ed claims, "This cat can't outrank the old Colonel, it just wouldn't be respectful. So, he will be 'The Major'."

In the end Anne will sell the Aerostar in September of Pat's sophomore year at college for $354. By then it will have struggled through its last summer of transporting Pat and Rachael the two miles from the house to downtown Boyne City to their work. Pat will be scooping ice cream and paddling fudge at Kilwin's chocolates. Rachael will be across Water Street at Bali and Beyond stringing beads and selling home décor.

The van's sliding door will fall off occasionally that summer, but the two will muscle it back in place each time. The asking price will come about as Anne will want to attend the annual Walloon Writers' Retreat in her search for help in publishing her memoir. The registration fee will be $354.

With no extra money hidden anywhere, in or outside of the bank, Anne will turn to Ed in desperation and ask, "Honey, would it be OK if I sell the old van and use the money to go to the writers' retreat the end of the month?"

"Sure. But how much do you need? That old thing isn't worth much except for parts."

"$354."

Grinning from ear to ear he will answer, "Honey if you can con someone into giving you that much for the van you are welcome to the money."

The ad will go in the paper and two buyers appear. It is the second man, who patiently out waits the first that will end up handing Anne $355 cash, saying, "Keep the change and thank you."

Tantrums, Housework and a Gift

Learning to look before leaping

Why is it when you are certain you're right about something that you are no where near the truth? Anne has stubbed her toe against this more than once. It's unlikely she will ever learn to look before she leaps.

I would be lying if I led you to believe everything settles into normalcy for the family. We almost make it but there is the problem of Laura's raging tantrums. As a ten year old she can really throw them, becoming furious over what appears to be nothing. Then it is pure rage in all manner and form; screaming, pitching things, kicking and eventually sobs.

Years ago when our Nancy was a pre-schooler and I took her to the grocery store with me I had to deal with her sessions of kicking and screaming on the aisle floor. I desperately wanted to walk off and leave her as if she was no child of mine. The youngest of four Nancy was the only one who would throw a 'if-you-won't-buy-it-for-me-I'll-have-a-yell-and-scream-fit-right-here-and-now.

Up to that point in my parenting I had observed other children pull such a scene and thought; boy, if that kid was mine he'd get a good whack on his behind and straighten up. How can a mother let her child act that way?

But Laura's outbursts are not like Nancy's. She is older and she's at home. I call Mary's friends, Lynn and Corrine. They think it's Laura's way of handling the grief of her mother's death. I emphasize because there are times I want to scream out about Mary's death, to kick something, throw myself in Ed's arms and cry. But I don't. I'm an adult and have the children's grief to assuage.

I ask myself, if this is deep grief how am I to help Laura? She resists my efforts to hug her and help her through her anger.

In desperation I decide to do something I never thought I would. I turn to psychiatric advice. At this point in my life I hold such medical practitioners on the same plane I assign to professional business counselors. In other words, pretty low on the ladder. I see them as opportunists, ready to say whatever their client wants to hear. My past experience with one was a disaster. He had his mind made up I was in the wrong without bothering to question me. My need for advice drives me to call and make an appointment. Feeling stupid to have to resort to professional help I am reluctant to make inquiries among my friends as to who they might know. I resort to the Yellow Pages, settling on a husband and wife team who say they work with families.

The office is in Petoskey. Doctor Frehling and his wife are in practice together, but he is the one who invites Laura and me into his office. He is only one-third as old as I am, which is always a bit unnerving. I reassure myself it only means he has had a more recent education and therefore must know more than someone my age. I admit there is nothing superficial or intimidating about his manner. I can't imagine him being involved in any kind of subterfuge. I like his friendly, laid-back manner and best of all, Laura seems to be at ease as they sit face to face, almost knee to knee and talk about who Laura really is.

In less than ten minutes he says, "Laura, I'd like you to go back out into the visiting room while I talk to your grandmother. There is a favorite book of mine on the blue table I think you will enjoy reading."

"I saw it when I was waiting to come into your office. It's a favorite of mine too. I'd like reading it again." Said Laura.

Smiling, Dr. Frehling closes the door behind Laura and turns to me, the grandmother. The smile deepens as he says, "Laura's problem isn't her mother's death, it is you."

For forty-five minutes I listen to the wisdom of a man I think too young. Will I ever learn not to judge those I meet or see by appearances alone?

Dr. Frehling continues, "Laura sees you as a threat to her jurisdiction. Much too early in her life she was thrown into a situation where she felt it was up to her to care not only for her mother but also for her siblings. Laura's step-father accelerated the whole load by demanding such menial tasks from her as a weekly mopping and waxing of the kitchen floor, doing the laundry, folding it and putting it all away in an orderly, prescribed manner and having the house picked up and vacuumed daily before his arrival home from work."

I understand immediately what he is saying. I had been privy to Larry's expectations, but had stayed out of it. After all, he was Mary's husband and none of his mother-in-law's business. I suspected his red hair was a flag of warning of a nasty temper. The hole his fist had made in Laura's bedroom door was no accident. I knew Laura was frightened of him. Patrick was intrigued with his step-brother's tales of keeping an iron skillet in his jeans so when his dad hit him with the ping pong paddle it wouldn't hurt. Mary had become unable to cope with her husband's problem because of her cancer and I hadn't realized it. I sit in Dr. Frehling's office remembering Larry. Guilt floods me. I promise myself the children will not be visiting their step-father for a very long time.

Dr. Frehling adds, "Laura sees you as her competition in taking care of herself, her sister and brother. Let her do as much as she wants without keeping up with the unreasonable demands of her step-father. Be patient. Praise her for what she accomplishes but lead her back into her childhood with childhood things to do. Have fun and good times. It won't cure itself tomorrow, but time will bring healing."

He is right. The family chides me for babying Laura; treating her specially and having her as my favorite. I stay with the program without telling the 'why' of my behavior. If the doctor's advice is to work it must be carried out without sharing the reason or Laura might hear about it and the plan could fail. I add another secret to my collection.

I rummage through the attic until I unearth a huge bag of dress-up clothes. Thankfully I am a pack-rat and never throw anything away if I believe it might be useful eventually. Some of the articles in the bag date back to Mary's and Nancy's early years. I have photos of them out in the front yard on Holland-Sylvania Road outside of Maumee, Ohio dressed from head to toes in clothing that had been mine, my mother's and even my grandmother's. I give this treasure to the girls. Even Pat gets in on the act a they create a series of plays to which Ed and I are invited. The costuming is fantastic.

Ed hangs a swing in the apple tree closest to the house, right outside the girl's big bay window. It is made from a sturdy rope threaded through holes he drills in a length of two by twelve. It becomes a favorite place to sit with a doll and dream.

Even the Chestonia post office plays its part in establishing a world of childhood within our household. Usually Rachael claims the role of postmistress on the premise it is her closet into which the post office window is set. Laura and Pat are content in writing and receiving volumes of mail. Rachael understands the other two must have their turns dispensing the mail. I suggest she do this before they have to beg for a turn. Peace reigns.

Sometimes I am in the kitchen cooking and one or more of the children appears to help and learn. This leads to learning how a table should be set and how the preparation of a meal is a study in time management so everything can appear on the table when it should. It isn't very long until Ed and I find ourselves invited to dinner in the girl's room. When handing us the written invitation Laura quietly suggests, "It would be nice if you and Gramp would dress. This is a special occasion, your 49th wedding anniversary.

Ed finds no problem in donning a suit and tie. I add jewelry to my good dress and apply makeup. Neither are part of my daily routine.

The bedroom is far from finished. Although the wallpaper is hung and its Raggedy Annes and Andys dance about the room the woodwork is unpainted and there is no carpet on the concrete floor. A card table is set in the room's center complete with a cloth, flowers and candle. I note the good silver and dishes are in use. Pat, our seven year old maître d' hotel seats us, pulling out my chair for me. He, too, is in his best attire and a towel is folded across his arm. He lights the candle and pours our water as he wishes as a pleasant evening. No smile appears on his face, but his chocolate eyes are dancing. He excuses himself and disappears up the stairs toward the kitchen.

We don't see the girls during our dinner. It is Pat who carries each course down the stairs and sets a beautifully presented dish before us. It is Pat who clears away between each. Everything is delicious. Small hors d'oeuvres precede a garden salad with its own vinaigrette dressing. This was followed by wild rice stuffed Cornish Hen with mint glazed carrots. The climax was chocolate cheese cake and coffee.

I glanced at Ed and ask, "It appears you have been doing a little grocery shopping behind my back, yes?"

I get back a broad grin and, "No comment."

As the last plate is being removed Ed asks our waiter if he could summon the chefs to our table. We want to congratulate them all on one of the finest meals we have ever enjoyed.

Eventually they will all be using my sewing machine and helping me nourish the flowers we brought form their mother's in their new back yard. Slowly I manage to turn Laura's self-imposed need of 'being in charge' back into the world of childhood

Laura and Anne bond. They'll become daughter and mother/grandmother. This is such a special word that it should be in the dictionary. Being a mother/grandmother is being a person who has been given the gift of second motherhood without the physical passion or pain of it all. Suddenly the gift of a child is received long after the possibility has faded. Like Sarah and Abraham, Genesis 9:18 of the Bible, it is so unbelievable Anne and Ed often laugh at its happening. God smiles. It's a gift of balm, which subjugates all the hurt that went before, whether loss, disappointment or unutterable pain to leave peace, joy and love.

Let's also include the word father/grandfather, for Ed echoes Anne's thoughts. So far no one has come up with shorter titles, but we are working on it. For the three grandchildren their second-time-around parents are simply Gram and Gramps.

Rachael, Grace. Laura, Ed and Patrick, Anne at Nub's in 1994

Social Security, Skiing and Tears

It's not a matter of money, age or how, but of love

To me it has always been obvious Ed spoils Anne. He probably always will. Anne believed when they married that hers was a husband as close to perfection as God makes a man. That belief has never left her. When Anne told Ed Mary had asked them to raise her children he never said, 'Let me think about this for a few days." His answer was immediate and with no conditions, "Sounds wonderful, Hon."

It is Anne's brother who suggests that they take six months to think about whether it is the right thing to do. He wants them to really understand what they are getting in to. He is looking into the future and seeing the big bucks it will all take. Ed's and Anne's perspective is different. They know the children can't hang in limbo for even a week as the adult world ponders the pros and cons of their living arrangements for the years ahead. The ongoing trauma that has been their life has to end immediately. It isn't a matter of money, age or how; but of love.

Where this love is going to land them down the road is of absolutely no importance to either of them. They never sit down to calculate how old they'll be when Laura will graduate from high school, let alone how old they'll be once Patrick completes his college years. Even when people tell them how wonderful they are they never catch on to what they're referring to. There'll be all kinds of red flags ahead, but Anne tunes me out. There's nothing for me to do but step back, figuring she'll work it all out in her own way. Only Heaven knows how that will be.

Having taught school and even having my own business I tend to be an organized person. I have to admit that my house doesn't always affirm this, but basically it is true. I keep files for all kinds of printed material that comes my way. Things like how to use and maintain my vacuum cleaner, washing machine, dishwasher, sewing machine, computer, alarm clock, microwave, the hand sander, miter saw, the Focus, snow blower and so on. I have to admit that my one fault in all this is that I forget to toss out the information on something when it dies and goes in the trash.

I truly appreciate these 'how to' pamphlets and printouts. I even have some that go back to the days they weren't published in two languages. Today if you happen to pick up some directions and start reading from the wrong end you find yourself in another world. It does have its side benefits as I now know a few Spanish words, including *Attencion*, which I have come to believe means 'may we please have your attention'.

There was no printed pamphlet entitled 'Options for the Orphan' handed to Ed or me when we went through the court procedure of becoming the grandchildren's guardians; and, very importantly, their conservators at the same time. Not even an 8 ½ by 11 inch sheet of paper; pink, white or green was available with bulleted information. There was nothing for us to return home with which we could study and eventually file for future reference.

Ed and I are aware we could have adopted the grandchildren that day, but we think it is important for them and the Cassidy clan that they keep their parent's surname. At least it is one thing that belongs to them and their parents that should be theirs forever.

Neither Ed nor I think about other orphaned children. That there are millions of children left parentless every year floats above our heads. The words foster care and institutionalized don't enter our minds. Information on any other kind of care is kept on the restricted list. Neither of us is to know of the other options our government holds for children without parents. There isn't even information on the choice of care we chose. I have no court handouts in my files concerning the rights of orphans. Of course, this excluded the Government's own expectations.

Something doesn't figure here for me. Isn't a child as important as a hand-sander? Don't they need the correct care and maintenance? Where's the eight hundred number to call in case something doesn't work as expected? One thing I do know is that something very important is missing.

As time moves on Anne will discover a huge governmental body which spreads its tentacles across the United States into every county. A staggering number of well educated people work within their appointed cubicles. These are persons who have committed their working careers to the care of those who desperately need help in living their lives; not least of these are the parentless children and youth. It is a profession that gives and gives despite the governmental bureaucracy that seeps in its doors. Eventually

Anne will stumble across these people and her way will be eased. She will then learn of foster care and the plight of its eighteen year old in America.

The children's Social Security Insurance checks begin to arrive somehow with no prompting from Ed or me. The system shifted gears once Mary's death is reported. It is impressive. Mary had explained the procedure to me soon after Patrick was born, otherwise I would have no idea how the amounts are calculated.

A family is allotted a payment for each of the first two dependents, after that the whole amount is lumped into one and divided among the total number of children. Thus with the arrival of Patrick six years ago the same amount was received as before his birth. But now as then it is divided evenly among three children instead of two as it had been previously. A strange ruling, but certainly it is beneficial to the government. To me it appears to defy the intent of the whole program.

Shaking my head I think. It's as if the mother is to buy the same amount of groceries but serve smaller portions. And, of course, pass down the outgrown clothes and shoes. What if there are seven instead of three? I wonder about my government. It seems to punish those who need the most help.

I plunge right in trying to stretch the grandchildren's income to embrace the increases I experience in my daily pursuit to feed, cloths and care for the children. I'm constantly reminding myself of the lifestyle that would have been my grandchildren's if their father and mother had lived. I'm determined to obtain the same level of living a young attorney with a wife who teaches would expect to give their children.

The fact that neither my husband nor I are in the ranks of the employed doesn't enter the equation. I simply accept that there is no way to increase the family income. There's no way to explain this thinking on my part except to believe it has an awfully lot to do with my faith. Remarkably I never flounder in my belief that all will work out as it should. My father, Tracy once told me when I was a young girl that I could accomplish anything I wanted to if I was willing to work for it. Since that time I've changed his advice to include 'and believe it possible'.

After being away from the ski slopes for thirty five years, Ed and I still have our contacts among those in the business. At one time we had operated a very small ski resort and Ed had moved on to be the assistant manager of one of Michigan's largest ski areas. Because of his connections my husband knew where to ask questions and discovered we could outfit the kids and ourselves for skiing inexpensively at the annual National Safety Patrol's ski swap in Battle Creek.

It is with a sense of holiday that the five of us climb in the Areostar the year after Mary's death and head south to the middle of the state. Our destination is a small mid-state ski area's lodge. Within its rustic log interior a type of managed pandemonium holds forth. Equipment is stashed in every nook and corner. It leans, hangs and stands around, behind and over rack after rack of hanging clothing. Like a smashed rainbow colors leaps at us. Bright red, purple, orange green, yellow, blue, stark white and black like the darkness of a deep hole fill our vision. Men and women in the burnt orange jackets and sweaters of the National Ski Patrol are every where among the shoppers. They are fitting boots over heavy socks, helping a person shrug themselves into a puffy down jacket or carrying a pair of skis out to a car.

None of us are aware we haven't moved more than ten feet from the entrance until a ski patrolman descends, with a wide grin, stops, holds his hand out to Ed and says, "Hi there. I'm Franck. Looks like you have some people with you who want to ski this winter. Need some help?" Then turning to a woman who walks up he reaches out to her and says, "And this is my wife, Marcy. She's the expert in kids' gear."

Ed does the introductions. We each have our chance to say hello. Ed explains to Franck and Marcy that none of us are strangers to skiing.

Pointing to the three grandchildren he explains "Their mother taught them to ski as soon as they could stand upright. Our daughter grew up on skis, too and was even a member of the Ski Patrol."

I watch the man and woman's faces for the expression I always see when realization that the kids are orphans hits. I see it this time, as I expect. But they say nothing to any of us. But there is a concern that descends; the three grandchildren will receive wonderful attention and care. Their equipment will be the best deals Franck and Marcy can locate today. It is their way of doing something for the three, something that might make the grandchildren's' lives a bit better.

I want to give the couple my thanks but don't know exactly how. Anyway, it hangs in the air between us. And, of course, there is the resultant regard for Ed and me. It is as if they are placing golden crowns on our heads, again. I squirm at this attitude but accept it. There isn't time to explain we don't see ourselves that way at all. We are certain if the circumstances were reversed Franck and Marcy would do the same for their grandchildren.

Ed helps Franck find and fit boots. There have been unbelievable advances made in them since the days the two of us wore laced boots. Now there are buckles and shapes that resemble the outfits worn by Bat Man and Super Man. There are even white and pink boots for Rachael and Laura. Mine are all white, Ed's are gray to match the overall-type ski pants he buys. Marcy and I have the fun of helping the kids find what they like in the clothing department. It is back and forth between Ed and Franck with skis and poles and Marcy and me with jackets, hats, mittens and pants.

It is only when Pat tugs on my sleeve to whisper, "When are we going to eat, Gram" that I realize we have been shopping for over two hours.

After looking at my watch I answer, "Me too, Pat. I'll go see how soon Gramps thinks we can call it quits here. Have you got everything? How about a hat?"

"I'm all done, Gram. Remember you helped me pick out my hat right over there?"

Pat points to a trunk overflowing with hats of all kinds and colors. But to tell him I remembered would be a stretch. Too much is going on here I think. I just nod at him and head for Ed.

The fact that everything is used, although in good condition and has been sold to us at give-away prices doesn't make any of the items we carry away less than new to us. We are wrapped in our excitement. We load up our gear, Ed carrying my skis, boots and poles with his. Laura, Rachael and Pat carry their own equipment, boots dangle in bags from their arms while I stagger under bag after bag of clothing. Franck and Marcy, one on each side hold the big double doors to the outside open for us, calling out their wishes for great skiing. They glow with the knowledge they have helped another family get out on the slopes; the intent of the annual sale.

Once the ski slopes open in December we climb into the Aerostar after church to drive north through Petoskey and on toward Harbor Springs where Ed turns onto Pleasant View Road and the three miles on to Nubs Nob. Arriving with brown bag lunches we eat in the community room of the big, log ski lodge A blazing fire makes even our home made lunches the best. It is a quick gulp meal as all five of us are anxious to move out onto the slopes, greeting the winter day and beautiful snow. Sounds like a dream doesn't it? And it is if you discount the hour or so before church when I work in the kitchen getting breakfast on the table and packing our ski lunches. That hour is the most hectic of the entire week. Elsewhere in the house the children are dressing for Sunday School and Ed, already dressed for church, is in the garage collecting ski equipment to pack in the back of the van. The kids are urged to get all their gear out into the back hall for Gramp. I call down stairs reminding them this means not only warm underwear but ski pants and jacket, socks, boots, hats, gloves, scarves and goggles. It all goes into their backpacks to be changed into once we reach the resort.

As everyone piles into the van just seconds before we must leave to make it to church on time Ed and I are checking gear and clothes. That we pull it off is just short of a miracle. That period of time on a Sunday morning when I finally get us all into the van is the hardest work I do all week. No wonder so many young families chose not to bring their children up in the faith they profess to embrace. Getting there can mean traveling through a veritable war zone. I know the reason I can persist is because Ed is right by my side all the way. Too often it seems the church part of life falls on the mothers.

Ed and I are eligible to ski for nine dollars a season as 'Over Seventy Club' members. The children ski free on the beginners' slope. This all makes skiing financially feasible for us. Of course, by next year they will all be ready for the main slopes, but the area has special price breaks even then.

Ed displays his natural prowess on the slopes, yet his seven year old grandson stops on occasions and gives his grandfather some pointers. Ed cherishes the advice. At seventy five he has the grace and drive of a life long athlete. I am in awe of Ed's ability, having never quite moved much beyond the beginner runs myself. I am content to look up the slopes from the lower levels and see him there with all the twenty, thirty and forty year olds. I remind myself that Ed is mine. I have the piece of white paper home in my dresser drawer to prove it.

I know it should be framed and hanging on our bedroom wall but I am the world's worst procrastinator; I've been putting off this little chore for fifty-two years.

Anne smiles out loud. As she explains it to me this is when she smiles a huge smile but doesn't break into laughter but just lets it boomerang around inside of her. She does it a lot. Like now, as she remembers the days Ed, their kids and she operated the small ski hill on the southern edge of Boyne City. She took care of the office work and ran its small restaurant while Ed with Tom and Dave's help saw to the operation of the lifts, the slope conditions and that stuff. At six and eight Nancy and Mary ran the candy shop. They learned really fast that if they each ate a bar they consumed their profit.

Anne seldom got out on her skis, but the rest of the family lived on theirs. While Anne tended to the operation of the day lodge; cooking the hamburgers, selling tickets and answering the phone they polished their skiing skills. Their four kids, except for Nancy, became members of the National Ski Patrol which attested to their abilities. Nancy skied for fun. Tom skied with grace. Mary and Dave were hard skiers. Ed was both. Anne vividly remembers the few times he fell, usually forward with so much force he ripped his bear trap bindings out of the skis. Not a casual thing to do. He seemed indestructible. Of course, Patrick has no knowledge of those times as he watches his grandfather ski the slopes at Nubs Nob.

It's a blue skied, sunny day in January almost a year and a half after Mary died when I finally crank up my nerve to ride the chair lift to the top of the main slope with Laura. The ascent is slow. I keep my eyes on the disembarking platform straight ahead as I maintain a continuous line of nervous chatter with my granddaughter. This is all in an effort to ignore where I am, how high I am and where I must go. My nerves are a wreck. In getting off I manage to let the chair clonk my head and knock me flat. Floating back into reality from where I landed in a bank of snow I look up into assorted faces peering down at me with great concern. I spot my hat ten feet away. There is no pain, only acute embarrassment. I reject the sympathetic and concerned ski patrolman's offer to take me down the hill on an evacuation sled. Declaring myself OK I put my skies back on, vowing to make it to the bottom but to never leave the safety of the Bunny slope again.

It is then I'm told my granddaughter, midway in our uphill trip had fallen forward off the chair to land skis first in a deep pile of snow fifteen feet beneath the lift. I had been so intent about my own problems I hadn't felt her leave the chairlift or heard her cries, if there were any. I can't begin to describe the guilt and disbelief that engulfs me. The fact she crawled out of the snow unhurt and laughing alleviates some of my self blame. In fact it isn't long until we are all convulsed in laughter over the whole episode. My goose bump was the only injury.

Eventually the kids coax me into riding the chair with them again. Their constant attention and instruction gradually put me at ease and I am able to enjoy the long, twisting outside runs. I gently snowplow or parallel ski to my heart's intent. It becomes enough for me to traverse these beginner runs and the lower levels, wave to my family as they cross the bottom hills to climb back on the lifts and repeat their flight downhill. Their happiness makes my day.

Eventually, despite the fact Ed is the older I find my knees giving me problems. It becomes next to impossible to get back up if I take a tumble. It is then I take to the lodge, sitting next to the large stone fireplace and its warm blaze with a book. I'll put it aside now and then to gaze out the large windows and watch my family, Oh, Mary, you and Pat must be bursting with joy, watching all this. What a wonderful start you gave your children. It will be your legacy to them for all their lives. Did you know? I think you did.

Ed's and my tears will always be somewhere within us waiting for a word, a thought, a gesture, a laugh or glimpse of a memory. There are time we cry with each other. Or one of us as the other comforts. We'll struggle with tears when someone talks about their memories of Mary, Tom or Pat. Yet neither of us break down and has a long, hard cry. Our pain is overshadowed with the joy of having the children to raise.

It's our kind pastor, Rufus Spaulman, who tells me, "Don't fool yourself, Anne. It will never get any better; I don't care what others may tell you. It just doesn't." Rufus had lost his older brother to leukemia.

The pain stays. Somehow knowing it will always remain helps. What a gifted minister to be able to say what he knows to be true. He proves what Jesus, through our Bibles, tries to tell us over and over, love never ceases. If you love someone that love will always stay with you.

Ed and I learn how to cry. We learn to let the tears flow and how to change the conversation, look away, not let the memory come all the way into the room with us. Besides we both understand our tears are not for ourselves, but for the children and Sue Ellen who have the rest of their lives to live without what should be theirs. And the reason we understand the enormity of the loss for Sue Ellen is because in marrying God gave her Tom to be hers to be with her until death should part them. And of course, none of us think that is likely to happen before old age appears on the scene. The same is true of our relationship with our parents. It is beyond human understanding when that gift becomes less than believed to be. When a spouse, child or parent leaves way too soon, it stretches the human capacity to accept. It is only the knowledge that we are promised yet another life with those we love that we survive. There is no doubt in my mind about this.

As for me; there's a strong desire to believe Anne is right.

Patrick and Laura in Washington DC—1992

The Capitol, Gift Shops and Squirrel

There is something about challenging a child

As Anne watches the children move out of sight it is obvious her thoughts are much the same as mine. She's asking herself if this, the first time the grandchildren will be each other's keeper; will be a lesson that will stay with them all their lives. Once Ed and Anne are gone the grandchildren are going to be alone together. There may well be spouses and children by then, and of course, always the extended family. But for those times when a special listening ear is required we believe they'll need each other

I'm in the kid's bathroom doing my routine cleaning and polishing when I hear Ed walk through the door behind me. On my knees working on a high water mark on the tub I am surprised at his presence as he has been intently at work on something at his desk up on the living room balcony. Since the grandchildren arrived it has become a favorite retreat for both of us. All our files and records are up there, separate from those of the children. Not even an extension phone is allowed within its confines. It is our world apart from that other world in which we live in 99% of the time.

As I turn and look up, Ed says, "Remember our conversation last September? The time we talked about what we wanted to see happen for the grandchildren?

My thoughts fly back and bring the talk to us. "Not every word, but enough to recall what we decided. Why?"

"I've been working on an idea. I'd like to run it by you. You have time?"

Looking at the unfinished tub I know it will wait for me, no matter how long I am away. Housework never disappears. "How about right now? You have my curiosity going."

The big grin appears on his face and grabbing my hand he pulls me up beside him. Then it is his arms and a quick kiss. "I think you will like what I have."

As I step up the last step I can see a map on Ed's desk. It is one of those huge oak office desks that comes with the angle companion for the typewriter and associated equipment. Doc, my brother, had given it to Ed some years ago when he moved into new offices in Toledo. Compared to me Ed is a real neatnique.

Ed pulls up an extra chair and side by side we examine the map. It is of the US.

Pointing to Michigan and Boyne City he runs his finger down to Lansing. "We'll have to drive this segment of the trip, but from Lansing on we'll go by Amtrak all the way to DC."

I look at him, "Sounds like we are going to the capitol. When and how do you propose we do this? What about the kids?"

"That's the whole point of my idea, Snork. You said you thought we should travel with them and I thought what better place to start than our nation's capitol. I am thinking we could do it this summer after school is out, of course."

I am so surprised I can't say more than one word. "How?"

Another big smile. Somehow I have asked the right question. My reaction is right on the money. But the word money is where I am stranded. I know there isn't enough to pay for five of us on such a wonderful journey. It would take at least a week and all I can think of is the cost of the meals. Seven days times three meals is twenty-one times the five of us is 205. Before I can multiply that sum by a cost factor I hear Ed.

"I have all the reservations ready to confirm. We can do it because the children are all under twelve and we are over sixty-five. Amtrak allows us all to travel on reduced rates. Even hotel rooms are available on family plans with free breakfasts. I am thinking we can pack lunches; there are parks all over the place in Washington. Remember, Snork, I lived there for over three months during the war. In the evenings we can go out and have good dinners. It will be fun to take the kids to some really nice restaurants. What do you think? Should I confirm the trip?"

It's a good thing I am sitting down. I had no clue Ed was even giving a trip a thought let alone had it all planned, neatly tied up in a big red bow for me. There is no reason for my surprise. I have lived with this man plenty of years and should have known he would be moving ahead on our decision to travel with the grandchildren. Hadn't he agreed with the whole idea way back there in September of last year? No, this is his way. While I am re-organizing my life with the grandchildren, solving problems and working out solutions he has been busy too.

Excitement envelopes me. Once again I am in awe of Ed. What a wonderful man, husband and grandfather he has become. The years have embellished every one of his fine qualities.

My happiness calls up the tears that lay so close to my world. Tears are so strange. They can wrap themselves around terrible pain and unbelievable joy simultaneously. That is where I am as I turn to Ed and say, "Oh, honey, what a guy you are. Of course, I want to go to DC with you and the kids. They'll be so full of questions when we tell them that you better have an answer for every single detail."

"I know that, Snork. I also know that you have questions at this point. So if the bathroom can wait a bit longer why don't I go over the trip from start to finish, outlining my suggestions on where we can go and what we can see. I suspect you will want to add your own ideas. I'm sure the kids will want to make some changes. This is as much their trip as it is ours."

Four months later on the ninth of July, 1993 well after school is out, we're on our way. Once again the Areostar is carefully packed. Each grandchild has their own suitcase; inexpensive ones we find at Penney's. The contents have been their choice beyond a basic must list I furnish them. Ed gives each a camera. An amateur photographer, he seldom leaves home with out his Zeis he's had since he was a teenager. By the time we return home each of the children will be schooled in the world of photography, recording those things about the trip which especially means something to them. My part in all of this will be to constantly watch that the cameras are not left someplace.

The trip to Lansing seems to take forever, but it is when we find ourselves standing track side in the shade of Lansing's little depot that time truly drags on and on. When the train's horn is finally heard in the distance, echoing above the state capitol building and the Michigan State campus it is then that we can believe it is coming. When we see it advancing in a purposeful manner around a bend in the track some two blocks away we can't absorb the immensity of the enormous mass of black moving toward us purposefully as a bullet toward its target.

I look at Ed. This is his love; his world; that of the train. I hope the trip will be everything he foresees it to be. I know it will be for the grandchildren, now 7, 9 and 11. Hopefully more than they can even dream as they stand excitedly besides us watching the enormous engine puff and grind itself to a ponderous halt ten feet in front of us and our baggage. None of us are aware of the 85 degree sun soaked air of the almost noon time. Ed automatically checks each of us for our cameras, bags and whatever else we might have elected to lug onto the train. He greets the conductor as our turn to climb aboard arrives and then stands back to allow the man to help each child up the steps and finally me. We are each wished a wonderful time on our journey. Then told to watch our step as we walk across the rough platform between the cars to make a turn to the left. Ed has arranged for us to travel in a Pullman car. We'll occupy facing pairs of seats which will magically transform into a double set of bunk beds at the end of the day.

The last time Ed and I rode a train was in Europe with our friend, Grace. It had been a cog rail that carried us up a mountain side in the Alps. I thought I was excited on that day but today is far more so as I see the looks on the faces of Laura, Rachael and Pat. This is their first train ride. The same look of joy is spread all across Ed's face as he ushers us to our seats and begins to explain to inquisitive Pat just how the seats will turn into beds after dinner.

The girls listen, but their eyes wander to check out the fold-down tables, the velvet curtains at the small windows and the water tap with drinking cups at the far end of the car.

Laura asks, "Where is the dining car?"

I answer, "We'll have to ask the conductor when he comes by to punch our tickets. Once the train is out of the station and city I am certain you can walk back or forward to find it. It will be good to locate it as we'll have dinner there tonight."

There is something about challenging a child with a new experience. Right under my eye all three children mature as they enter the world of travel. We set only a few rules, they went along with the packing process. The first one is the most important, it is ages old.

"Stay with someone in the family. There will never be a reason for you to leave by yourself at any time. Even using the toilet must be done with another, if no more than standing outside the door. If a stranger or even someone you think you know quite well asks you to do something for him or her or go with them for some reason, do not do it. This means even if they say your grandmother or grandfather has asked them to tell you to do it. The answer must always be 'no'. If it is a friend or relative they will understand if you say you have to have the permission of your grandmother or grandfather. If they get upset with you then they aren't the friend you think they are. If by any chance one of you becomes separated from the rest of us stop, look around and find a safe place to wait while we come back to find you. Cities are very large and many, many different people live in them. Almost all of them are good, kind and caring. Even if one of them wants to take you someplace else while we are looking for you just tell them, thank you, but I have to stay where I am. They may decide to stay with you and that would be fine. Once we are in Washington you will all have the name of the hotel where we will stay and its telephone number. If you should call us and we aren't there leave a message with the desk clerk who will be the one who takes all the hotel's incoming calls. They will be certain we get your message. Questions?"

Once we are moving through the country side past farm houses, fields of corn, tiny villages and occasional crossings Ed gives the kids the nod to go check the train out.

"Walk, don't run. Behave as if you are in a stranger's house and keep your hands off things that don't belong to you, understand?"

There are three nods as the grandchildren head down the aisle, matching their strides to the sway of the car. We know we will get a full report on their return.

As Anne watches the children move out of sight it is obvious her thoughts are much the same as mine. She's asking herself it this, the first time the grandchildren will be each other's keeper, will it be a lesson that will stay with them all their lives. Once Ed and Anne are gone the grandchildren are going to be alone. She knows they must be together. There may well be spouses and children by then, and of course, always the extended family. But for those times when a special listening ear is required they'll need each other.

Our supper experience in the dining car diminishes in importance to that of getting ready for bed. Not even the fascination of watching our waiter navigate half the length of the car swaying with the train's side to side motion as it streaked through the country side rivets the children's attention as does the metamorphosis of four seats changing into two curtain engulfed bunk beds. The fact the whole process dates back over one hundred years only adds to it magic. And that the inventor was actually a Mr. Pullman who gave his name to the car we stand in increases the children's sense of discovery.

We tuck the three grandchildren into the lower bunk. It is wider than its upstairs counterpart. And because I sleep so soundly Ed opts to cling to the outside edge of the upper birth. This way he can hear if any of the children call out during the night. What he doesn't realize is that he has given me the side of the bed which includes the protrusion of a metal box about four inches high and ten inches long. It is the box which from the exterior of the train displays the illuminated numbers of our particular rumbling giant. I find it necessary to keep myself in a semi-circle all night long. If I relax and endeavor to straighten my body I am immediately jabbed into remembrance.

Ed sees to it we are all up, washed, dressed, fed and packed almost an hour before our arrival at our destination, the Washington D.C. Union Railroad Station. All ten of our eyes in their assorted blues, brown and green stare in wonder at the magnificent building. It has been restored to the days of its glory in the eighteen-hundreds. The high vaulted ceilings, glass and beautiful wrought iron work affirm the human ability to create unique beauty which can well vie with Mother Nature herself. The enormous building surrounds us with practical design that performs the services for which it is intended. Behind us the covered entry and departure tracks allow the massive engines and cars to receive and discharge their passengers. People from all over this country and others far across the seas surround us. Obviously some of its over thirteen million visitors a year take this route frequently since I see them purposefully head out for some destination, seemingly unaware of the building they pass through. I wonder if I could ever become that oblivious to its grandeur. Ed has told me there are over one hundred places to eat and shop within its two levels.

My mind goes back to my grandparents day and everyone one around me is suddenly clothed in the uncomfortable attire of the 1880's. But I am quickly brought back to the present when Rachael asks, "Grandmother, look over there. See the shop with the doll in the window? Can I go look at it?"

Sure enough, the first open door in the cavernous terminal is a small gift shop bulging with all kinds of temptations. Ed had given each of the children fifteen dollars as theirs to spend on this trip. I suppose Rachael has found her treasure already, less than a hundred feet from the train. Leaving Ed to make arrangements to have our luggage stored temporarily in a locker, I head off with the kids.

But it doesn't happen. Rachael is not ready to part with her money this soon. Much as it is love at first sight between she and the doll, Pat and Laura persuade her she had better hold off.

"Gosh, Rachael, what if you spend your money and see something later that you like better?" asks her brother.

"Yeh, I wouldn't spend it so soon," Laura joins in. "It'll be here if you decided it is what you really want to buy. I'd wait, if I were you."

Reluctantly Rachael sets the doll back despite the clerk's pointed last remark, "Well, deary, you know I can't hold this for you. It might not be here if you wait."

The words are like an arrow straight to her heart. Rachael pauses, then manages to turn her back and walks away.

We let the children choose in which of the restaurants we'll buy lunch. It is Italian. Our hotel overlooks the large park directly in front of the station. Its towering trees attest to the years the city has served as our country's capitol. I think the short taxi ride to our home away from home is the first such ride for the children. The three grandchildren do not miss any of the procedure Ed uses to hail the cab, help the cabbie load the luggage, give him our hotel name and once there help the man unload and pay him the fare. They take in the procedure with the doorman and the valet next. Once up the elevator to our room and the transfer of the luggage from the luggage trolley and the tip to the valet, the three disperse to check out the room and its contents.

When he sees all of us have had an opportunity to use the bathroom and get our things stowed Ed asks, "Well, gang, how about it if we head out to the Space Museum?"

And so it is, day after day; one government building after another, one museum after another, until we are as full of history as a Thanksgiving turkey with stuffing.

Despite the ride in a mock space ship and the Wright Brother's first plane, the exotic flowers in the Botanical Gardens and the monuments and chiseled words of our unforgotten leaders it is the albino squirrel which will become the most unforgettable moment of the trip. It had come up to them as they sprawled on the grass under the huge trees in the park within sight of the rail terminal and their hotel. Enjoying their sandwiches, chips, cookies and pop the little snow white creature arrived to beg for a handout. Its bright pink eyes pleaded.

Fortunately one of the new cameras preserved the moment. To this day when someone comes across the picture in the DC photo album it brings the whole episode back.

Rachael remains on her very own mission throughout our stay in the capitol. When we visit the Smithsonian's skeleton collection she just about has to be bodily removed from the institution's gift shop. She hasn't forgotten the doll in the railway station. As Laura and Pat slowly spend their money; a little here and a little there, Rachael clings to her fifteen dollars. Every museum, every monument with few exceptions have gift shops and my youngest granddaughter searches each.

The day arrives all too soon that we have to leave. It is hard to tell whether we hate to return home or whether we are glad the time is on hand. But there is no choice. The tickets have today's date. Getting ready to return to the station is much easier and goes much faster than when we had first set out on our adventure. There is no doubt about it the grandchildren have become good travelers. I am proud of them. They haven't begged for anything and have been better than Ed and I when it comes to walking the miles of sightseeing my husband set up for us. Even so, we'll leave far more behind us unseen than seen.

We have extra time when we arrive at the terminal. This time we all know where we are headed. This is true for Rachael, especially.

"Can Laura and I go ahead to the gift shop, Gram?"

I watch them head in the shop's direction, Pat along side. She is heading out to buy her doll.

After Ed has the baggage all together down by the train he turns to me and says, "Better get the kids. The train will pull out in ten minutes."

When I reach the gift shop I ask if everyone is ready to go and am surprised when Laura answers, "Gram, Rachael can't decide whether to get the doll."

Knowing our time is down to minutes and that trains leave on schedule no matter what, I tell Pat and Laura to hurry down to the train and tell Grandpa Rachael and I are coming, not to worry.

"Your Gramdpa is waiting for us." I say to Rachael. "Rachael, you are absolutely out of time. Either buy the doll right now or not. What is it going to be?"

With tears streaming down her cheeks Rachael turns to me and says, "I just don't know, Gram. I think I want the doll, but fifteen dollars is a lot of money. I guess I'm not going to buy her."

We grab each other's hands and run as fast as we can. As we round the corner we see the conductor reaching down to pick up his little step. Ed is watching us run toward him with a look of utter disbelief. His granddaughter has no doll in her arms.

Sitters, Fudge and Casseroles

No one stood on the shore and wished Bon Voyage

Neither Ed nor Anne ever had any reason to anticipate that the arrival of the grandchildren could change their lives so profoundly. It was as if, one by one each tie line which secures them to their world is slowly and slyly cut; the two set adrift in waters completely uncharted. No one stands on the shore and wishes them bon voyage. They merely shield their eyes against the distance and say a quiet prayer. To them, Anne and Ed are leaving, probably not to return.

Our social life does a nose dive.

Not that we are all-the-time-goers. Actually both Ed and I love being home. We always have. Of course, this fits into my reclusive life-style perfectly. And although Ed is a real people-person he is even more so a 'nose-in-a-book' type. We have the books to prove it. But this doesn't mean we don't get out to sports events, a good play or movie and party once in a while. And, of course, with my love for cooking we enjoy having others in for an occasional dinner or cookout. And we hit the restaurants whenever we have a spare nickel. Boyne City has amazing places to eat and represent a broad range of cuisine. However, now that there are five of us and not just two dining out is a bit too rich for my budget. I keep it for very special occasions.

These days, before I can accept any invitations for Ed and myself to spend time with friends a sitter must be found. This isn't easy as it has been years since we've have needed one. Thinking back I can remember a couple of times we arranged to have a sitter for our dog when we had gone on long trips. That was different as it only involved feeding and walking. They aren't likely to get into the medicine cabinet and take an overdose or fall on a pencil point.

Now I find myself at the mercy of Mary's friends to supply me with names of possible help. I feel guilty as I don't want to take a sitter away from them when they might need her.

In the midst of this dilemma and soon after the grandchildren moved in a church member stops me following the service. Much to my complete surprise she volunteers to be a sitter. Iris is a woman whose own children are grown and away from home. She is a born caretaker and her offer is from her heart. The kids come to adore her. Among other things she will frequently make fudge for them while on duty. Iris's is the perfect velvety-smooth mouthful of yummy deliciousness one would die for. The kids never get home-made fudge from me as mine always granulates. Grainy fudge is absolutely the worse.

Iris stays on call for us until the day comes when she judges the three are old enough to care for themselves. Iris makes the decision more easily than I do. But by this time Ed's and my lives have changed. It is as if we are in some state of limbo. We are in a never-never land between the parents of the children who are our grandchildren's peers and those friends who are of our age. We have evolved into a place where we no longer quite fit either group. It is an intangible which dwells in the minds of those who watch us as we move into our new parenting role. We, the grandparents, are perceived as not quite like who we should be or once were.

Of course, we are older, but everyone else is also. It isn't a matter of aging, it is more a matter of being out of step with the world around us. It is as if the band is out on the field at half time and every single member is doing Script Ohio except Ed and me. We are the couple down on the field in each other's arms dancing to the music which belongs to the days when we first met. Everyone is hearing the same music but interpreting it their way.

Those who know us come to the conclusion we are way too busy for anything but the job of taking care of the grandchildren.

For some reason Anne and Ed both forget the children are growing older and will slowly become more and more capable on their own. They will discover more of each day will belong to them alone. But that day is over the horizon, out of view. There's no way for me to nudge Anne and disclose my insight. She seldom has the time to tune me in anymore. This will also improve as the years go by.

The group that would have been Mary and Pat's ages is obviously not a fit for us. We are just too old. To them, Ed and I all but speak a different language and certainly live a life style apart from theirs. Even though we are attending school functions with them, cheering at the sports events, working at band fund raisers and painting scenery for the drama productions, as the kids' grandparents we remain just that. We are out of place. Even though both of us gobble our dinner, leave the dirty dishes on the table and drive like mad to make the event, as they all have, we are different, not the same. Oh, the others are all supportive and gracious, but Ed and I aren't on their invitation lists. They wouldn't know what to do with two seventy-year olds. It would be like entertaining their mothers and fathers. It never enters their minds that Ed and I have a lot to share and even things we might like to ask.

Our friends, on the other hand have put us on the unavailable list. Without inquiring they decide as parenting grandparents we are way too busy to have time to play cards or go to a show with them. What would they do with the three children? Set up another card table and set out the scrabble board? It gets so ridiculous that the women at the church who gather to do funeral lunches and have bake sales no longer ask me to donate a couple of pies. They are so certain I'm up to my neck with laundry, cleaning, cooking and all that great stuff that I can't find the time to do anything else.

More than one asks me, "You are planning to have some one come in at least once a week and help you, aren't you, Anne?"

The question seems to be directed at some other woman, not me. I can't imagine having to live such a scheduled life or where the money is supposed to come from; certainly not from Ed's and my or the children's Social Security income.

The only real change I make is to resign from my position as gallery and shop manager at the McCune Arts Center in Petoskey. But it is time for me to leave. I had taken the job five years ago to be out of the house once in a while after Ed retired. But that need certainly no longer exists. With a buffer of three young children neither of us have to ever worry again about the necessity of having time apart. Instead our focus has become on finding time when it can be just the two of us for a few hours.

Kathleen, the children's aunt who lives in Rochester, Michigan wisely recognizes this need. It awes me that she perceives our need for time off. After all, she is Mary's generation and how could she possibly understand a couple of oldies like Ed and myself. Annually she invites the kids down to visit their Cassidy cousins while Ed and I reclaim each other. It is then the we seek normalcy by going off to an Elder Hostel. Within each session we find an entire week in which to fraternize with those of our own ages. It seems like a slice of heaven. But even on these occasions once the 'cat is out of the bag' about our parenting three grandchildren we are set aside in a special place in each Elder Hosteler's mind as being different than they see themselves. I understand. It isn't until you are tapped on the shoulder to step forward and begin something you never, ever dreamed of doing that you are able to understand it can be done. And beyond that, you learn it can be the stuff dreams are made of.

Not being in my shoes, my peers can't be expected to know that how I live my life has not drastically changed with the arrival of the grandchildren. I still let the laundry wait until Tuesday or even later if there is something interesting to do outside of my household chores. I have always lived life with the doors open for the unexpected opportunity. It isn't that my house is allowed to become too dirty or overly messy. It is that to me the house is just that, an inanimate companion, not my top sergeant.

To me, our house is where I hang my paintings and Ed's photographs. It is where our books line the shelves and vases of flowers vie with the wallpaper with the happiness of color. It is my kitchen which smells of good homemade soup or pies baking in the oven. It is a place for family to be comfortable and belong in whatever way they choose. Foremost of all it is my husband's domain because I love him. It is one way I show him my love. The same is true for our children and now the grandchildren. My house says "I love you all".

So, living in this in-between place has become a world of windows in which Ed and I look out in contentment and peace. We find the answer of fitting ourselves into the lives of others is totally our call. I come to realize they are not comfortable interfering with Ed's and my lives. To them it appears to be a terrible amount of work and responsibility. So our friends retreat, waiting for us to call. I no longer hesitate to do so. At one time it would have been impossible for me. My shyness would insist that if our friends wanted us they would ask. Now I know better.

In less than three years riding the school bus will become difficult for the kids since after school activities beckon them. Ed and Anne become chauffeurs. In addition to their sports programs, a piano teacher is found so all three can continue in their music. Laura is the only one of the three who will continue her piano studies up into high school. Patrick and Rachael find their creativity in other venues.

Rachael is the little artist. She has the eye, heart and mind for visual art. Anne sees to it that all three children receive paint boxes and learn the principles of art. She does this in their daily life as she guides their choice of color when their rooms are wallpapered and clothes chosen. They discuss why some of the things they see fall short of being beautiful. Anne's own paintings hang on the walls with the work of other artists and photographers. She frames and mats the children's work as it comes home from school.

But their love of music can not be enriched by Anne. Somewhere between the music she hears in her head and reads on the page and what comes out of her mouth is a disaster. The family all laughs when she tries something as common place as 'Happy Birthday'. It is sufficient if she bakes the cake.

Patrick finds his world of music in his voice. Like his father and grandfather who both sang with Boyne City's Snow Belt chapter of Barber Shoppers, Pat will sing. His voice will be rich and wide in range as he enters college. He will tell Anne she shouldn't be able to detect his among all the others in the Alma Choir and Chorus, but she will believe she can. It will give her goose bumps as all great voices do. She loves music and her inability to sing leaves her in awe of those who not only can sing in tune but on key. It is all beyond her. She remembers her mother's melodic whistling, but suspects she inherited her father's gene. She never heard him sing.

Within three or four months of the children's arrival the dryer quits. I can't blame the poor old thing as I have been using it more in these few weeks than I have in the whole preceding year. There is always laundry coming and going in some form or another. I thank heaven for all the no-iron stuff. But buttons still come off and mysterious tears appear as if by magic. The kids have two responsibilities in the matter of their laundry. The first is to see their clothes are put in the clothes hamper when they require washing. Secondly, they are to fold, hang up and put away their clean clothes. Their is in the hands-on part and mine's the machine end of things. I think myself pretty clever and the kids seem content. Of course, Ed continues to have his processed the entire distance as I feel it is too late in the game to make changes in his department.

I notice a great difference at the grocery store. There are times I think one basket will never hold it all and the sales slips will be long enough to drag on the floor. I confide in Ed that I think we should have bought a cow the first week the grandkids became ours.

"We would have been further ahead in the years ahead. Heck, a few chickens would help also."

Ed's reply is just his usual slow grin. It dismisses my whole idea.

I never add candy or soda to the grocery list. Such goodies are kept for special times when we all travel together.

In some ways it excites me to once again make casseroles; those wonderful concoctions of meat, vegetables and pasta, potatoes or rice. I even locate some of the large lidded dishes which have been packed away for years. Ed is euphoric when I set my pork chop, green pepper, onion and rice medley smothered with tomatoes before him. As Ed has done our entire married life he serves each of our plates. I once again become a wizard with sixteen ounces of ground beef. And I don't reach for the Hamburger Helper. I find those pre-prepared shortcuts to cooking only add to the cost of a meal.

More exciting to Ed than the casseroles is my return to baking cakes and pies after these past years of fruit, cookies or ice cream.

A little background information is needed here that explains my strong commitment to eating healthy foods. Way back in 1916 my mother graduated from Ohio State University in home economics. She knew her foods and was fascinated by their preparation. Unlike the majority of women of her time Mother climbed aboard a train alone that year to head for New York City to study culinary arts under Fanny Farmer. Ms. Farmer was the lady of Fanny Farmer's Chocolates everyone was so crazy about back then. Mother was a true woman libber far before they banded together in the later 1900's. I admit to feeling quite proud of the old gal for getting out there and doing what she wanted to. Even today it isn't the easiest thing to actually do, no matter how much a gal may dream of it.

During WWI Mother served with the Red Cross in South Carolina in a TB rehab center as a nutritionist. This was before my father claimed her as his own. The snapshots of the time show Mom on the front porch of a hospital barracks, the only woman among a dozen or so army clad masculine figures. I believe Mom was a real swinger. I have my mother's small, brown leather-embossed address book filled front to back with the address of guys from PFC's to Majors. My father's Fort Sill address is in their midst. Because of this I know the two were in contact during those months. Not by telephone or e-mail, but by letter. I like to think they were pretty mushy letters. Both my parents certainly were capable of it. I wish I had known her then, but I was destined to arrive properly some seven years later. So, Mother's food pyramid was part of my growing years and since has played its part in Ed's and my four children and now Mary and Pat's three.

I expect my grandchildren to eat balanced and nutritional meals. Ed's rule is, "If your grandmother spent her time making this meal then you will eat it."

I temper my husband's military-like commands with my own instructions, "Try one good sized bite and if it gags you then you don't have to eat any more." No one has gagged at the table.

A surprise 51st wedding anniversary at Presbytery Point in 1994

January, Pigeon Holes and Medicaid

It's such a labyrinth out there

Anne admits she doesn't see any difference in today's children than yesterdays. To me there's a great difference in her perspective. Her rose colored lenses have changed in hue, although she isn't certain she can describe the new color. It's obvious; it's the color of wisdom. She still embraces life and those in her world with love, concern, hope and empathy. She has learned to be comfortable around others by accepting the fact they may disappoint her. At the same time she prays she won't disappoint them. It is such a labyrinth out there. She holds on to her faith much tighter than in her earlier life. It has proven indispensable. Admittedly, all this holds true for me, although this rollercoaster she and Ed have me on has me holding darn tight. Makes me wonder what dips and heights are ahead for us.

The government reports fall due in January. What a month to pick. Don't men understand that Halloween, Thanksgiving and Christmas don't just happen? By January, women, the planners and doers are ready for time off. At least I am. Instead, I must spend the month carefully filling out both the court's progress report and that of Social Security. Oh, I understand there are those guardians who find Social Security an open invitation to use the money for something not at all beneficial to the child for whom it is intended. And I realize the authorities have no way of knowing I never tried to steal a cookie out of my mother's cookie jar. I would have been caught when I might accidentally push it off the counter, causing the jar to break in a hundred pieces with a loud crash. No, I understand.

Still it is a lousy job. Once I do it I know I have no other choice. It would cost a sizable amount to have a lawyer have his secretary do it for him.

To work on the reports, I sit at my small Queen Anne's desk I bought for a song at an auction up the Maumee River. It was found in the little town of Grand Rapids, Ohio soon after Ed was discharged from the Army Air Corps in 1946 at the close of World War II. I remember the elm shaded side yard of an old farm home about a half mile south of the town. Enough people milled around among the sale items or stood fanning themselves under the trees for me to wonder if anyone was left in their homes. Ed had known a few of the townsfolk and farmers as his father had grown up there.

Both his grandparents were dead but aunts, uncles and cousins were everywhere. On the way through the town, all three blocks of its business district, Ed told me about the State Park. It lay just beyond a couple of blocks of homes on the western edge of the town. The park's north boundary was common to the banks of the beautiful and historical Maumee River. Stories of Mad Anthony Wayne's Indian battles and the Erie Canal were all part of the wide river's lore. Ed had been spoon fed on these happenings. All were part of America's westward expansion through Ohio and Indiana. As a teenager he and his best buddy, Stan, had paddled their canoes up river to Defiance. Originally the location of a fort, its very name spoke of our forefathers' will to claim the land. On the two friends' return they had used a portion of the old Erie and Miami canal to exit. It had come into disuse shortly after it was dug in the late 1880s. His grandmother's land had been left to the state on her death. The park bore her name, the Mary Jane Thurston State Park.

At the auction half a dozen cousins came up to shake Ed's hand. Nodding to me when Ed introduced me they quickly returned to reminiscing about the old days when Ed would visit. I watched one slap Ed on the shoulder and comment, "See you've got one in the oven. Didn't waste anytime, there, Coz." Only half way along in my first pregnancy, I had thought no one could detect any sign of a baby being on its way. Ed's grin at his cousin and side glance my way let everyone know his pride.

The auctioneer was well known in the area. In fact, so much so he was able to throw in a local's name now and then as he rumbled through his sales harangue. This always brought a response of laughter from the crowd and a good natured slap on the back for the person targeted. Thin as he was the sweat poured out from under his mop of red hair, down his cheeks and even off the tip of his nose. The neatly ironed bandana handkerchief he pulled out of his overalls soon became a sodden, wrinkled wad. For some reason he reminded me of the illustration of the Tin Man in Frank Baum's Oz books. He had the same disjointed look. I wondered if he, too, oiled his joints each day after his shower.

As usual the prospective buyers had to wait as all the junk and small items were sold. Often by the box full. Or even, "What am I bid for one hoe? The other five will go for the same. Buyer take one or all."

Ed found a good sized drill bit and a coping saw he bought to carry home to hang in the garage. I checked out the dishes but let the pink flowered tureen go to a higher bidder. I really didn't want it that much. Ed had been eying the Ladies Auxiliary's long, white clothe covered table with its sandwiches, cold drinks, cakes and pie with home made ice cream for over an hour when he suggested that the two of us support the hard working women. Each of us enjoyed a generous slice of apple pie complete with a large scoop of vanilla ice cream. After we had taken our leisurely lunch break we returned to the bidding scene.

It was mid-afternoon by then. The auctioneer had worked his way over to the larger pieces of furniture. He leaned against a walnut headboard propped up beside a small desk. The desk's wood was dark. Later I learned it was mahogany. It was love at first sight. Right there in all the heat I knew it had to be mine. Whispering to Ed my desire to buy the desk I had his immediate approval. As he stepped a pace away I understood the bidding was going to be up to me, win or loose. There was a twinkle in his eyes and a grin lurked on the edge of his mouth. My husband was going to let me sink or swim on the bidding all by myself. This was to be my victory.

Fortunately most of the crowd had dispersed. The heat had increased to the point not a leaf moved on the big elms. It was the wringing wet type of a-thunderstorm-is-brewing late August afternoon so common to northwestern Ohio's flat farmland. The heat made the townspeople think of their own cool parlors. With drapes drawn and blinds pulled they could sit with an iced tea or glass of lemonade and review the gossip they had heard at the auction. Having lived in the San Juaquin Valley of California during Ed's last three years in WWII neither of us was minding the heat as much as the local folk.

I began to bid in earnest having observed the protocol of the event during the day. I felt comfortable with the silent lifting of my hand. The lack of oral recognition of a bid was perfect for my shyness. Glancing over at Ed his eyes told me he knew his wife was ready for the battle. There was no doubt in his mind I would get the desk. I just knew how he felt about me. How easily it happened was a surprise to us both. An older man, probably in his fifties, was the only counter-bidder. He soon developed second thoughts about the desk's feminine size and backed away from the bidding. Much to my surprise, I found the auctioneer pointing at me, saying, "Going once, going twice. Sold to the lady in the white blouse."

A few minutes later Ed surprised me by bidding on a chair. Again the end of day bidding was slow. He walked forward to claim his purchase and carry it back to me saying, "Here, you'll need this to sit on at your desk."

Ed found his cousin, Ralph, back by the barn with some of the men. Three of them offered to help Ed with the furniture we'd bought. An old canvass was found along with a couple hanks of rope. By the time they had both pieces of furniture lashed down to the top of our '36 Ford the distant thunder was rolling to the southwest and an occasional flash of lightening was visible. Uncle George called out to Ralph, "We'll hear the corn growing tonight, son."

I had heard stories of farmers laying in their beds on summer nights and listening to their corn grow. In Ohio it grew to well over a man's head. Small tots had to be watched carefully less they disappear into a cornfield, unable to find their way out. Ed had told me of a time when he was in his teens when this happened. He had helped walk the rows searching for the child. It had taken over five hours and night was closing in when they found her. Exhausted, tear stained and dirt smudged faced, she was sound asleep beneath the corn. As a married woman I re-evaluated the story of 'listening to the corn grow'. I figured, from the size of many of the farm families the father often did more than listen to his crop grow. He must have been busy planting his own seed in a fertile field.

For most of our marriage our furniture has been all hand-me-downs or gorgeous finds at sales. Some pieces will probably not make it while they suffer through yet another family The desk and chair still sit in my bedroom. My fondness for the desk centers around its pigeon holes. There are six. Two are larger than the other four. From one I pull out pale green cancelled checks. From another, light yellow bank statements. From a larger drawer my probate court and Social Security file folders appear. With these stacks of pale blue, light yellow and buff I am ready to create the annual reports. It will not reflect the colors I see before me, but rather will appear on ordinary white. Not the most stimulating palette for a creative venture. In my mind any reports to the government take a lot of creativity. I believe they should not only tell all the financial facts, but most importantly should reflect the mental and emotional stability of our charges. After all, raising a child is far more than clothing it as one would a lifeless doll. I see every child as a future adult. Each is unique in the way they will chose to live their life. However they require the same basic instruction about making that choice.

Although excellent in math for the sake of time I capitulate and purchase a calculator with a tape. The tape will become the substantiation that my figures are undisputable. I fear the day when an angry government official might challenge my work. Check by check I pull off what it has cost to feed, cloth, shelter, educate and entertain our little flock of three. The bank statements are to corroborate income as well as expenses. Anyone who tries to exist on Social Security can attest the costs always exceed the income. To balance the whole fiasco I simply shows a deposit to the grandchildren's account from Ed's and mine's to equal the difference. The final figure turns from red to black. The reports balance as did the ledgers my brother and I kept for our father years before. The thought brings a smile to my face and heart. I remind myself, "I've got to call Doc and tell him about this. I know he will get a laugh out of it. I don't know how Dad would react if he were still alive, but I think I could make a good guess."

The bottom line is never disputed. After all, the government could care less what is happening to Ed's and my nest egg. In the end Judge Landers will call Ed and me into his chambers to tell us what a bright light we've been. In his entire case load we have been his ray of sunshine. Suddenly my January marathons with the adding machine seem worth while. The Judge has bought my creations.

Although the legal echelon has evolved a system that succeeds for itself it fails miserably for the orphan. Oh, the court visits the home situation. Thank heavens they didn't check Anne's and Ed's until after the kids had moved out of their temporary basement sleeping quarters. And Anne always sees to it she defines their progress in school, church participation as well as the support given by visits from their father's family and theirs. None of this is a part of the report form. It is attached as a letter by Anne. It is her idea alone to do this. It is not expected. Of course, she is asked to report on the children's health and she does all that. Not even then is she alerted to the existence of possible Medicaid for orphans. She never has a reason to look into any government assistance. She thinks it only kicks in for the really old folk in her country.

Perhaps this sounds stupid and Anne isn't. It's more that she grew up in the depression when there was no government aid and everyone just managed as best they could. There were a lot of favors exchanged when others did for others what was within the scope of their skills and means. Then during FDR's many work projects, you were expected to work to earn what you needed. And people, for the most part chose to work. It often proved to be the first rung on the ladder to a return to self sufficiency and pride.

When government relief checks came into existence those who had lived through the bad times saw them as diminishing to a human's self esteem. So it is that neither Anne nor Ed considers there might be more assistance available for the children than the government's Social Security plan that both their parents had supported. To Ed and Anne Social Security is not a hand-out. It was meant to be the grandchildren's in the event they should ever become orphans. It is generally believed such things almost never occur. Even when it does it's to someone else. Someone unknown. Neither of us discover until we're way down the road that there are literally hundreds of thousands of parentless children in the US.

Because of this Anne is oblivious to the availability of additional money for doctor bills. It is only after a broken arm, then a toe, special care for a lazy eye and all the other routine health care for growing children that she accidentally discovers help. The three should be under the care of Medicaid. When she asks the staff at the County Court House why she had never been told of its availability they suggest, "The doctors should have told you."

Amazed at such a pass-the-buck reply she says, "I hardly think the doctors in this country should be considered responsible for telling their patient of possible financial assistance from the government. After all they aren't on the government's payroll, at least not yet."

The loss of money Anne and Ed experience before they accidentally discover the availability of Medicaid is sizeable. What's the old saying? 'There's no use crying over spilled milk. I'm not all that sure. Maybe others should hear this and benefit from it. I certainly hope so.

A Bully, Faith and a Change
Staying as close as Velcro

Anne and her brother, Dave, grew up in a family where they watched their father, Tracy and his only brother drive a wedge of silence between themselves. The reason was never revealed to either of the children. The loss of years of companionship and family fun left a deep impression on them both. They've stayed as close as a couple strips of Velcro all their years. Always there for each other although life styles and politics have been at opposite poles. Doc, that's what we all call Dave, installed an 800 telephone number when they first became available so his sister could call him as often as she might like or need. He could afford it at the time and knew his 'Sis' was counting her money. This relationship budded back in their early years when Tracy dispensed a weekly quarter allowance to each. There was one restriction. At the end of the week they were to present ledger books which would document how the money was spent. The columns had to balance. It was then Dave and his sister learned to get their heads together. They saw to it their ledgers were in balance even if it meant shuffling their money back and forth. Tracy had no idea what a lesson he taught his two. At that time Anne never suspected she would use such a trick to balance her household account and then her reports to the government.

One part of raising our own four children I remember and have no desire to repeat is that of being an arbitrator between their arguments. With this in mind I sit the grandchildren down and explain there is just one thing they may not do in Gramp's and my house. They may not fight. Ever! If they have a disagreement about something they must talk it over like sensible people. They are never to take sides against each other.

The request is taken to heart and the three set out to solve their differences in a manner most grownups could benefit from observing. This ability transcends into their daily lives and they are often the peacemakers.

Patrick is in the second grade when he comes home from school to tell me, "Grandma there is a big boy in my class. He is bigger than any of us and he is mean on the play ground."

I answer, "He is what is known as a bully, Patrick. They are usually kids who no one wants to play with. To get attention they do something mean to someone. Why? Is he bothering you?"

"Not until today, Grandma. He slugged me in the eye."

It's then I notice one eye is reddish. "Did you ask Mr. Ladd to help you?"

"No, I just did what the Bible says to do. I turned my face and told him to go ahead and hit me in the other eye."

Astonished I ask, "Did he?"

"No, he just looked at me kinda' funny and walked away. He never came back, either."

Thinking about his reply I can all but see the expression on the bully's face when Pat called his bluff. I wonder if the toughy learned anything. As a teacher I have seen such confrontations result in surprising friendships. Of course, there is the realistic side of me that has to think, "Thank you Lord that Patrick doesn't have two shiners and a bloody nose."

Perhaps more than anything else Ed and I see an entirely different world in communications today. Long distance phone calls were next to taboo during the post depression days. My father would set an egg timer in front of Mother if she called her mother, my Grandmother Eisele, in Columbus, Ohio slightly over 130 miles to the south. Even as our children grew into adulthood a long distance telephone conversation remained a luxury. Not so today.

What of those young Pony Express men who in the early 1800's rode their horses so gallantly and courageously from station to station dodging Indian arrows? What would they think if they happened upon a chat room today? The nearest thing they had to one would be back in Ed's parents' day, the rural party line. It's a different world out there now in the ether waves. New inventions are fast making the radio and the TV surrender to the internet and the DVD. But then, the internet is similar to the party line in many ways. However, the party line had its built in censorship in Aunt Sallie or Uncle George. Today's chat rooms can turn as vile as the participants choose.

And I can't omit the cell phone. My granddaughter, Melissa's looks small in her palm and is fascinating with its pictures and is light as a feather. The big black telephone that sat on a small, one-drawer walnut stand in my parent's front entry hall was a monster in comparison. I remember its being about ten inches tall and standing on a round base that looked like the business end of a toilet plunger. At its top was a daffodil shaped mouth piece. From its neck a straight handle with a flared end hung from a bracket. My mother or father, because my brother and I never answered the phone when we were small, would pick up the whole telephone, remove the handle and holding it to their ear, speak into the mouth piece, "Hello, this is Trace" or "This is Helen". The telephone was heavy to hold and was dusted weekly just as if it were a lamp or chair. I am willing to bet no one even thinks of dusting their cell phone today.

My friend, Doug, startles me every time I call him. He answers, "Yes, Anne, what can I do for you?" This could have never happened with the heavy black telephone that sat on my parents hall stand. Like so many others he has caller ID and it spooks me. I can't help but think, all this and we are still burning fossil fuels?

Come on, out there, when are you control inventive geniuses going to let the rest of us have it a little easier paying our bills? If possessing far more than your share of the world's wealth is your goal, as it seems to be in so many cases, why not become the wealthiest person on the earth by making it a better, easier and safer place to live?

It's because our sons and now our grandchildren stand by my side that I know as much as I do about my computer. Back in the eighties our Tom tried repeatedly to explain to me that I should have a one. The who idea intimidated me unbelievably. First of all, they cost an arm and a leg, at least in light of my budget. Plus I had absolutely no understanding what went on inside their neat boxes. On my Remington typewriter I could see exactly what transpired when I depressed the 'A' key or any of the others. An arm swung up to hit the ink ribbon and imprint the 'A' at its end onto the paper I had rolled into exact placement on the machine's heavy rubber roller. There was absolutely nothing secret about the whole process.

In the end Tom won out. He arrived one day with a computer for us. He had assembled it. It was a gift. At that moment I knew Tom thought his mother and father had the ability to move into the modern world. It was a Kaypro and has long since been replaced. Ed never took to the new thing. He was too easily discouraged when a wrong key was touched and all sorts of strange happenings occurred. I regret I didn't push him a bit more, but with the arrival of the grandchildren it became too easy to think I just didn't have the time to work with him.

I am the first to admit that what I know about my computer I could put in my grandmother's thimble. And her fingers were small. I can't even wear her ring on my pinkie thanks to all the orange juice, cod liver oil and veggies my mother forced down my throat. If the computer and I come to a stalemate over something I believe it should do, and it disagrees, I click on my e-mail and reach out to our Dave, or our son-in-law Paul, or one of the grandchildren down on their college campuses for help. I am aware there is a support team available through the manufacturer of the computer, but I much rather hear a familiar voice to that of a stranger. My family has yet to ask me to push 1 for Spanish, 2 for shipping or 3 for the next menu of choices.

As frustrated as I become I know I wouldn't want to live my life without it. I have re-established contact with friends of years past. It is unbelievably wonderful we are able to 'talk' to each other more than we were able to way back when.

One friend, Ellie, lives in California and shares her poetry with me. This is so special. Ellie is severely crippled with arthritis and must write with her thumbs. In her words the computer has given me back my life. Another recent discovery is the daughter of Ed's roommate from his OSU years. Ed and Art lost track of each other after their graduation and induction into WWII. Thanks to the search engines available on the web Art's daughter has found Ed. She was able to share where her father had been, what he done down through the years as well as a recent picture of Art. Unfortunately he died a few months before the contact was established, yet it was wonderful for Ed to hear about his good friend.

The grandchildren have their own web sites and stay in touch with other people they have met on their trips abroad and in this country. In our younger years such contact meant hours of writing letters for Ed and me. Unfortunately, during our life, the pressures of earning a living and raising families diminished the time we needed to stay in contact. Way too many friends were lost. Just not enough time to write the letters we would have liked to.

I wonder if the day will arrive when someone will ask, "What do you mean when you say, postage stamp?" Another bit of communication from the past that is fast becoming extinct could be the fountain pen. I remember the ink bottle I kept on my desk and having to fill the pen. Mary's Pat had a collection of such pens that we are keeping for his son. Some were quite expensive when his father bought them. Some were gifts.

So, the kids have their cell phones and laptops, although as they become more involved in research and college papers they are replacing them with desk-tops. Even I have to admit I reach for the e-mail more frequently than I do the telephone when I want to share information with someone. It makes no difference whether it's something I'm doing or something I need.

I haven't become an on-line shopper. Probably because I have never been a true shopper. Buying something always has had to do whether it is something I need, not what I might want.

Anyway, I love the hands on feeling of holding what it is I'm buying, even if it is just the glossy cover of a new book. I admit, a book fits the classification of something needed, not wanted. Then I appreciate sharing a smile and some general comment with a sales person. The kids, all three, do a lot of window shopping on line even though their limited funds don't lend to much in the way of purchasing.

There are similarities with today's world and those of the past. Mom Thurston, during her early days as a housewife and mother in the '20's and into the 40's would telephone the local grocer and meat market, place orders and they'd deliver. The shops were no more than three blocks away. The delivery saved her carrying her food. She didn't drive and like families in those days if there was a car, the husband drove it to his work. Only the wealthy owned more than one automobile. She didn't learn to drive until she was well into her sixties. The merchants kept a running tab for their customers and it was settled once a month. This simple small town system preceded the UPS and Fed Ex, Master or Visa cards. Strangely enough without the aid of TV ads, the businesses flourished.

Today there is overnight delivery from wherever and instant credit unless you max out your credit cards. Even the banks allow a customer to withdraw money from their establishments after hours and on holidays without having to use a gun and mask. People ask Ed and me in all sincerity if we find raising children today harder than when we raised our own. We know the real question being asked is, "Are today's kids different than kids were back a generation?"

I can truthfully answer, "I haven't noticed anything more difficult."

This is absolutely true. Children haven't changed. You can't give them too much love as long as it is non-possessive, or give them too much trust and understanding. You can't buy them too many books, take them to the library too often or read to them too much. You can't teach them their responsibilities as a member of God's world too diligently. It is in their childhood children need to learn there is a higher authority and love beyond man's ability to understand. They have to have this knowledge with them throughout their lifetime so life itself never becomes too much for them to handle. Ed and I talk about this frequently.

We happen to be Protestant. It was what we were born into. I have for a long time realized I could be of any faith if my birth had been of different circumstances; by other parents than those who were mine. But in my heart or some place within myself I recognize the fact that the faith of my parents passed on to me has made the living of my live not only possible, but one of continual joy no matter what has fallen out of the sky onto my head.

I have taught Sunday School over fifty years. I can't imagine any child growing into adulthood while having to live without an understanding that there is Someone or Something standing by them all the way. I am blessed as Ed shares these beliefs and has always attended church with me on a weekly basis. I believe that there are far too many women who sit alone in the pews as their husbands strive to find all the answers to their life within themselves. Could this have anything to do with the discrepancy in the expected longevity of life for the male and female? I believe it must be a factor.

If Anne listens to me on this she will discover complete agreement on my part.

After saying all of this about raising children today as compared to yesterday I must be honest and admit one thing. There are a couple of major differences that have had a profound impact on the ease with which I have raised the grandchildren, my second round of being a mother. This time around I have been post-menopausal and there have been no PMS outbursts of anger over some stupid thing. Add to this that the children were past potty training and beyond teething. It goes without saying it has been blue skies and clear sailing all the way.

George W. Carver and Computers

The best glue between generations is peanut butter

All his grade school years Ed only lived one block from school, so he went home for lunch. Anne always seemed to live out of the range that permitted noon meals at home. For her it was a lunch bucket, complete with thermos. Her mother, Helen was innovative and creative. Lunches were not only nutritious but good. That was all back in the '20's and 30'. These days it's different. There are no lunch boxes, just squashed paper bags in backpacks or cafeteria hot lunches of unbelievably strange combinations. The only glue between the generation gap Anne discovers is peanut butter. How she admires George Washington Carver. He is her hero.

Not aware of the national free lunch program that had evolved in the sixties I decide one place to cut corners on the cost of feeding five is to pack the children's lunches as Mother had for me and I had done for our family of four. When it comes to brown bagging not much has changed. The choices remain pretty much the same with peanut butter and jam (or without) and baloney and cheese (or one or the other alone). There is still mustard, mayonnaise and lettuce in the way of fixings. I suppose if I want to bring the meat and cheese up to today's ethnic approach I can choose salami, smoked turkey or chicken and pastrami plus a zillion types of cheese. All I have to do is check out the local Subway and a number of ideas can be nailed down. They will be road tested since the local teenage crowd always seems to have representatives in the place. It is amazing the items chosen to be placed together in one sandwich. Today's stomachs must have layers of tough skin to insulate them from the choices made. Any home economics student could ace their final paper by doing research at Subway. They could develop charts on what cheese is chosen with what meat and with what condiments and other additives.

I stand beside my kitchen counter and visualize fascinating graphs done in vivid colors of mustard yellow, catsup red, lettuce green, olive black, pepper orange, and those little sliced yellowish ones, cukes and so on. A horizontal bar graph of preferred dressings could be overlaid with simple line diagonals representing the many meats. Maybe even the cheeses could be shown by placing dots in the proper places. Blow this whole thing up to a room sized presentation of four by five feet, frame it, and I believe it could cop a first prize in any local art show.

The mainstay of a packed lunch remains the cookie. It is here there has been a major change. Where once there had been sugar cookies, brownie bars or peanut butter cookies the number one, two and three choices today are the chocolate chip variety. Mine are made without the nuts because Pat doesn't like them. Omitting them not only pleases him but cuts back the cost. The cookie jar can empty itself magically between any given noon and the following a.m. When this happens I open the cupboard door over the stove and pull down the box of graham crackers. Next a small can of prepared icing is taken from the refrigerator. I cross my fingers that it too hasn't emptied itself, and then proceed to put a generous amount between two cracker halves. I've never had any complaint on this last minute act of desperation of cookie substitution.

This too can be varied depending on what frosting is on sale when I stock up once a month. Of course, chocolate is everyone's favorite, but vanilla, lemon, confetti, caramel etcetera are all acceptable. Using chocolate grahams or cinnamon is OK, too.

I stay away from junk foods like any kind of chips or cheesy things on the theory they offer next to nothing in the way of nutrition.

Truthfully, she doesn't want a bag of them lurking in some kitchen cupboard where she can gorge herself on them.

Another staple is fruit. Apples, oranges or bananas are the favorites, although the banana must be almost green or it gets too squishy and comes back home with the bag. Sometimes there will be grapes when they're in season or on sale. I seldom bother with carrot and celery sticks because all too often they end up coming back to me at day's end.

She thinks the kids are too lazy or too much in a hurry to want to chew them. Anne suspects they are in a rush to get out on the playground. You understand this is just her undocumented thinking.

One thing that doesn't fly is leftovers from dinner. Please, no fried chicken leg or sliced roast beef. And no fruit Jell-O or applesauce, thank you. Ready made pudding cups, tiny containers of applesauce and Jell-O or pre-packaged crackers and cheese and other such prepared foods such as beef jerky and miniature candy bars I regard as too pricey.

The edge I have on all other mothers packing three school lunches each morning is my inexhaustible supply of plastic bags. They are all that remain of my P's and Q's quilting business with the exception of thousands of spools of thread and even more thousands of quilting needles. The last two don't figure into school lunches, but the first does, big time. Every lunch item can go into its very own plastic bag before being inserted into the regulation brown paper lunch bag. There is no early morning, not quite awake yet, struggle with plastic cling wrap, which like craft glue, manages to stick to everything. There have been moments when I have peered down to see thumb and two fore fingers on my right hand completely bonded together. This is difficult because I normally use that hand to hold scissors to cut things. Efforts at cutting with my left hand can be downright dangerous and at the best ineffective. No, thank the Lord for my plastic bags.

Boxes of them are stored in the garage and will be there until the day I die. I have tried diligently to give them away to one enterprise after another, but with no success. Individuals who accept them only take a few, declaring they could never use a whole box of 5,000 bags. They were originally used to enclose quilting patterns. I wonder why I don't just heave them? I can't. The Great Depression days have left such an indelible impression on me that I absolutely can not consider throwing away anything with an obvious use. Doing so is to throw money to the wind. Besides, there is no way my ancient Scots ancestors would let my soul rest if I should do such a dastardly thing.

As the kids move into their teen years they will from time to time pack their own lunches. Unlike younger moms Anne doesn't have a job and is not rushing around the house trying to get herself off to a place of employment so she has the time to fix the lunches. It is just part of her morning routine. Granted she's often the chauffeur both coming and going but that doesn't take much energy. The car starts itself and even though her hand is on the steering wheel, she knows and it knows, the way to and from the school. After all, how many trips does it take to figure out the shortest and quickest way between two spots? If Anne can't remember one of the children will let her know. Today's kids have built in computers. In earlier days they were referred to as our minds.

The car itself is nothing but one giant computer. The day will come when Ed and Anne will drive a Focus, engineered to function in a large city, not a small town where everyone knows what everyone else is doing. So the car will think every time it's parked at the bank, or grocery or wherever, it's being left. Left in the world of auto thefts, it deducts, so it automatically locks all its doors without ever bothering to ask Anne if it is necessary. This really annoys Anne as it means she has to remember to take the keys out of the ignition every single time she climbs out of the car or the darn thing will lock her out.

And there'll be that cute panel beneath the clock and radio which can be pulled out and carried with her. By removing it the clock and radio can't be stolen. The problem is no one will bother to tell Anne or Ed about it. Once it's accidentally loosened, no matter how hard they'll try none of the gadgets will work.

Sometimes Anne thinks, Ed and I have lived beyond our allotted time.

An Offer, Water Pistols and Customs

Prayers said, gifts given, help extended and smiles

In fiction and news articles for years and years small towns have been beleaguered with accusations of gossip, mean tempered behavior and interfering in everyone else's business. Yet, those very residents who are the targets of such remarks are the ones who step silently forward to tend the wounds of those who suddenly become the victims of sadness, loss and pain. Such is Anne's and Ed's experience as they receive support in the raising of their grandchildren. They find arms around them, prayers said, gifts given, help extended and most of all smiles wherever the two might go in the town. Even from those they can't call by name. One does not raise a family alone. It would be crazy to think of doing so.

The support that becomes Ed's and mine after the children move in doesn't die off in a year or two as one might expect. It continues, year after year, flowing in from all sides. From Mary's friends, their church, Pat's family and ours it is without end. The variety of outreach is indicative of those who extend it. There are no words we'll ever find to express the appreciation we feel.

The offer of help that amazes us the most is that which comes from Dr. Jim, Mary's and the children's physician. He had guided her through her illnesses. During the second year the children live with us, Ed and I decide to take them to Dr. Jim for a check up as prescribed by the probate court. As Jim stands beside his desk and greets the children he turns to us. An expression of disbelief works its way into the his eyes.

"Are you and Ed raising Mary's kids?"

Ed's answers, "We certainly are. We'd have it no other way," Ed's reply does nothing to remove the look of disbelief.

"I'd like to talk to you while Sue is giving the kids their shots."

I see a look of panic fly across Laura's face and reply, "Can we do it after the shots? I really want to be with them to hold hands and stuff. Afterword they can stay in the waiting room while we talk."

So it is agreed.

I follow the kids as the nurse leads them into an adjoining room to check their height, weight and other essentials. Laura doesn't relax a minute, her mind is glued to the shot that has been promised. And I am right there with her. I dread the whole thing just because I know how it grabs her like a horrible monster. All I can do is put my arm around her and say, "This nurse is one of the very best, Honey. She knows that children don't like to have shots so she has practiced and practiced to be able to give them with just a little prick."

Laura can't even work up a tiny smile. She isn't buying my words.

I have to give her credit, with tears streaming down her face when her turn arrives, she is silent.

After the shots are given and they go into the waiting room to get their jackets, Jim turns to us and says, "If at any time, Anne and Ed, as these children grow older and into their teens you feel the responsibility is more than you can handle, call me. If anything should happen to one of you and the children want to stay in this area, my wife and I will take the children into our home and see that they are college educated."

It is my turn to stare in awe at this kind man who sees so much sadness and suffering and yet can reach out in such a generous way. There is no doubt in my mind but what he would do exactly as he says and do it in the very best manner possible

I flounder for words. "Jim, what you have said is so wonderful a thank you is not enough. It is my hope that both Ed and I can run the course with these three, but if for any reason we aren't able to I promise I will call on you."

At this point I believe Anne comes the closest to being speechless as at any other time in her life. For the doctor to consider those possible times when she and Ed might not be able to fulfill their commitment to their Mary was staggering to her. His thoughts are of possibilities that she has not stopped to think of herself. That they might ever happen is beyond her ability to anticipate. I watch as she assimilates Jim's words and accepts the fact he is speaking from observations of his profession. Rather than feeling appalled at what might be she feels reassured and comforted by the doctor's up front reality and his solution. It is hard to say, but at that moment I saw a seventy year old woman mature another degree.

Probably the most fascinating thing to the kids is the support of my nephew, Doc's youngest son, Chris. He is Mr. Wall Street with his good looks, brass buttoned navy blazer and impeccable manners. In his late twenties Chris works for an investment firm out of London, England and Milwaukee, Wisconsin. On an annual basis he makes the trip over to Michigan to attend a conference at Shanty Creek Resort near Bellaire. At one time Ed had been its assistant manager and it seems so strange to us to think of Chris as a guest there.

After the conference closes Chris drives his rental car north over the back roads of Antrim County's forested hills, through the small town of Central Lake and on past East Jordan on the South Arm of Lake Charlevoix to spend an afternoon with Mary's three kids.

He comes loaded for bear. Literally, gun in hand he steps from the car in his white shorts and navy T, calling out for the children. One look at him standing beside the car less than fifty feet from them is the kids signal to disperse in all directions. Yelling out strategy they disappear around the house corner. Chris is in hot pursuit. I move out of their way, knowing their first stop will be through the back deck door, into the kitchen in a bee line for the junk drawer where they keep their guns. All three of them try to paw through its contents at the same time. This high excitement has nothing to do with fear; it is all about ecstatic fun.

"Hey, let me get them," Pat demands. "I know where they are—way in the back."

With that said his hand pulls one out and Rachael reaches for it. Turning she calls out, "I'm filling mine in the laundry sink."

By this time Pat has two guns.

"Here' he says to Laura.

"Thanks," she replies. "I'll use Gram's sink. You use ours."

They are wise enough not to try to load their pistols from the same faucet, so there is dispersal to the bathrooms. I catch glimpses of Chris circuiting the house, waiting for a door to burst open and the firing to begin. He won't come in. And the kids know this. But it doesn't slow the process down at all. They can't get out fast enough to tangle with this crazy adult I have told them is their cousin.

It is three against one, in and out of bushes, behind the maples and pines, over the fence and out into the old orchard. The whoops and hollers bounce off the house. Guns are reloaded from buckets of water I fill and leave on the deck when the coast is clear. It is my effort to expedite the confrontation.

The warfare only worsens as the years go by and more sophisticated guns become available on the market. The large, double barreled pump variety of brilliantly colored plastics guarantees all those involved will be completely soaked.

It is only when exhaustion sets in that Chris calls kings and collapses on a deck chair, wringing wet. After that first war I buy myself a small derringer-version water gun to keep in the kitchen junk drawer, just in case. I know it will happen. Eventually I will be challenged. I can hardly wait to see the look on the kid's faces when I pull out my weapon.

It is just a matter of when. In later years when Pat comes home on break from college and can't stand not having a gun battle he simply pulls out the kitchen spray and lets Anne have a squirt when she least expects it.

The down side of water pistols is that she has no way to keep hers loaded; in readiness, so to speak. Now there is a challenge for an inventor somewhere. Anne would appreciate it. Water pistols are where Anne's affection for guns ends. She's fortunate because Ed is a non hunter. He couldn't stand to kill an animal. It is strange Anne has such deep anti-gun feelings as both her father and brother hunt. Dave uses a bow now. She remembers walking as Tracy's bird dog through the lowlands of the Maumee River when little. She was on one side, Dave on the other, back a few paces. They were to scare up pheasants or flush out rabbits. It isn't about shooting animals and birds that bothers Anne; it is about shooting people accidentally or on purpose. Anne doesn't fear a gun, but certainly does people.

David is Chris's older brother. Yes, I have three David's in my immediate family; a son, brother and nephew.

The other side of the conservative coin Chris represents is the side his brother, Dave does. His has a tie-dye business that he earnestly pursues year in and year out, following the top rock bands and selling at major craft shows across the country. Equally handsome with his long hair pony-tied and Heidi, his wife and their three beautiful children he produces the most unique tie-dyed garments I've ever seen. They are works of art, which Heidi designs and Dave dyes. One of their favorite trade stops is Michigan's Blissfest, which is held north of our place about thirty five miles. Its location is a farmer's field carved out of our forested land and within view of Lake Michigan. A Mecca for couples of the 60's and their families, they gather to camp, party and listen to bands from their era.

As the grandchildren push their way into their teens Dave sees that Laura, Rachael and Pat have passes to the event. If any of them want to help vend the clothing they are put on the payroll. The older the kids become the more they enjoy working Dave's booth with him.

On the Cassidy side of the family the entire clan rallies around Ed and me with their offers of help. Patrick's sister, Kathleen and her husband, Fred treat the children to vacations down on the shore of Lake Huron or in the malls of the Detroit metropolitan area. During their visits they come to know all their cousins, aunts, uncles and have time with Grandmother Cassidy. Kathleen does this so we can take a week or so off to be with each other, unattended. This is her thoughtful idea, something I might yearn for, but never suggest. Each time is like a honeymoon. A couple of times we enroll at an Elderhostel and spend the week with peers doing things that such an age group finds interesting. What a change. It's a trip back in time for a couple who are already reliving their life.

During one such stay with Aunt Kathleen and Uncle Fred in Rochester, Michigan, I decide to treat Ed to a trip to Nova Scotia. It is something he has spoken about for years and which we've never managed. We come to the conclusion a pop-up trailer will enable us to travel and camp with the kids in the least expensive way.

The pop-up we hunt down is old, but in good shape and available for a fraction of the coast of a new one. Buying it reminds me of the time we bought the Areostar. Because it was being displayed in its owner's side yard completely extended it was just a matter of seconds before we heard Pat call out, "Hey, Laura and Rachael come see the inside of this thing"

Ed and I turned away from the owner to see Pat's head poking out of the camper door.

"Pat", Ed called out," I don't remember your asking if you could go in the trailer. Don't you think it would be good to do so?"

Looking from Ed to the owner Pat asked, "Is it OK?

As soon as the owner's head nodded Pat's was out of sight.

I could hear Laura and Rachael discussing the merits of the little stove and sink. Then there was the surprised voice of Rachael, her head stuck out of the door and her eyes on me, "Gram, there's a refrigerator."

Seasoned travelers, we figure the pop-up would save us motel and restaurant costs. For a family of five this could certainly amount to a large outlay of cash, less than the trailer's cost. After leaving the grandkids at Kathleen's Ed and I head north into Canada. Our route takes us by way of Sault St. Marie and then eastward across the southern edge of Ontario, across Montreal, veering north onto the island. A week flies by all too swiftly as we move eastward from one wonderful Canadian park to another.

By pre-arrangement we arrive at the Halifax airport to intercept the children who were put on board a plane at Detroit Metro by Kathleen. Although it was to be Pat's first flight and he was somewhat apprehensive about changing planes in Boston, the girls had convinced him it would be a cup of tea.

It is a small, quiet air terminal, Ed and I watch as the plane arrives on schedule. Passengers enter the building, collect their luggage and leave. The sudden burst of their excited conversations enter the small terminal with them and then follow them out into the afternoon. The last bulging suitcase disappears through the door and the waiting room becomes vacant. We see no sign of the grandchildren.

As is so often the case in small airports once a plane unloads, reloads and takes back to the air there is no employee visible.

Neither of us can think of any reason for the children's failure to show up and are uncertain what to do. Leaving to look for them elsewhere doesn't seem to be a wise option. If they missed the plane certainly someone will step forward with information. After double checking for someone to question and finding no one Ed convinces me the only thing to do is to sit and wait. It is late afternoon and the building becomes one big echo with its silence. Just the movement of Ed's boot sounds like the rush of a large truck toward us. Somehow the building, although filled with benches, and surrounded with booths and counters offers no break in the passage of time. Too far away to hear its ticking Anne watches the hands on the big circular clock check off the minutes. The plane had hardly paused before it had taken back to the air and flown out of sight.

I note Ed hasn't closed his eyes. There is no thought of a nap. There is nothing relaxed about the large body on the bench beside me. He too is listening. Something has to move, some sound has to happen. The children have to be somewhere. Maybe the telephone on the desk across the room from us will ring

We hear a sound. It is the door to the back of the building from which the passengers had come out. Ed's and my heads turn. Ed is on his feet first.

It is Patrick who emerges from the swinging doors at the side of the waiting room twenty five feet away. He is accompanied by a uniformed man. The man is not too tall, but a somewhat heavy formidable man with dark hair and a grim, almost angry appearance. On second look I observe that Pat doesn't appear too happy either. Ed, standing watches as the two approach.

It is strange neither of us rush forward to take Pat into our arms. It is the demeanor of the man. Obviously something isn't as it should be. Besides, where are the girls?

It is Pat who speaks first, "Grandpa, this man won't let us through customs. He says we are runaways. Laura and Rachael are back in there crying."

I watch Ed assimilate Pat's words and at the same time appraise the man before him. To Pat he says, "It's OK, Pat. I'll talk to this gentleman and we'll unravel the problem."

Turning to the red faced, custom official he asks, "What's the problem?"

"I'll tell you what the problem is. It is you and the likes of you turning loose kids like these with no passport and expecting the rest of the world to care for them. How am I to know they are even yours? How do I know they aren't smuggling drugs or running away from home?"

Obviously the man is in a rage. Ed and I are the offenders. But Ed is wise and knows he must not join in the anger and name calling. Somehow he must calm the man down and get to the heart of the problem.

"What is it that I can do to help?"

Deflated over my husband's lack of desire to fight with him, the agent eases his anger against Ed by telling him exactly what it was we hadn't done. As the words fly out of the agent's mouth we learn our error. Contrary to our years of traveling without passports back and forth across the US-Canada border at the Sault we have done the unpardonable by sending our grandchildren over the border into Halifax without passports.

Unable to believe my ears I blurt out, "But they have their identification. They have their school ID's, their Social Security cards and other things."

Turning to me the customs agent is overjoyed I've tried to defend herself. He has been unsuccessful in getting a rise out of Ed but now I've swallowed the bait, hook and all.

"Lady, what do you think a passport is for? It is to move across the border. That is not what a Social Security card or a school ID is for."

Ed intervenes. "What is it that we can do to be able to take the children with us?"

I am relieved that Ed has come to my rescue. I don't say a word but continue to look at the man standing glued to the floor in front of us, legs splayed, hands clasped behind his back. Poor guy, he must have had a fight with his wife before coming into work today. Or maybe she is the one I should be feeling sorry for. At the rate he is going he better change jobs if he doesn't want to have a stroke or heart attack in the near future. How sad to see a man so out of place in his work.

Ed has asked the question the agent knew would be his to answer. Of course he is going to release the three to their grandparents. First he needed to rant and rave at them and let them know what terrible examples of grandparents they are. Besides, they need to know you don't tangle with a custom's agent who has had as many years on the job as he has. Before he hands the grandchildren over he extracts from Ed a promise the children will never again travel outside the United States without passports. Hands are shaken.

It is then I notice Patrick has disappeared. Once he was satisfied his Grandfather was indeed going to make things Ok he turned back through the swinging door to emerge with his two teary-eyed older sisters. The hugs are terrific and the smiles that break thorough are magnificent. Looking over the three heads I beam my thanks and love to Ed. He is always my hero.

Besides his five sisters the grandchildren's father, Patrick Cassidy, had two brothers, Paul and Peter. The three sons were the oldest of the Cassidy children. Of all the Cassidy aunts and uncles it is Peter who shows up for graduations. I love him for it. Years before when he and his Sue were dating they had accompanied Pat and Mary with Ed and me on a camp-out off the Algoma Central Rail Road in Canada. I remember the stillness of the lake which we portaged to get back to our camp spot and the forests around it. The first evening, after our dinner was cooked and the small campfire burned down to flickering hot coals the six of us watched an almost full moon ascend over the dark spruce forest. Then we heard the haunting cry of a loon pierce the air. It has become another memory I have framed and have hanging in that part of my mind which I designate as my art gallery. The area is next to the library where I shelve one memorable book after another.

Now whenever I see Pete there is the same look of loss in his eyes that our own David carries in his. Pat was Pete's oldest brother by less than two years. Tom was younger than David by less than two. Neither Peter nor Dave have ever found a way to fill the void their brother's unexpected deaths left. This haunts me, for I know they never will. Half of their lives will be lonely because the first half was so very, very full. Both have solid faith and through it handle their loss as well as possible. But I suspects it will be only in the end the light will return to their eyes.

Dave sends Anne flowers periodically signed simply, "Love from the Kids". It is his way of telling his mother that Mary and Tom are still here for her; that all four of her children love her. I wonder if he can even come close to knowing how much the flowers mean to his mother. He must, or they wouldn't arrive.

Among Mary's close friends are Julie, Lynn and Corrine who never let loose of the children. They become as an extended family, remembering holidays and birthdays. All elementary teachers, they determine which teacher each grandchild will have as the years go by. It is only the very best of each grade level that is selected. I am told over and over that any time I need anything I am to call. And I do. It is a wonderful backup when I ask myself 'What would Mary do?" By calling them I know I'll be given the answer Mary would have come up with.

Our daughter, Nancy, lives too far away for me to seek instant advice. Her profession in the ministry has called her to serve churches in southern Ohio, Oklahoma and then Iowa.

Grace Otte, life long friend of Ed's and mine is the sister I never had. She is also another Grandmother to Mary's children. As a mother she raised her five children alone and now claims seven grandchildren. She has adopted our new family. Whenever we can manipulate schedules she is on hand for birthdays and other celebrations. Many times it is Grace's council which eases my mind as I search for answers to decisions that have to be made.

As Ed health deteriorates his concern about the future household finances quietly slip into Anne's area of responsibility. She begins to struggle with the mountainous job of making decisions on her own. It has always been Ed's part of their marriage as his education was in the field of business. For Anne, her money management studies began as a child of the depression with the ledger her father had her keep. With her frugal nature, which she attributes to her Scots heritage Anne seeks every possible way to stretch the money available to her. She is determined to meet the goals she and Ed set for the grandchildren's growing up years. She finds one way after another to permit Ed and her to travel with them to give them the life she believes their mother and father would have provided. It is Grace who, time after time listens to Anne and me as we run our ideas by her.

Our church family, individually and as a group is always there for the children, without a doubt one of the greatest things it does is to reach out to the community with a youth program. The church, like so many mainline protestant groups had dropped their ministration to children about the time they really needed support. The time when questions suddenly rear their heads into their not quite adult lives. Moving on into the teen years is a giant, uncharted step. For the church to initiate such a program takes a lot of soul searching. Despite the worries about where the money to support the need would come from interviews for the position of Youth Director begin.

The final selection is a middle aged woman. Highly qualified, having worked in the Chicago area with troubled youth and holding the educational degree to support her interest Faye is hired. What no one on the committee knows is that Faye's husband, Jon, will be her constant support and co-worker throughout her time with the church.

Together they open the doors of their home and farm to the youth of Boyne City. Word gets out and the numbers swell. The farm offers the room for noisy, violent games of volley ball, hide and seek in the surrounding woods, limitless water gun battles plus wonderful camp-outs complete with bonfires, guitars and food. Jon becomes the mentor of a group of boys who are fatherless for one reason or another. Among them is our grandson, Pat.

In turn, Faye is the love of every girl she reaches out to. Rachael and Laura look on her as a second mother. She is the model of good grooming, gracious manners and above all else openly declares her faith and love of the Christ. Prayer is always an answer for whatever may need resolving. Together Faye and Jon exemplify a Christian marriage which reaches out beyond its own to others. The teens all know Jon and Faye's is a second marriage and seven children are part of its bonding. From the experience of becoming a family Jon and Faye have learned much that they can share with those they embrace.

It's after Jon announces to his 'boys' and 'girls' he has prostate cancer that he shares with them he and Faye are selling the farm to move to Ann Arbor, Michigan. There they will live close to the University of Michigan's cancer treatment center where he can benefit from their continuous research. Pat helps in the move, becoming the recipient of Jon's golf clubs and other treasures. Ed and Anne understand why Pat develops his interest in cancer research. Three times he has been made aware first hand how devastating the disease is. First his mother, then his Uncle Tom and now Jon.

After Laura graduates from college with her masters in the German language she'll decide to attend Asbury Seminary. The church will establish a scholarship fund to help her meet her expenses of studying Hebrew to teach the language at a university level. With her fluency in German she'll become a student of the early writings of the Bible. With knowledge of Greek and Hebrew she'll hope to continue that study as well as teach.

Paul Cassidy, the children's uncle, is always available. Every year he helps Anne with the reports she must complete. It is Paul who takes care of Mary's estate and sees that the children's portion is put into a trust for them. It will become theirs when they turn thirty. The age arbitrarily agreed upon as Ed and I realize we may not be here in person to help them by then.

It haunts us that unlike most others the three grandchildren will not have that bridge of having their own parents beside them throughout their adult life. Ed and I know first hand how much our parents did for us during their thirties, forties, fifties and even sixties. It is a terribly sobering thought that Mary and Pat, and we as their backup will not be here for Laura, Rachael and Patrick during that forty year span of their lives. It seems once an orphan a child is destined never to have a whole family as long as they live.

Ed and I have trouble with this thought. It hangs in our minds, nagging us, even begging us to find a more equitable answer than the one we see. Sometimes my mind seems as if it is a mass of fuzz, heavy fog or thick smoke, or maybe all three when trying to figure out a better answer. It is as if the answer is right in front of me if only the air around it would clear. I talk this over with myself. It is a problem I know I need help with.

Ed and I pray that through wonderful marriages the grandchildren will come to know parent-in-laws who will be there for them. But what really gives me peace is knowing they will have each other and memories of these great years together. And that God will stand at their sides.

One does not raise a family alone. It would be insane to think of doing so.

Encyclopedias, Cell Phones and Red Satin

Too often one thing is said and another done

All too often parents move into a state of extreme anxiety as their children leave the nest. This is hard for me to understand. It can't be their inability to trust their children and the choices to be made. Maybe even more it's about the parents' trust in themselves. They start to have second thoughts about whether they've really taught their children the values they set out to. Too often one thing has been said and another done. As their adult child walks out the door this suddenly becomes visible to the parent. Their sense of a job well done wobbles in their minds. Normally there is no second chance.

I can be standing almost anywhere and hear my dad say, "Use you mind, Anne; just use your mind."

Today I'm far more likely to say to one of the grandchildren, "Go check it out on the computer if you want to be sure."

In fact, one of the biggest laughs Ed and I have as grandparents is our buying a set of Encyclopedias in 1991, the first year the kids came to live with us. We probably should cry rather than laugh as it was a huge hunk of money. At the time we were certain it was the right thing for the three. Before the year was gone the books did nothing but try to collect dust in the tiny library. Oh, they were impressive bound volumes with gold lettering. The inside of each heavy book was beautifully illustrated but all this was nothing compared to the equivalent on the Web today, three years later. The sad part of it all is that they can't even be given away. Part of the past, the set is a dead issue.

Which, for some reason makes me wonder about the pay phone. Does anyone still use one? With a cell phone as close as a purse or pants pocket why would anyone look for a phone booth to make a call; especially in a strange area at a not-so-great-time-of-the-day. Even such terminal locations as airports and train stations don't seem to require the pay phone. The once upon a time phone booth has shrunk to a small shield on each side of a wall hung phone. Its purpose is to grant the caller a place of privacy. However, today those who are in the midst of cell phone calls are walking about, phone glued to an ear as they check their passes, buy a cup of coffee or look in gift shops for a book or magazine. Perhaps the need for privacy disappeared with the advent of the diamond studded belly button. Boy, I think my age is showing here.

Neither Rachael nor Laura indulge in body piercing. Probably due to the fact they know they are OK as a person. We always extend our complete trust to them. First we discuss how to determine what the right decision is and why it is right. In doing so the we expect the children to recognize the right thing. When Patrick, at twenty, decides to grow his beard he understands he doesn't have to ask permission. He knows we expect him to make such personal choices on his own.

The subject of trust can't be over emphasized and part of being able to trust is being the good example you teach. In other words, Ed and I try not to say one thing and do another.

The kids will learn Ed enjoys a beer when he goes out to eat. But that is where it ends. Not two beers, just one. Sometimes it is ale for me or a glass of wine. It is our belief that as the children move into adulthood they will understand why their grandparents limited themselves and will do the same.

This understanding will manifests itself at the time of Rachael's Senior Prom. Always an out going, fun loving person she is surrounded with close friends in high school and dates off and on. As prom time approaches she and I go to pick out fabric for her dress and a pattern. A small size eight and five foot seven Rachael is a knock out in the red satin gown she makes. Nothing frilly about it, the gown simple hangs by two spaghetti straps from Rachael's shoulders and follows the lines of her body to the floor. Her sewing skills are evident as the gown appears to be anything but homemade. Rachael's dress is her dream. She is a perfectionist and anything she sets out to do must be done right.

Generations of sewing skills are evident and I think of my mother's stories of the days when a seamstress would arrive twice a year at my Grandmother Eisele's home in Columbus. She stayed for two weeks and helped make dresses for Mother, her three sisters as well as my grandmother.

The memory is interrupted by Rachael, "Gram, you wouldn't believe how much some of my friends are paying for their prom dresses. Two have spent over $200! Mine has cost me just over twelve dollars, pattern and all."

"Knowing how to sew is a wonderful way to have the clothes you like when you can't afford to buy them. Besides it's fun," I answer.

As Prom time approaches I'll finally ask, "Who is taking you to the dance, Rachie?"

"Oh, I'm going alone. I'll hang out with my friends."

"Oh, Rachael, your prom? You don't mean it?"

"Grandmother, if you knew what will be going on at the parties after the prom you would understand. I just don't want to get involved in all that stuff. I don't see any fun in it."

Trust.

Needles, Red Wine and Cabbage
Living in the world of tomorrow

Anne has lived to see such unbelievable advances in the realm of medicine. It is as if she's living in a tomorrow's world. It seems only yesterday that as a young child her TB shot became horribly infected. The scar on her upper left thigh is the remnant of that vaccination. Today a mere scratch is all that is required. Two years later, at seven, Anne was privy to the death of the beloved son of the next door neighbors whose house was just on the other side of a privet hedge in Maumee, Ohio. He and his older sister had been playmates of Anne and her brother. The death was a result of a bout with a deadly strep infection at a boy's summer camp. Today there is penicillin. Medical science has always fascinated Anne. She would have studied the profession if she had thought her parents would have permitted it. Anne's Uncle Uri, was the horse and buggy doctor in Sylvania, Ohio when she was little. He probably had a lot to do with her interest. Dave, her brother, did head for the field of medicine until the military service decided it needed dentists more during WWII. He became a dental surgeon.

During the short time Mary was a widow she relied on the county health service for the children's immunization. Usually held in area churches they were easily accessible and I would go along to help her with the children. I remember no difficulty as the girls faced the nurse and accepted the shots. And of course, Patrick as an infant seemed oblivious to what was happening.

This memory makes it hard for me to understand why I'm having such a difficult time getting Laura to go to the doctor with me. She has a fever, sore throat and is really not well. At ten she is a big girl, well on her way to being the five foot eleven that she so wants to be. And she is strong. I can't carry her. My only option in getting her to go is with her agreement. There is no way I am going to bodily drag my granddaughter to the car and then into the doctor's office.

Laura's fears verge on absolute terror. It is the 'why' I can't understand. She isn't stubborn and doesn't challenge my requests as a rule. She is always her grandmother's helper. This action doesn't make any sense at all. And, of course the fact Laura feels lousy can't be helping.

So I sit on the edge of her bed and talk; first to calm her down, get the sobbing stopped, the nose blown and the sore throat relaxed. We talk about the fever and sore throat. I tell her about the days when I was a little girl and how all too often the doctors didn't have the wonderful medicines of today and children stayed sick for long, long times. I explain infantile paralysis and how it no longer affects children thanks to a vaccination that all receive.

"Have I had it, Grandmother? The shot?"

"Oh, yes, when you were a tiny baby. In fact you have had a number of other vaccinations also."

"Were they done with needles?"

"Yes. Using a needle is necessary because the medicine must be injected into the blood. I even have had shots for poison ivy for which I am so grateful."

"Will the doctor give me a shot today?"

"I don't know, Laura. It is something he will have to decide. Sometimes pills work, other times a shot is better. It just depends."

"Well, I'm not going. I don't need to. I'm feeling better."

With that Laura closes her eyes and pretends to go to sleep.

I remain on the bed beside my possum playing granddaughter and think.

Lots of kids are afraid of getting shots, but not to this extent. This fear is so real. It is so overwhelming for Laura. Why?

Suddenly it hits me; I understand. All three of the grandchildren have watched their mother for over two years go in and out of hospitals for treatment. It always involved needles sticking into her arm or body in some manner or form. They had watched the areas where the needles were inserted redden and turn painful and have to be re-inserted. In their quiet observation they had understood the whole process had been hard for their mother despite her smiles and laughter. They had not been fooled. Laura, the oldest has retained vivid memories of those days.

And in the end all the doctors and all their needles, all the caring nurses and their injections had not saved their mother. To Laura needles are to be avoided at all costs since they serve no purpose whatsoever.

Reaching over to Laura I tell her, ignoring the closed eyes, "I understand, Laura. You have seen way too many needles in your life time but if it hadn't been for the medicine they allowed the doctors to give your mother she would not have lived as long as she did. And to do so was her dearest wish.

The eyes open a bit and look out at me.

I continue, "Come on, we'll go to the doctor today and I will tell him how you feel about needles and we'll see what he can do to help you get over this throat infection. It is the best way for you to become well. It's no fun being sick."

It takes Laura years to conquer her fear of needles. In fact, I doubt if she ever will completely. But she makes herself face doctors and their needles when she must and that is all that can be asked.

On the other hand, Rachael, takes her health issues in stride. She had eye surgery before she turned one. Once being born with a 'lazy eye' was a life sentence of being cross eyed. A disconcerting affliction, which makes it difficult for others to look at you because it appears the eyes are looking off into two entirely different directions; one at the observer and the other at the sky, ground or whatever.

By the time she is eight and living with us the surgical treatments have almost completely adjusted the discrepancies in Rachael's eyes. She wears glasses to complete the process. It is only when she becomes overly tired her eye tends to become lazy and drift out of its corrected position. To me it's a miracle that such a beautiful child can be given corrected eye sight and not live her entire life as a freak of nature.

Of course as she grows into her teens Rachael will move one step further and set her glasses aside, preferring to wear contact lenses. They are another awesome progress medical science has attained since her grandmother's childhood days. Without all the medical innovations her granddaughter wouldn't be such a beautiful blue eyed blond young woman. She is Anne's and Ed's sunshine.

With Patrick it is the male side of the story. Although not at all fond of needles he takes them in his stride. His awareness of the world of medicine increases with the discovery his youth group mentor, Jon, is a victim of prostate cancer. It draws him steadily into a deep interest in medical research. Part of his acceleration into research is the world of computers. He sees in them the tool that is required to move more quickly and to penetrate far deeper into the unknown. Not a day goes by that this is not demonstrated as the media reports new findings, new discoveries, new answers. And we are inundated with drug ads on TV.

And, of course, with Pat there is the humorous. There is a time in his mid-teens when Patrick goes onto a two hour feeding schedule as his body suddenly realizes if it is to attain the expected Cassidy size it must get going. Ed and Anne hear the refrigerator doors opening and closing all hours of the night and day. His grandmother finds herself trying to manage two carts through the grocery aisles as she buys bags of food to lug home.

In the process, Patrick attains his six foot four height and fills out nicely. He discovers soccer and can no longer find his shoe size in the local stores, but must look on-line for his size fourteen. Ed, who has had big feet all his life, discovers his size 12Ds are no match for Pat's. In the process of his feet's growth Pat learns the hard way that his foot will no longer fit on the stair steps. He breaks his toe running up stairs one day after school.

Somehow the whole growth spurt will stop as fast as it had appeared. Patrick will work with weights and watch what he eats to keep himself where he wants his weight to be. Anne stands back on the sidelines knowing all three children have been taught what they should eat to remain healthy. She realizes the nutritional story is changing as today's research broadcasts new information on the food pyramid of her mother's day.

Anne will decide that at Ed's and her ages they'll stick with what has brought them this far with whatever else might sound feasible. In an e-mail from Pat he'll alert her to the advantages of dark purple/blue fruits such as purple grapes and blueberries in the area of brain support. She'll wonder if red cabbage and eggplant fit the category also.

She and Ed like them all. Anne prepares a German dish her mother taught her when she was little. Chopped red cabbage is braised in water until tender; vinegar is added with a dab of butter and brown sugar to glaze it. Bratwurst and spaetzle are the finishing touches. Ed and Anne can pledge their brain power with a glass of red wine and dive in knowing they're eating healthy.

The backyard project—1993

Gym Set, a Wheelbarrow and Septic Tank

It is far more likely to understand the work of the hands than that of the mind

Memory is one of those things which comes as part of our package, like breathing. It is just there, filing things away for us, which would otherwise disappear like the evening sun or summer's last day. One's memories are unlike that of someone else. Just because two of us participate in the same event is no assurance our memories of it will be anything alike, especially when it comes to the details. In today's world it is far more likely we understand our hands better than our minds, even though we use both extensively and for a great variety of purposes. Like breathing, our memory is pretty much taken for granted until it ceases to function properly. It is then we understand what a precious thing it is. Unlike breathing, there are no oxygen hook ups to help us along. Anne will become aware of this as she and Ed age.

The spring following Mary's death the five of us took on a major building project. As I think back it is hard for me to know who was having the most fun, Ed or the kids. We'd driven up to Home Depot and returned with an outdoor home swing and slide set, that are frequently seen in backyards. This one had an upper fort deck with a yellow, red and blue striped canvas top. In addition to the slide and swings there were gymnastic rings, an overhead bar and an access ladder. Ed also bought the makings for a big sand box. Patrick is a car and dump truck fanatic. I suspect he'll outgrow the dump trucks but never the cars.

The assemblage of this outdoor recreation center in all its complexity was no challenge for Ed. He is a I-can-do-this-if-you-will-just-leave-me-alone type. That time I wasn't the one who was trying to help him, it was his three grandchildren, ages seven, nine and eleven. The grandkids were way ahead of their grandfather throughout the whole effort. Actually, they about went crazy when Ed explained that the posts had to not only have holes dug but they must be set in concrete.

The mixing of the concrete was presented in lesson form by their grandfather. It was formulated in his old, leaky wheelbarrow with the use of a hose, bucket, garden hoe and shovel. Ed heaved the opened bag of mix up in his arms, pouring it in a huge cloud of white dust into the old barrow. Pat stood near by with the hose in hand, directing it away from his feet. Once Ed gave the word Pat was in his glory helping to slosh the Redi-Mix Cement from front to back in the wheelbarrow. Then with Laura's help he wheeled it over to a hole his grandfather had dug with the post-hole digger and dumped it in. I am certain he saw himself as one of those gigantic spiraling mixer trucks that roam the highways during construction season. It fascinates the artist in me to see the open expression of wild creativity displayed in the designs displayed on their rotating surfaces. Who paints them in purples, oranges, yellows and whatever? Certainly not the burly, work clothed men who drive and operate the large and strangely shaped machines, or do they?

In awe at Pat's strength I thought, I'll bet the day will come when he will stand taller than his grandfather does at six feet two and will be able to out do his grandfather in just about anything.

Rachael was shown how to tamp the cement down into the hole around each pole with the shovel handle so all the air will be released. It was just the job for Little Miss Perfectionist. The whole process of setting the gym supports in place became a well organized operation that not even Ed could find fault with. The children studied the level as Ed explained why the posts must be just so.

"If they aren't set upright straight the pieces of wood that join them at the top may seem too long or too short and we'll be in a mess. We have to do it right now so we won't have problems later," he explained.

They understood. The posts stood sturdy in their concrete anchors, exactly six feet apart about ten feet from a copse of young maples in a spot where the children thought it should be. It was under the small trees that they built the sand box. All was in comfortable sight of the back deck. I felt I needed to have the whole structure where I could keep an eye on the children. The swing and slide were one thing but the rings, parallel bar and high fort floor were something else. I didn't want any broken bones.

Although heavily used the whole play set still stands today, some four years later, as if it had just been put in place. I have learned to relax about its potential dangers and seldom am aware the kids are even playing on it. I have learned to trust them in what they do. Besides, it seems there is always something else demanding my attention. Today It's a visit from the septic tank man. We've been having problems for a while with toilets not flushing right and have come to the conclusion the septic system is overdue for some care. There have been five people using it these last four years rather than just two. And, oh, boy the laundries!

Mr. Radly arrives mid-morning and drives his big truck around the south end of the house, past the garage, through the field and into the area he remembers where the septic system was installed. The drain field extends out into the side yard beyond the garage and play area. Of course, the first order of business is to open the tank. This becomes a problem. No one remembers the exact location of its lid or had thought to mark its place. Years of grass and weeds disclose no sign of the tank's top.

Mr. Radly, prepared for just such a thing, retrieves a long rod, a probe, from his truck and systematically begins stabbing the ground. The kids are fascinated, especially as he works himself closer and closer to their gym set.

Ed and I become more and more concerned and upset with ourselves that we hadn't thought to mark the opening. We had been so certain we'd remember its location. Then the sound of the probe hitting the metal manhole cover causes five heads to turn and look in amazement at Mr. Radly. He stands, metal rod in hand, bent over under the gym set, behind the slide. He looks at everyone with a big, relieved grin. The lid is dead center between the four uprights Ed had set so securely in concrete.

How he had dug the four holes and didn't once hit any part of the septic tank is nothing short of a miracle. There can be no other explanation unless you call it just dumb luck. But to me that doesn't seem to fit.

A month later I get the three children aside and tell them about an idea I have. It involves the small storage barn the church owns next to its Sunday school entrance. Not really a barn, it is a small shed which can be bought at lumber yards ready to assemble. Designed with a hip roof it looks like a miniature barn. They can frequently be spotted in backyards.

This particular one is stuck back in a recess near the rear entry, but is still visible from the street to anyone. It had been set in place about the same time the church updated its building to meet the handicap access law. The ramp ascends up one side of the church to a side entry. It had been painted a dull brick-red to complement the brickwork exterior of the old church. There must have been leftover paint as it was also used to cover the outside of the little barn-like shed.

None of this has bothered me until the paint began to chip and peel. The ramp was eventually repainted. In fact this has happened twice. But the little shed is ignored. All this prompts me to suggest to the three grandchildren that the four of us take some brushes and go in to remedy the situation. I grab some scrapers off Ed's workbench and head for the hardware store. There I buy a gallon of exterior latex enamel. It matches the ramp's brick-red. In an afternoon's time the shed is scraped, cleaned and repainted.

The whole thing is a secret mission. The grandchildren are sworn to eternal secrecy. I impress on them the painting was done because it needed being done and because they were able to do it. The important thing is to know they had accomplished something helpful, without being asked, being paid or thanked.

As time passes I begin to wonder if anyone ever catches on that the small building has been painted.

Books, Headaches and a Trap Door

The mundane world of daily chores is easily forgotten

Anne has always been able to empathize with an addict. Whether they are the gambler, the overeater, the drunk, the smoker, the zealot or whatever it might be someone can't live without. She has always thanked the Lord that her addictive passion has been for something truly wonderful rather than life threatening. Anne is a reader. The mundane world of daily chores is easily forgotten. Anne wears no wrist watch. She can't leave a book alone. Nor can she resist purchasing a book whether at a rummage sale where she has found the complete sets of Zane Grey westerns and Mary Robert Rhinehart mysteries, estate sales, secondhand stores and yes, even book stores. And as the hand fits the glove she has come to love to write. I don't know which is more exciting for her, to enter another's world as she opens a book or to enter a world of her own creation as she sits at her computer keyboard.

As a child I learned at an early age a book is a place I could enter to disappear, leaving the world outside to wait for my return. Perhaps more for me than most other youngsters, books became my close and trusted friends. They were non-intimidating and safe harbors from the world that demanded all too often I relate to an individual never seen before. My phobia of shyness was acute. The teasing of relatives and friends thrown my way intensified it as I grew.

In Maumee, Ohio in the late 1920's my parents lived directly across the River Road from the Lucas County Library. The library was new and every alcove beckoned me, a six year old, to explore the brightly jacketed books on its shelves. Best of all there was a weekly story hour. As soon as I learned to read I devoured the Oz books. For today's kids it is the Harry Potter stories. And of course there were all the classics; Little Women and Little Men, David Copperfield, Tom Sawyer and other favorites. There were always two more books to read beyond the one I was permitted to check out. I have never caught up.

Destined to never leave my shyness behind, I have learned to live around it. I have become unbelievably ingenious in ways to hide it from those life sets in my path. Only Ed has known my secret. In his love for me he shares and helps me with the burden. He has become my front man, the person who stands between me and others. Never once does he insist I grow up or act my age. Instead he tells me how wonderful I am and how much he loves me. This is all I need to have to attend social occasions; even an evening with another couple. I have learned not to bolt. But there are times I go through all kinds of terror making myself become the person I'm positive I'm not.

It will be the fall of 2001 Rachael leaves for college. Shortly after her departure Anne will drive to her first Walloon Lake Writers' Retreat. It is something she's wanted to attend in the worst way. Yet as she leaves her car and climbs the steps to the beautiful log lodge on the lake's edge it takes only one glance through the large glass doors to stop her dead in her tracks. Inside she sees those who would be her co-students and instructors welcoming each other over an amazing array of tantalizing food. They're laughing and conversing. She knew in advance she wouldn't know anyone at the event. Yet even that preparation isn't enough to allow her to open the door and join such a group.

Instead Anne will turn around and run down the steps, stumbling across the long stretch of lawn and onto the stony parking area. Climbing into her car to leave the grounds, tears of anger and disappointment stream down her face. After driving two miles on the way home Anne pulls into the driveway of a farm house, turns off the car and literally talks out loud. In her anger she reminds herself she is seventy-eight and a grown woman. That if she is ever to write a book this was where she must begin. She coerces herself into believing she can enter the lodge by visualizing Ed at her side. She will let him lead her through the evening. Drying her eyes, replacing her smeared makeup, turning the car on and backing out into the road she heads to the retreat.

Anne treasures the friends and support she finds among the group. No longer intimidated by the authors that assemble to teach, she remains in awe of their success and complete lack of self-importance. They arrive from all over the country; New York, California, Atlanta, Ann Arbor; the east, west, south and north. It is obvious writing is their passion. Because it is hers also she becomes one of them for those magical hours she listens to their instruction, reading and life stories.

The year Anne is persuaded to write her memoir she takes Ed with her for the first time. Together they attend the last evening's 'read' and dance. She knows she is there only because of him. In all truth she will be showing him off to those she's come to know.

Today every room in Ed's and my house has books. Without saying, the children are read to every night as they are tucked in bed. I had read 'The Crooked Man' and "A Million Cats' to our own four until I knew the cadence of each story by heart. Now I have pulled them off the shelves and started again with the grandchildren. Even the ancient Oz books are still there along with Ed's life long collection of the American Heritage, my Zane Gray's and Mary Roberts Rhinehart mysteries. Countless volumes on Lincoln and the Civil War along with book after book on the American railroads stand shoulder to shoulder with hundreds of contemporary writers, both novelists and non-fiction.

Reading is always a learning process. As we have become older and wiser we're able to sort the believable from the ravings of a troubled person. But I believe children move right into a world of fantasy, whether good or evil. It is here parenting begins when the very first read-to book is held beside the bed, pages turned, pictures studied and words heard.

The grandchildren listen to books that spread across four generations and eventually they'll take their own choices with them to a favorite reading place and begin to explore the world of current literature.

After one bedtime read, probably Silverstein's poems, we say prayers and I reach to turn off the light but am interrupted by Pat.

"Gram? I think I have figured out where headaches come from."

Not prepared for such a scientific discussion I sit back on the bed's edge and reply. "How's that, Hon?"

"Well, you know how you start thinking the minute you wake up in the morning?"

I nod.

"I believe that starts your mind going and it keeps circling just like a clock all day, picking up speed as it moves. Now, if you're having a really busy day that requires a lot of thinking and your mind is going to pick up so much speed it's going to make your head ache. You think this might be it?"

The theory is so simplistic I smile. Our six year old grandchild has thought out the origin of headaches in a manner that not even the most advanced scholar could more clearly state.

"I think you have nailed the whole thing right on the head. Now slow your mind down and get the sleep you need for it to function tomorrow or you may find yourself with a headache."

It is the same with the girls' love of Rob Dahl, of Peggy Parish's *Amelia Bedelia* and Maurice Sendak's *Where the Wild Things Are*.

The house is all but wallpapered with books today. The kids have their own collections. Anne can't throw even one of hers away, planning to re-read it sometime.

She loans books, but is so possessive about them the recipient senses they will suffer dire consequences unless they are returned. They always are. She convinces herself that although she can't take them with her at the end of her life that they will be there waiting for her. Wherever There proves to be. To know she'll have the time to read those she has always wanted to but never has had the time to, is a wonderful thought. Plus to read her favorites over and over for eternity is a heavenly thought—sorry about the pun, but I can't leave it out.

Much to the kid's delight Ed installs a two-way radio set in the grandchildren's rooms to connect with our bedroom some sixty feet away. It is at the other end of the long one-floor-before-the-kids-split-level-addition-is-added-on home. Normally a sound sleeper during the night, I must rely on Ed to hear an approaching thunder storm. It is he who gets up to close the windows. There's no way either of us are going to sleep through a child's middle-of-the-night barfing session or coughing fit. Unfortunately, the children feel the sets should also transmit between their rooms. They don't understand our concerns. Rather they envision all the kinds of fun they could have with the equipment.

One day the three in all seriousness come to me with a plan. It would allow them easy access to each other by eliminating the need to use the stairs. They propose a trap door be built into the Rachael's closet ceiling to open into Pat's floor above. A ladder would allow access and egress. Their eyes shine. As an adult I can't quite see the need. They are young and energetic. There is the direct stair route immediately outside each of their bedroom doors which accomplishes the same purpose. However, the child in me can't help but be privy to the fun the secret passage could be.

I let myself go as far as to visualize myself pulling my mature body up through the small square opening and into Pat's room. The hole would be square because it would have to be cut between the ceiling/floor joists, which are the traditional sixteen inches on center. I consider my diameter and wonder if I'd make it.

Pat would be peering down at me, calling, "Come on, Grandma, it's easy. Don't be afraid." And the girls would be encouraging from below. Probably pushing.

Then I think how to explain the idea to Ed. I know there will be no trapdoor. He's way too practical to see the need. And from his point of view there would be none. It is only from the kids perspective such a device would be beyond description in the living of life. I can't think of a way to justify my refusal. I don't want to use Ed as my reason. So I suffer as I watch my image as the greatest of all grandmothers shrink before me. I know it will take something fabulous to erase the trap door idea from their minds.

It is then I remember the Chestonia Post Office in the garage. Ed and I had carried it home from an auction in the small Michigan town of Alba some fifteen miles north of Mancelona back in the mid sixties. A beautiful piece of maple, the post office was made to set in the wall of the town's general store. There it was accessible from either side by the residents of the tiny turn-of-the-century lumbering town. The mail could be inserted into the individual cubby holes by the clerk on one side and withdrawn from the opposite side by a patron. Quarter inch iron bars set in each opening much like in a jail cell protected the mail boxes which were numbered in a beautiful gold calligraphy.

Not aware of the request to open the closet ceiling to the room above Ed finds the post office a great idea. He is glad to finally have a spot for it. After he cuts an opening in the wall between Rachael's closet and their hall the three excited grandchildren and I help Ed slip the post office in place. A half dozen well situated nails hold it tight. The three grandchildren play 'mail' by the hour. Rachael is often the postmistress. After all it is her closet that was invaded. Pat and Laura write endless letters to mail and later receive.

Anne's reputation is saved. Fortunately e-mail is not yet on the horizon, at least not within any of their vision.

Bricks, Pudding and a Log

What we see and hear as children can become who we are as adults

When we are children so much of what we see and hear becomes who we are as adults. At marriage we bring such a mix-match of traditions together it can be difficult to combine the pieces. But persistence, a bit of letting go and holding tight creates a combination of its very own to be passed on through future generations. This evolution of family traditions has been a special challenge in America, known for years as the melting pot of the world. The extensive use of the word aliens by our media today causes me to shake my head. What else are any of us? The American Indian with Alaska's and Hawaii's natives are our country's only exceptions.

Thanksgiving was Thursday. The family had the usual turkey dinner with all the fixings. The really big thing about the holiday for the children is the two days off from school. For Ed it's all the great food and the history behind the day. To me the whole affair is like a gigantic red flag being waved across my brain alerting me of what lies ahead. Christmas.

No matter how our pastor and others may try to keep the Christ in Christmas and Santa Claus off in some far corner I know they're fighting a losing battle. In fact I sincerely believe they have forfeited their childhood for the adult world of thought. They are completely missing the boat, having somehow lost the whole idea that the Christ brought God's love to the world and within our human limitations, mankind endeavors to mimic that gift in a gesture of gratitude. For that one brief day the world witnesses the gift of love. We in turn give to those we know and even to the stranger. I believe the challenge lies within each of us who are parents to teach our children why we give gifts. It has nothing to do with want lists but everything about the love God brought into our world the night His Son was born.

Granted the media hype gets sickening and down right repetitive and deadly. It doesn't change a thing I do or a gift I give. I tune it all out selectively; keeping the music. The festive lights, the ribbons and glitter affirm the music in my soul as I set about creating or selecting the gifts for all those held dear. I'm blind to gimmicks and have a deaf ear for extravagant sales pitches. There is no denying the wonder of young children as they are swept up in this sudden world of doing for others. This becomes the driving force for me.

Christmas never becomes a wish list. Rather it is an ongoing plot. Everyone tries to covertly discover what it is they can give to others that will reflect how much they care for them. With my eye on the budget I'm pressed to find ways to make the day as special for the grandchildren as I believe it would have been if their mother and father were with them. I solve the dilemma by getting each a modest gift from Ed and me much as I do for our other four grandchildren. Then I look for something special, something their parents may have put under the Christmas tree for each of them. I use money from our investments for the gifts. I know very well what I'm doing but pretend it's Ok. After all, the budget survives.

But the gift of love is not always easily accomplished. Christmas is proof of that as we ready the presentation over a period of days. The celebration becomes difficult as to how love is and should be preserved. Tradition eases the struggle for many. In our family Christmas has been celebrated on Christmas morning for as long as our memories go back. For my brother, David, and me it meant a long, cold trip of over one hundred miles to Columbus, Ohio where Grandmother Eisele waited for us.

Our father would endeavor to break the hardship of the slow drive in his olive green, red pin-striped Reo four door sedan. He carried hot bricks out of Mother's gas oven in gloved hands to the kitchen table There they were wrapped in layers of newspaper and taken out to the car. He placed them on its floor. Dave and I were also wrapped in layers. Underneath everything we wore was long underwear covered with cotton stockings, pants and leggings. The upper half of our bodies was covered with sweaters, coats and scarves.

We were so enveloped in clothing we became stiff, all but unable to bend enough to sit on the car seat. Hats, mittens and scarves topped it all off. All of these were made at home with knitting needles or crochet hooks. On our feet, over our shoes, were galoshes. These were placed on the hot bricks. Then a thick quilt, also homemade, was thrown over us, closely tucked in around our legs and arms.

There we were mummified up to our chins in everything our parents could think of to keep us warm. Why all this? Simply because Dad's beautiful Reo had no heat and Twinsulate, Dacron and other such materials had yet to be dreamed up. For half the distance, down near Findlay, the feet stayed warm. The last half was terrible as the cold penetrated through the layers of clothing and toes and fingers turned numb. My brother and I knew how much they would hurt once we retrieved them from all their wrappings.

These memories make wonderful stories to tell the grandchildren. To them it must seem of another world. Even Ed and I admit, looking back, that it really was. Today's travel is so very different. But some things like visiting relatives over the holidays remain constant, thanks to tradition. We pray it will continue for generations to come. I still make Christmas cards the way I have for all the years of our marriage. Now they are mailed out with the grandchildren's names included. For a couple of years I used photographs taken by Laura. My favorite is the one she shot of Major when he was a kitty. He had crawled into the Christmas tree at its base and worked his tiny body upward until she caught him peering out between the needles near the top; his big, bright green eyes reflecting the tree's lights.

I always serve Grandmother Cook's plum pudding with its hard sauce perfectly laced with brandy. Patrick loves to set it ablaze and carry it onto the table. Stockings are hung from the mantle and unlike magazine photos they are not matching. They represent no theme other than Christmas. Each belongs to a particular member of the family and at one time had been sewn or knit by someone just for them. The tree is decorated by all who care to assist with a hodge-podge of old and new, bought or handmade ornaments. Each year's tree is impressive and may be set in a different place in the house. It is an annual decision dependent on that season's desire.

I remember the first year the grandkids were with us for Christmas. The holiday closely followed on the heels of the moving van's dramatic arrival. The tree stood on the corner of the tiled floor area at the base of the stairs. It was a wonder any balls survived, considering the number of times an ornament seemingly hung upon a branch slipped off to fall on the floor. There it shattered into a jillion tiny pieces of glittering colored glass on the dark charcoal grey ceramic tiles. Voluntarily, the six, eight and ten year old trimmers had murmured, Whoops in a sympathetic chorus as they contemplated its broken beauty beneath the green needles of the tree's lower branches. There were no bare footed grandchildren or grandparents that Christmas.

This holiday season, three years later, the kids request a really tall tree. The ceiling is ten feet above the tiled floor. Out in the Jordan River Valley Ed discovered a tree farm a couple of years before. This year when we reach it everyone sets out to find just the right Christmas tree. The snow is deep, over the tops of boots. It is only a short time before the nineteen above zero wind works its way between the layers of sweaters and jackets, up the sleeves and around the ears.

Mittens are tucked over the sleeves, caps are pulled down over the ears and every button is fastened.

Seeking a tall tree, their goal for the year, the kids are drawn to those which rise above the others. Often they prove to be in the fourteen foot range. Before toes freeze and fall off, the three kids gather in earnest discussion about how to find the right one. A plan is set in place and they take off down separate rows, calling back and forth to each other as a possible candidate is spotted. It works. The perfect tree is located near the back fence. It stands straight, not too fat and at least nine or ten feet in height. Ed joins the excited group and insists it will be too high, but he is over ridden by his grandchildren. I keep silent, but inwardly have to agree with the kids. The tree looks perfect. Pat and Ed take turns flat on their stomachs in the snow sawing the beauty down.

Like monkeys I have watched and laughed over at the Toledo Zoo, the kids crawl in and out of the van securing the tree so it won't fall out despite its long protrusion from the open tailgate. The half hitch knot their grandfather has taught them is diligently used. The frigid December winds whip through the van during the entire trip back to the house; picking up clumps of snow from the tree's branches and flinging it down necks and into faces. Everyone is excited about the thought of having a tree that will reach the very top of the room; with the exception of Ed who is visualizing it protruding through the roof.

The German heritage, some would call it a tendency to be stubborn, in Ed insists the tree is too tall. There won't be room for the angel to fit on the top. Once the kids have helped him drag it into the house, through the living room and into the stair hall Ed tackles what he terms the worthless bottom branches. They must be cut off to rid the tree of those near-the-ground, almost dead ones. In the process and despite the kids' howls of pain, he proceeds to remove part of the lower trunk. The result is a disaster. The tree is eighteen inches shorter than the grandchildren had envisioned.

Ed, realizing the damage is irreparable removes himself from the scene, leaving me to somehow bring peace and joy back to Christmas. There is no feasible way the amputated limbs can be glued or nailed back onto the tree. Instead, with the children, I go out behind the garage. With their help I dig into the snow until some left over cement blocks from the house's building days are uncovered.

Cold, heavy and wet they are carried inside and stacked four high to form a base for the tree. By means of fishing line and ladders the tree is guyed from its upper branches to the ceiling, walls and window jambs of the corner in which it sits. So, for all intents and purposes, the Christmas tree hangs in place this year rather than being held by the usual floor standard. But it does appear tall.

The blocks are hidden from sight by a tree skirt improvised from a pair of old red drapes. The gifts which gradually appear beneath the tree, almost complete the illusion of a nine foot breathtakingly beautiful Christmas tree. In the spirit of

Christmas, Ed is forgiven and for years to come the section of trunk he removed will be tied with a large red velvet bow and presented to him as his Yule log.

And so a tradition is born—not that of cutting off the bottom off the tree, but of unpacking the severed tree trunk, resplendent in its crimson bow. Before placing it on the hearth the children run up to Ed to ask, "Remember this, Gramps? It's the Yule log you made."

Poor guy, he is never to forget the year he cut the tree too short.

Intergenerational, Snakes and Stars
Deep in the heart of Texas

It's always been a question to me whether Anne has understood how fortunate she is to have married Ed. Oh, there's no question but what she thinks he is the most wonderful man on the earth but the thing is, does she understand his love for trains and ships has made such a difference in their life together. It was because of his studies in international traffic that he was spared the experience of ever having to take part in the actual combat of WWII and the Korean War. It was during these two hitches in the Air Corp that Anne first began to assimilate the how's to travel. Because of his knowledge of transportation Ed was always able to see that Anne and their children traveled with him. They both came to take it for granted.

They have grasped every opportunity to travel that has been presented to them. Their sojourns have always been of their own doing. Ed would make all the arrangements and Anne would create ways to save money along the way; always with an eye on their limited budget. More often than not this meant camping. Their first tent was a drab canvass, floorless model from WWI, her father's. Their smallest has been the three once, bright orange nylon, backpack version used on their Canada sojourns when they climbed off the Algoma Central Railroad to portage back into the wilderness with their beloved Old Towne canoe. The exceptions to this are the times they traveled on the request of the U S military and the Alaskan cruise their Dave and Cathy gave them on their fiftieth wedding anniversary. Both were strictly first class. The neat part of all this is that every trip was mine, also.

I have been daydreaming today. Actually I have been for some time now. I suppose it is because things have settled in a routine which has become normal. It isn't because my life has returned to its old one. That will never happen, but it has formed a new river bed which it follows day after day. We have all been caught in its flow long enough now that we know all its bends and rapids, its smooth runs and its music as it rushes us along.

As a result I have long moments in which my mind can roam, either backwards or forward, whatever its pleasure. The arrival yesterday of the 1995 Spring/Summer issue of the quarterly Elderhostel News brought back memories of the Elder Hostels Ed and I have attended, the places we visited and the people we met. Each one was a special time of learning. I have to admit they are one part of our short retirement years I miss and would love to be able to continue. I hope someday we can.

One thing I discovered in this current issue is what are called Intergenerational Elder Hostels. They are sessions for grandparents to attend with their grandchildren. The problem is the cutoff date is age twelve. Laura was thirteen last July, which makes us ineligible. One southwestern Texas week-long hostel sounds especially great. It is to be held on a working ranch; one which has been in a family since it was homesteaded back in the late 1800's. The short descriptive narrative about a week's activities cries out to me. Oh, if I had only known about this last year when Laura was still twelve.

I think about age limits. They are arbitrary efforts by mankind to stop or start a particular service. Didn't the psychologist direct me to return Laura's childhood to her? A ranch trip like this would be another wonderful way to do so. My desire to take the trip with the children heightens my imagination until I become so enamored with the whole idea I decide to call the program and see if the twelve year age could be bent. I hear my mother saying, "Nothing ventured, nothing gained."

My request finds itself rerouted directly to the owners of the ranch. After Mrs. Prude listens to my tale of Ed's and my raising the three orphaned grandchildren and my deep desire to spend a week on the ranch in August she doesn't have the heart to refuse my request.

"Mrs. Thurston, we would very much enjoy having you and your husband and grandchildren visit our ranch this summer. From what you say I am certain your oldest granddaughter won't find our activities too childish for her."

I thank her and promise to call back with our final decision as soon as I talk it over with Ed. I know before I bring up the whole idea that Ed will be as excited about the trip as I have become. I find him at his desk. Opening the catalogue to the page where the details about the Prude Ranch Intergenerational Elderhostel is featured I point to the information on the trip.

Ed quickly reads through the descriptive blurb, looks up at me and says, "When are we leaving?"

"As soon as we find out if the kids are interested in the idea," I respond.

Before any of the three find their way into bed tonight they have their camping gear out of their closets and spread across their bedroom floors. You wouldn't think the trip was over three months away.

To keep travel costs trimmed to a minimum we elect to drive and camp along our route. The Aerostar once again proves its value as Ed and the kids stash all our gear in it the day before we leave. It gets harder and harder every time we decide to go off camping. The kids are always bigger than the previous time and there is more gear also. But somehow the four manage to push, squeeze and tug everything into the van and still leave enough room for five bodies. Of course, Major and Bucky are left at home with a visiting caregiver.

We head diagonally across the States traveling southwest for the land where the stars shine big and bright at night. Along the way we stay at state and national parks and sandwich bits and pieces of our country's history into the vacation. Bits of trivia lodge in our minds; not all lakes are crystal clear, there are miles and miles of country where a tree as we know one can't be found, the sky often is cloudless day after day and people drive their Cadillac over ninety miles an hour at the minimum down the arrow straight roads of Oklahoma and Texas while wearing their Stetson and probably boots

The ranch is all one could possibly expect. Stretching out across square miles of land that appear to be the leftovers from the fertile central plains. There the wheat grows like a gigantic sea of gold across Kansas, Nebraska and spills over their borders onto their neighbors. This is not the land of Ed's and my birth where the corn grows taller than a man and the soil is like brown velvet; where summer clouds roll up on the horizon and tumble in over the fields marking their arrival with thunder and lightening; or where the rain falls until it runs across the earth like a miniature river system.

No, the Prude ranch is a cluster of buildings under a grove of ancient trees. Back on a rise of ground behind the family home is a spread of small cabins like a brood of baby chicks snuggled around their mom. One of them becomes ours. I love watching the three kids invade it. Every nook and cranny is explored and bunks claimed. Ed and I look at the porch and know where we hope to spend some time. There are two rockers waiting for us and the view of southwestern hills is endless as it extends across the huge ranch.

On the dirt road which winds around the ranch's out buildings and eventually ends at the cabins we pass the corral. A large herd of horses bring their heads up to watch. I see a couple of men working with two of them. There is no doubt but what I am seeing two honest to goodness cowboys. The information on the ranch had stated that it is a working establishment and here before me is the proof. The hats are the real thing. By that I mean they are worn, a bit droopy and are smudged with the brown of the land. It is obvious they have been taken off frequently to mop a sweaty face and have for some reason or other landed on the ground a number of times. The rest of the clothing has the same used appearance. These are not Hollywood cowboys.

We meet the Prudes after lunch. The senior is ninety-four; a tall, weathered man of remarkable agility as he rides up to the mess hall on his horse. Mrs. Prude is a beautiful and stylish woman, and our gracious hostess for our stay. She and her daughter have a small dress and gift shop off the main lobby of the mess building. It is a bit of San Francisco and New York assembled to tempt every woman who visits the ranch. I can't believe my eyes at all of the lovely merchandise.

At the meeting we are briefed on our week's schedule. I know that we are going to be so busy that we'll have to rest when we arrive back home. Mornings we are to be separated from the grandchildren as they are led off to their own activities and we are turned over to Joe, our very own real cowboy who leaves his ranch duties to another ranch hand during Elderhostel times on the ranch. With Joe we'll study the history and lives of the American cowboy.

We assemble in yet another outbuilding not far from our cabin where we oldsters begin to get acquainted the. Hands are extended and shaken and questions asked.

"Where you from?" asked a mustached gentleman to the couple next to him. One of them answered, "Oh, we're from Kentucky. This is our sixth Elderhostel but the first time we have tried bringing our grandson along."

Then a rose cheeked, plumpish woman in her early sixties chimes in, "I did this last summer with two of our grandkids. I went in a covered wagon on part of the Lewis and Clark trail. Had a wonderful time. The kids think I'm the greatest grandma in the world."

Of course Anne is glued to Ed's side. Smiling and listening and absorbing the friendliness and warmth of her fellow elders. Nobody in the big room with its rows of folded chairs and walls of windows looking out across Texas have a clue she is shy. As Ed moves from one small group to another it is questionable if he remembers. It is then a short sidewise glance that he casts at Anne tells me he hasn't forgotten. He has just checked to see if everything is Ok for her. It's a lifetime habit with him.

I hear Ed saying, "We're from Michigan. Drove down with our three grandchildren." Then turning he introduces me, "This is my wife, Anne. Together we are raising our grandchildren. They were orphaned three years ago."

I immediately sense the change. All those within hearing range have turned their attention to Ed and me. Just like that, we have lost our identity as being their peers. Their brains are automatically reclassifying us into a category entirely new to them. Like the rare and endangered species of animals living in distant lands, we aren't entirely unknown. It is just that in their own lives we are the first of our kind to cross their paths.

"Oh how tragic. To lose both parents at such young ages. Was it a car accident?" Ed, in his wonderful way fields the questions until in the end our new friends know the circumstances of the grandchildren's becoming orphans and our involvement with them. There is no doubt in my mind but the concern that hangs in the air is genuine. But we are set apart and the brief time of being back into our allotted time as elders has dissolved and I am once again adrift in some strange land of limbo. I am that strange entity, a grandmother-mother.

Joe rescues the day by striding in the door and greeting all of us, his pupils for the week. He carries a guitar. He isn't tall, but his sinewy limbs, deeply tanned and wrinkled skin and sun slit, dark eyes tell all of us that this man is authentic. His has been a life that none of us know anything about. With his wide smile and cigarette tortured husky words Joe, from that moment on transports us into the world of the western cowboy, his heritage, his way of life, music and work. Joe sings songs, both new and old. His voice is strong and true. It's range includes the low and high notes the songs require and his boot never ceases tapping the beat. The morning hours fly by with the gregarious man. He appears to be ageless and I suspect he is truly much older than his appearance would have me believe. But from the stories he tells he would have had to been in the saddle at the age of one to accomplish all he claims. Maybe he was.

Lunch, like breakfast is made for those who have been out throwing cattle to the ground for branding, not a bunch of sedentary oldies. But we all dive right in, it is so good. After lunch is siesta time. Ed and I block out the call of the two rockers on our cabin's front porch and accompany the three kids to the large outdoor swimming pool near the ranch house. Walled in with rock and adobe it is Olympian in size. I have to admit the water feels wonderful once I make the plunge. Ed swims his lengths and the kids are swept into a game of Franco. Eventually I swim some laps and crawl out onto the concrete surround, find a lounge chair and simply bask in the mid-day Texas sun. I feel Ed's hand searching for mine and as we make contact he says, "Can you believe this, Hon? Here we are at a Texas ranch, poolside, and all because of three grandchildren." I have no answer. One isn't required. Ed knows I am feeling exactly the same way. I am in a world I never dreamed would be part of mine. This makes me all but believe I must be someone I don't know. Who am I?

I discover afternoons, after the hour of rest, are to be a series of well planed events for the grandparents and the grandchildren together. None of our grandchildren have ever ridden a horse. The first afternoon includes their initial learning session. By the end of the visit Patrick, Rachael and Laura will have participated in a rodeo competition, including caring a flag to a given location and implanting it in the ground at a predetermined spot. The fear that had brought tears to some of the children's eyes the first day as they saddled up and headed out on the trail had been replaced by a shine of sheer joy that Friday.

Another afternoon we all loaded up in open-sided busses to ride to the site of the renovated Fort McKenzie, which dates back to the days of the Indian presence in the area. The first Mrs. Prude had sold eggs and bread to the soldiers stationed there. Now under the guardianship of the National Park Service the fort is quite remarkable. As we enter its gated fence a wide parade ground stretches out in front of us. Around its edges we see assorted wooden buildings. Directly in front of us, at the far end of the parade ground is a small steepled wood-frame chapel. We learn later it doubled as a school house during the week for the children of the military families stationed at the fort. By the time the bus door opens our three disperse to the winds,

"Stay together and remember this is a national park.' Ed calls after their fleeting bodies.

A ranger steps forward and welcomes us, at least the grandparents who still stand by the bus. She has a big smile and I know immediately she understands children.

"They'll be all right. There are signs and information posted on all the sites inside the fort. You are all welcome to look around as you please. There are restrooms in this main building behind me. It also has my office, a first aid station and gift shop. Will you please be certain to register before leaving today. In an hour you will hear a whistle inviting you back to this area. We have a special event planned for that time. Oh, yes, there are sodas and snacks inside our main building here. Any questions?"

I can't think of any. Besides I have been watching the kids entering and then leaving one building after another while the ranger was welcoming us. At this minute they are just emerging from the little church and heading back our way, but it looks as if there are a number of places they have yet to explore. They appear half their sizes at the far end of the parade ground as they wave at us.

I turn toward Ed and ask, "Think we better intercept the troops?"

We meet at the solitary confinement facility about midway the length of the grounds. The three are standing around its edges peering down into it.

Pat turns to me and says, "Gram, look at this, they actually put a soldier down in here for punishment. All he'd get was bread and water. Can you imagine how hot it must have been?"

I don't want to look. I don't understand such things. How could such treatment produce any understanding of how to do something the right way?

The special event is held after we gather in the main building to eat our box lunches. Ranger Betty, as we have come to know her, blows her whistle and gathers us in family groups, or platoons, handing one of the children in each group a staff with a colored flag at its top and their list.

"You mission, today, troops, is to conduct a surveillance of the fort to determine where each of the twelve items listed on your orders is located. Once you have fulfilled your mission return directly to this place, the base of today's operation. The platoon completing their objectives first will receive a special accommodation. If you are ready you may begin when the whistle is blown.

There is a brief planning session as the three grandchildren read our list and plan their itinerary.

Laura suggests, "If we follow the list we will end up crisscrossing the parade ground a lot of times. That's going to slow us down. Let's put everything in order."

Rachael pipes up, "Let's start on the other side of the fort and end up here."

Within less than a minute we hear the whistle and are off at a full run. There is no doubt in Ed's or my mind but what the three kids know what they are doing. The parade ground, much larger than a football field is sun baked like bricks underfoot and every building around its perimeter has steps that must be climbed to access its interior and then to leave. The sweat is pouring down my face by the time we have crossed to the hospital and found our first answer. It is August. It is hot, and once back on the parade ground, all shade is gone.

I am not at all surprised the kids bring our platoon in first and accept our awards.

The following afternoon is a trip out to a ranger station in the desert to learn about snakes. The ranger gathers us together in a small, close quartered work shed. Everything about him is all regulation from his hat to his polished shoes, that is except for the white pillowslip he carries with the top wadded together in his right hand. It is bulky and seems to have a life of its own. From its depths he brings out examples of the snakes which can be found in this part of Texas. One by one the wiggling, writhing or even lashing reptiles are handed to the children. Each is beautifully marked in various manners; geometric markings, rings and stripes included.

I am fascinated as the snakes, all at least three feet long, stretch their lengths down an arm, across shoulders, from one youngster to another. Most of the adults stand with our backs against the walls of the shed, behind our grandchildren, perfectly content to observe and not participate.

Occasionally one grandchild will turn to his grandparent and offer his snake, saying, "Feel it Grandma. It's really cold. Why isn't it hot when its such a hot day."

It is then the ranger offers the explanation and lets the grandparent off the hook.

I shouldn't be surprised, but even here out in the middle of nowhere, somewhere in Texas, this little ranger's station has its very own gift shop. I buy a beautiful rounded flat pot full of cacti without considering how I might pack such a prickly thing hundreds of miles back to Michigan. Somehow Ed finds a protected nook in the van and it makes the long trip in tack.

The night before we are taken up to see the MacDonald Observatory to peer at the planets and stars through it large telescope the kids have a night out under the stars back on the ranch somewhere. Having been part of the snake show that afternoon all I can think of is some snake crawling into a warm sleeping bag during the night. But none of the grandkids bring the possibility up and I keep my mouth closed. I don't even bother Ed with the idea. I am sure he has thought of it and discarded the whole happening as highly unlikely. And even if it does happen I suspect it wouldn't cause a stir after this afternoon's handling of so many. Such a stranger in a sleeping bag would probably be rescued and passed around.

It will be years later when Anne is writing this story and Rachael is about to graduate from Michigan State that Anne will ask her about that night and snakes. Rachael will say, "Gram, we were all scared to death. We were told to check out the inside of our sleeping bags and look in our boots. We were up late around the campfire, sitting on our bags, but even so we all shook them out. If it hadn't been so cold I would have never crawled into mine."

Even at the observatory with its huge dome and adjustable instruments yet another gift shop awaited Rachael's arrival. For the first time in my life I have become aware of these little shops tucked away in corners of almost every national or state museum, visitors' site or historical area. And this is because I have come to see all of them through Rachael's eyes. Growing up without two coins to jingle in my pocket I look back at those times when I was Rachael's age and wonder if there just weren't little shops or whether I ignored them through my lack of purchasing power.

On our way home during a side trip to Carlsbad Caverns to see the evening bat exodus I discover the maple syrup in our food box has accidentally fallen over. Its sweet goop smothering the tape of Joe's cowboy songs, completely destroying my only Prude Ranch trophy. But no syrup can ever erase that special something about the land where the stars or so big and bright at night and of a kind host family that stretched their rules to allow us to have such a memorable week.

**Patrick, Laura, Rachael with Ed and Anne on
the shore of Lake Superior 1997**

A Storm, Whale and Bat

Being afraid does not equate to being irresponsible

*I have always known Anne has no fear of the great out of doors and all that lives
within it. She is far more leery of people than of wild creatures. It's the same with
night time. She has never been able to understand a person's fear of darkness. To her
it belongs to God with its quiet, its depth and width. On those nights when the stars
or moon add their beauty, her peace increases. To Anne being unafraid does not equate
to being irresponsible. She wouldn't think of intruding into any creature's world; just
as she would not inflict herself on a human being unless invited.*

Ed and I discovered Pukaskwa sometime in the '80s on one of our sojourns
up into Canada. The park isn't difficult to locate because it is before Marathon,
Ontario and just south of the main east-west highway that stretches out like a
long bungee cord across southern Canada, hooking the Atlantic to the Pacific
Ocean.

Expecting to drive into Canada for vacations days began for me back in 1931
when my parents, Helen and Tracy first took my brother, Dave and me north to
fish. The world we accessed was as far away as the moon to us and just as unknown.
We would sit for hours at the southern end of the Straights of Mackinaw waiting
for the ferry to transport us across to Michigan's Upper Peninsula. Sometimes
those hours in the car were unbelievably hot. With no air-conditioning, bottled
water or roadside park the time became endless and the tempers short. But with
Dad in the front seat Dave and I tried our best not pick on each other. We knew
our father would have no patience with us if there was any kind of ruckus. If

the waiting time ran on and on Mother would initiate word games and dig out sandwiches and cookies with a thermos of tepid lemonade.

Across the Straits our dad drove the last fifty miles of corrugated dirt roads north out of Iron Bridge, Ontario. This last part of the long trip took over three hours in itself. Along the way he guided the packed car across stacked timber bridges over many streams before pulling up in front of the washwoman's log cabin at Mountain Lake.

Then he'd announce our arrival, "We're here. Everybody out."

Along with Dad we'd unload gear while Mother took over the big black iron wood cook-stove. Then we'd all settled in for two weeks of the greatest fishing available.

The owner, a Mr. McElroy, Mac to everyone, swore he had our mom back on lakes that no white woman had ever fished before. Canoes were used. Dad teamed up with me and Dave went with Mother. Mac paddled one and an Indian, the other. No one growing up during that post depression era could have had a more wonderful time.

Ed's and my discovery of Pukaswka was truly a step back in time for us. The park is one of Canada's effort to preserve its natural wonders. Its boreal forests and forgotten caribou are near the western terminus of Lake Superior. It's a world with challenges that make any theme park second choice, even Disney World. It is not for the novice.

After leaving the highway just west of the White River and the huge gaily painted gold mines that have sprung up north of the road, Ed follows a well paved road south toward Lake Superior. A garbage dump is passed. We will return one night and watch in fascination from the car, with windows wound up, the foraging of the huge black bears and their cubs. There is such strength and muscle shown in their movements that it seems impossible anyone would challenge them in their search for food.

Once in the park Ed turns right into the small loop set aside for tent camping. Our returns become frequent enough we begin to think of one particular spot as ours. Last year the site was already taken, but when the people packed up and left the following day the grandkids picked up their self supported dome tent and walked it down the trail to their favorite camp area. They were afraid to take the time to disassemble it for fear someone else might drive into the camp and claim the spot.

Camp area #3 is our favorite tent site. It is laid out in two parts, which are joined by a short walk through the trees. The front half has the fire pit and table. The back has the groomed sand for the tents. It is here one night, with tents set side by side under the towering spruce all of us zonk out. The crisp northern air can bring instant relaxation and sound sleep. Suddenly a fierce squall blows in off Lake Superior. Known for its changing temperament the Great Lake has sent more than one freighter to its depths. No one knows how many Voyageurs and Indian canoes have also sunk, victims of the savage storms. The year around frigid waters, make human survival all but impossible.

The howl of the wind, the waves crashing on the shore some 200 yards distant and the snapping and creaking of the tortured trees wake all five of us. The crack, which brings us upright in our sleeping bags, is a spruce breaking off behind the tents. It is as if a gun has been fired. Everyone feels a bullet pierce their bodies, the sound is so close and loud. The earth shakes as the tree hits the ground between the two tents. Somehow the ten inch trunk falls straight and true in the foot wide space left between our tent and the children's.

Despite the cold driving rain and continuous twisting and turning of the other trees, Ed has everyone in the car and is headed out of camp in a matter of minutes. The only precaution against the gear becoming saturated is the time he takes to tie down the front flaps of both tents. There is absolutely no way my husband is going to tempt good fortune by weathering out the storm in the camp ground. Much to the delight of the kids a dry motel room in White River is available and all are back in bed by three a.m., although far from asleep. To complete the adventure Ed treats the family to huge woodsmen breakfasts in the log restaurant across the highway from the motel the following morning. This overnight fling in a motel followed by a restaurant breakfast is like a trip to New York's finest. The excitement is unbelievable. The crashing spruce is relegated to the past.

Although they'll never spend a night in the motel again it does become a tradition to break camp early enough on the last day of their visits north to have another huge backwoods breakfast on the way home. Served on platters, each includes pancakes, scrambled eggs, sausage, hash browns, toast and jam. The kids have hot chocolate with whipped cream while Ed and Anne enjoy decaf coffee, the old folks' drink.

Almost directly across from area #3 is the path through the woods down to the shore of Lake Superior. Not frequently used over the short camping season the trail follows the course of least resistance. It twists around any boulder in its path and jogs between tree trunks. It is only in the boggy area near the shore that the park rangers have improved the walk. There they have laid logs split lengthwise and face up to keep hikers out of deep mud. It isn't until the trail actually breaks out into the bright sunlight of the shore that any major obstacle is found. A wave tossed scramble of drift logs extends as far as the eye can see down the beach in each direction like a gigantic game of Pick up Sticks. Every summer they are different, dependent on the storms of the previous seasons. The logs are all clean eight foot lengths, which have broken loose from the lumbermen's river rafts to find their way out into the waters of the big lake. In places their tangled interwoven mass reaches twelve feet in height.

With all the side branches having been trimmed off by loggers, Laura and Rachael with Pat's help find the logs perfect to drag across the sandy beach. They build Lincoln Log forts by lapping ends at the corners. Working together they choose the logs they want and carefully extract them from the woven mess the storm waves have dumped them. It is drag and push to worm them across the sand to the spot they intend to build. Architectural design is considered along with the science of procurement and delivery. With no mechanical lift apparatus anywhere in sight the structures can only become as high as the kids can reach. With Ed's height and long arms the forts grow even higher.

Ed watches them and holds back on his offer to help or kibitz until the point where further progress is stalled. It is then he calls out, "Need your Granddad to help get the next one up?"

Access to the interior is through a tunnel dug in the sand underneath a bottom log. The slotted sunshine in the inside becomes shade for hot days.

However getting too hot is never a problem with the lake's cold 54 degree water breaking in waves on the shore. Some days the incoming water is only a ripple that scallops the water's edge. About ten feet off shore and in three feet of water the whale waits to take the kids on its back for rides. Not an adult whale it appears to be more the size of a teenager. A basalt rock formation that is almost black with the wetness of the waves rolling over its top, it has been scoured by decades of water and ice. It is the children who see the shape and roundness of a resting whale and name it.

Like a favorite pet, it waits for them each year, staying close to the sandy shore anticipating their screams of joy. The children play on it for hours while their grandparents wonder how they can stand the frigid water for such a length of time. One quick dip is enough for Anne. Ed sometimes swims out a few feet, but never far. There is the danger of an undertow in the small bay. The day following the five's arrival in 1994 two children were lost to its pull. The parents had left them in the care of an older sister. The tragedy haunts both Ed and Anne. How something so tranquil and quiet can be so treacherous is too incongruous to believe.

There are other trails that penetrate the wilderness of the park. One stays inland but follows the coast southeast to the White River, like its name it is one of Canada's fine white water streams. High in the air a primitive swinging suspension bridge crosses the rock strewn rushing river. To take the trail the hiker must check in with the rangers and on returning sign out with them. With the grandkids Ed and I walk the trail to the first camp area. Very primitive, it includes a smooth, flat granite boulder about eight feet above a small lake, enough grassy area to accommodate four sleeping bags, and an open roof, three sided privy. A bear proof food locker placed some twenty feet from the site and a breathtaking wilderness view. We have lunch there and then turn, leaving the rest of the trail to the river for the grandchildren to do at a future time. Then together or with others they can return for the strenuous hike and all its promised wonder. Its hard for me to admit I can no longer carry the gear for an overnight adventure.

The Park maintains both overland and water emergency personnel to dispatch in case of need. Weather is a constant threat, especially to those who set out along the rocky shore in a canoe or kayak. A place to beach can not always be located and when available is even then treacherous to the inexperienced.

Another trail heads out from the tent area to the northwest to Half Way Lake, so named by the early voyageurs as they traveled down from the north with their furs to access Lake Superior. It is back on the exposed granite of the land, which surrounds the clear lake waters that the five of us walk to in search of blueberries. Pockets of rainwater trapped in deer moss support the scrubby plants with their tiny leaves. Covered in berries the bushes themselves appear blue. Working together enough berries are harvested for me to make a pie in the camp skillet for dessert. It takes a while, there high above the sparkling lake, to fill the camp cups because pickers eat handfuls on the spot. So sweet and full of deliciousness, they are a wonderful supplement to the standard camp food of dried goods. No pie will ever taste better.

Laura calls out, "Don't pick them all. We have to leave plenty for the bears."

Ed assures her they won't mind as he looks out across the wilderness which extends its rocks, deer moss and berries to the very edge of the beginning of Hudson Bay country. What the campers consume will not bring on a bear famine.

There is something about the enormity of the park and all that it contains that causes a human being to relearn his or her need to co-exist with nature. Whether from a city, small town or farm the lesson is the same. In Pukaskwa man comes to understand his fragility. What becomes important isn't one's possessions, but what the mind can do to keep one well and content. Each of the five relies on the others to see that everyone is safe. The children learn the wilderness is a place of the unexpected to be respected and must be left as it is found.

It was in 1990, the year after Marry remarried, she, Larry and the children joined Ed and me on our annual sojourn to the park. It was Larry's first trip. An avid hunter and fisherman we assumed he would be a natural camper. But in the first evening as we sat around the campfire mesmerized by its movement of bright flames and the surrounding silence of the north woods he left to get something from his pack. When he returned with a bottle of Scotch in hand and offered Ed a drink I concluded he was uncomfortable about something. I wondered if it was being with us. After all, we hardly knew our new-son-in-law. Or, I questioned if his discomfort wasn't us but rather the surrounding wilderness. Something was begging him to drink to allow him to escape from where he was or the company he found himself with. It never entered my mind that this was a daily routine.

A little later that same evening it is around the camp fire that the bat visits. It was twilight, perhaps a bit deeper under the spruce, but not so dark things and people couldn't be easily seen. The fire had been lit not so much for light but for its warmth because there was a chill in the air that began to descend as sunset neared. The fire's warmth felt good on my back as I stood with Mary at the table preparing chili and instant rice on the Coleman stove. The kids at four, six and eight were all fire pokers. They found sticks some three feet long and contentedly sat beside the fire ring poking its burning logs and embers from one position to another. This sent orange flecks of flame and wood skyward like fairies on important errands to disappear into the dusk. Ed never relaxed as this went on; constantly expecting one of them to inadvertently burn themselves with the hot end of their stick. But they were wise enough not to do that.

It was when Laura put her stick aside and stood to turn and help her mother with supper that the bat flew into camp. It selected Laura's nose as a perfect landing spot. All six of us watched it happen. Any departure from the stillness of the wilderness, even the soft sound of tiny wings becomes an attention getter. It isn't that the tiny creature was noisy or that Laura let out a scream, but rather it was a change in the stillness of the campground. Silence hung heavy in the air as we stared in disbelief.

There our granddaughter stood with the little critter clinging to the very end of her nose. All our eyes were glued on it. Even Laura's appeared all but crossed as she looked down her nose into the bright little eyes of her visitor.

No one called, "Hold still. Don't move. Don't say anything."

Laura knew to try not to startle the little animal. Rather than hanging upside down it sat upright and stared up into Laura's amazed eyes.

Larry was the one who lost it. He simply went bananas. Yelling and screaming, "Get that thing off of her before it bites."

He began to circle the camp as if searching for a broom or some other device to knock it off Laura's face. In the meantime the rest of us, including Laura stood mesmerized. That is, everyone but Ed who simply approached Laura and shooed the bat away with a gentle wave of his hand. Unharmed the little creature circled the camp area a couple of times much to Larry's continued apprehension before disappearing into the night.

There wasn't a mark on Laura's nose.

As a junior in high school Laura will entertain her literature class one hour by reading her written version of that evening. Her classmates laughing aloud will congratulate her on her great imagination. It is only with difficulty she'll be able to convince them the happening is true. From that moment on they'll see Laura differently. She'll no longer be just the terribly shy high achiever they had known but someone who has great things to share; someone who can laugh contagiously to the point of tears; a girl who isn't afraid of a bat.

Rachael, Patrick, Ed, Anne and Laura—1996

A Safari, French Painting and an Omer

Caution can be inflicted not to avoid danger but to control

Children don't consider failure. Adult-like in so many ways, even the pre-school child will say and endeavor to do things we find totally unwise. And the surprise is ours when success is theirs. All too often we unwittingly predetermine what choice, direction or words will be theirs next. We inflict caution, not to avoid danger but to control. It is only when the child begins to mimic the actions and words of those older than themselves that the impossible disappears and caution defines creativity.

If the grandchildren had not become Ed's and mine to raise there are a number of experiences which would never have become part of our lives. An example is certainly the existence of the work of Odyssey of the Mind. The concept of a competition for thinking was born in the mind of a Professor Emeritus of Rowan University. He saw in children a depth of possibility that is overlooked in many homes, schools and communities daily, year after year. The idea, though embraced by many schools has been rejected by more as too time consuming and demanding of an already overworked teaching staff. All understandable reasons. It is also unknown by many parents today.

Often, school systems build huge sums of money into their athletic budgets and bombard their constituents into supporting large sport complexes. Busing to and from events is also included. Some students are not sports oriented, or limit themselves because of qualifications required for participation. Boyne City is one such school system. If the parents do not ask for Odyssey of the Mind competitions it is not offered to the students. The down side of this is that all too often the parents who would support the effort know nothing of its existence. It must be officially sponsored by the school.

The very small community of Vanderbilt, which is over forty five miles east of Boyne City between Gaylord and Alpena, out in the nowhere woods of Michigan participates in division competitions. Its schools endorse Odyssey of the Mind as an extracurricular activity. This system allows classroom space to be used after school and members of the teaching staff to coach. The teams they send into competition walk away with a large number of first place awards. Doing so, they become eligible to take part at the state level, which then offers the opportunity to travel to the national and even world events. All are unbelievable opportunities for the youth hidden away in such a small community all but lost in the forests of up-state Michigan.

In 1989 Ed and I learned about OM as Laura, a third grader in Gaylord's elementary school became a team member. She was the only girl on her team. The project they selected was that of building a structure of balsa wood and glue. At various stages in its construction it was tested to determine if it could support a given weight. The group studied all the information they could find on stress and angles of support. They then decided how to incorporate this knowledge in the design of their structure. Even the glue figured into the overall strength because of its additional weight.

The day of competition the concentration was so intense as the construction proceeded I found myself forgetting to breathe. Hundreds of pounds were supported before the tower collapsed.

There was no deference given to Laura as the only girl on the team. Sex had no bearing on the overall success of the exercise. Quiet words of encouragement circulated among the builders, interlaced with suggestions and appreciation of a piece of balsa placed correctly. The team work was so visible that the encouraging words became an eighth team member. I was seated five feet away. All I could do was watch and hope for success for the kids as they hovered around the ever ascending tower from its perch on a base that stood in the center of their construction circle. The work was deliberate and all consuming. Each team member knew the tower would collapse. It was just a matter of when. Would it be the small section of balsa they just laid on it?

Now, in 1994 with Laura turning thirteen I remember the exciting event and decide to see if I can coach a team for Boyne City. Ed becomes equally interested so we research the way to proceed. After contacting the area OM official we obtain school permission and form a team. I will be the coach. Ed will train to be a competition judge. A generous envelope of instructions arrives. We pour over them and they all appear well developed and possible.

Ed and I talk the idea over with Laura. She is excited and it is a green light for the her to round up a team.

Both Ed and I were in scouting as kids and cherish memories of events we took part in, especially the work that led to winning merit badges. It was all about using our minds and being creative. Odyssey of the Mind is similar but functions on a much higher level. In many ways it is a youth's version of the adult think-tank employed frequently in the corporate world to solve problems or create new products.

Laura has no difficulty in rounding up the necessary six to form a team of seven. With permission notes from their parents members are able to ride the bus to Laura's home after school with her. It is understood the parents will pick them up after the team's work sessions.

The team spends a lot of time getting themselves organized and then studying the various categories offered as projects. It isn't easy for them to settle on one, but eventually they select a problem based on the concept of a Safari.

The rules are very detailed covering everything from the length of the skit to how much the kids can spend on putting it together. Even items brought from home to use have to be appraised as to their cost and included in the final figure. I get the feeling some of the team members are realizing for the first time in their lives how fast the cost of such incidental items as tape and paper clips can add up. As the coach I'm not to perform any of the work, track the cost or throw in ideas. I'm on the scene to help maintain direction and enthusiasm.

There are times when I have to leave the room to keep myself from making a suggestion. But I'm obligated to let the kids do things backwards or upside down if that is the way they see it should be accomplished. It is OK for me to make such simple suggestions as having the team members stand across the room to look at their work, as if they were the judges. The same tactic is used to check their speaking voices and facial expressions. But all the scripting, construction or answers to the various required happenings come from the children's own creativity.

It fascinates me to see the seven feed off each other's ideas; how they decide which direction to go, how they veto another's idea and applaud a sudden thought when a dead end looms ahead. Even though I may race ahead of them with my own idea of how to satisfy a requirement I often find their solution, although not mine, is far more creative and unique. I'm in awe of their complete emersion in the project. There is no effort to be the big cheese, to hog the limelight or to always have one's way.

Every piece of the props must be transported in the Ford Areostar half way across the state to the place of the competition and whatever other car might be offered for our use, depending on what parent will go along to drive. Tools are packed to take in case of the need of a last minute repair. Extension cords, duct tape and other essential replacement or repair equipment is included, even a first aid kit. The team members elect to wear like T-shirts. They ask me, their coach, to wear one also. Their spirit is as high as that of any football or basketball team.

Everyone has his or her job to do and part to play once the starting bell is heard. There is no such thing as a stage crew or understudy.

The competition itself proves itself to be a day of continuous events as one after another teams from across the northern part of Michigan convene to put on their skits. The huge high school building is like a mall of performing theaters as room after room opens onto yet another performance. Visitors are welcome to observe as many of them as their schedules allow. Laura's team, although it wins no awards, leaves at the end of the long day content with their efforts and flowing over with the happenings of their day. We are all also dead tired.

Now, a year later all of the team have moved up into high school. There they become eligible fore the next level of competition. However some team members find themselves so involved in high school extra curricular activities that the thought of entering OM competition is given up, not enough of our original team is available. Disappointed, Laura asks if she can help coach a junior high team, her sister's, Rachael's. Knowing I will have Laura's wise help I decide to coach an elementary team for Pat and his classmates, also. The project choices will not be the same in light of their different grade levels. I'll stagger the teams' meeting days. The idea flies and we are full steam ahead.

The Junior High team chooses to compete in the Classic division, 'Great Impressions'. The instructions read, "For this problem the team will select a drawing or painting by a French Impressionist artist and write a poem relative to it. The team will also select a poem by a famous author, create an original drawing or painting that relates to the poem, and present the poem and work of art. Time limit is 8 minutes. Materials used cannot exceed a $95 (U.S.A.) value'

The painting chosen is The Card Players by Claude Monet. It is presented by the team as a four by four foot copy, faithfully reproduced in acrylic paints by one of its four male members. He is an art student at the school and familiar with the medium and technique. I'm entranced as I watch the gangly teenager confidentially reproduce Monet's work on a four by five piece of plywood he cuts to size as Ed stands by to be certain he handles the power saw correctly.

The rest of the team plunges into preparing all the other criteria set forth by the rules. The basement room which had been the children's first bedroom becomes the team's work shop. Once again it is cluttered from wall to wall. They meet the deadline.

Meanwhile, Pat's team struggles in their selection of a project but finally settle on The Tall Tales of John Jivery. The instructions state, "In this problem, the team is to create and present a humorous performance about an original tall tale. The tale will include a team-created hero or heroine that performs an incredible feat, a unique explanation of how something began or came to be, and a surprise for the audience. The time is 8 minutes. Materials used cannot exceed a $100 (U.S.A.) Value."

For a group of Michigan students who have been spoon fed on the story of the giant wood cutter, Paul Bunyan and his enormous blue ox, Babe, putting their heads together to come up with their own tall tale is the perfect problem. One of the criteria is there must be a vehicle which moves a minimum of ten feet without the use of an engine or the driver's feet. Pat is elected the driver and his method of propulsion becomes a large black toilet plunger. What seems a brilliant idea backfires as the gym floor on which the team's skit is enacted is highly varnished, shining like a mirror. Seated in a small red wagon, his feet braced against its inside rim and knees tucked under his chin, Pat grips the plunger in both hands and pushes onto the floor with all his strength. The black rubber end on the long handle refuses to get a grip. The theory of movement by suction goes out the window. Although no prize is won it is an audience grabber as Pat valiantly plunges the floor generating a barely perceptible movement.

The team is scheduled for 4:15 in the afternoon, the last performance of the day. This last notch is hard on the participants as they must wait all day to perform. The first group presents theirs at 8 a.m. Presentations follow throughout the day at twenty five minute intervals. There is no time allotted for a noon break. Lunch is whenever a group can find the time. Almost any hour of the day teams can be found in clusters on the hall floors. An obvious effort is made not to block the passage of others. They may be eating, snacking or enjoying a cool drink, even catching a short snooze. Invariably some or all of a cluster will be critiquing a competitor's presentation or seeking ways to refine their own. In all instances they sprawl on the linoleum tiles as only kids and teenagers can manage. Their body language does not speak of nervousness or panic. Ed and I elect to take such breaks in the cafeteria, seated in chairs at a table. There we share stories of our coaching efforts with other coaches. There are some great stories; we are amazed how long some have been involved.

On competition day everyone is free to come and go between the various divisions to watch. The doors are closed during the actual time of participation. Audience responses are similar to those seen at tennis matches. Silence prevails except when laughter is generated. Applause is sincere and freely given to competing teams no matter if they are in direct line for the same award as the on-looking team. Skill and creativity are appreciated no matter where they are found.

Set up is not part of the allotted performance time although it is also time restricted. It is fascinating to watch seven team members work together with sets made from everything from corrugated cardboard to PVC pipes. Sound systems involve lead cords, microphones and music tapes. Props can include everything from furniture to rolling stock. It becomes obvious before the day is over there is nothing a child's mind can't imagine and somehow bring into reality.

The degree of sophistication accelerates as team members become high school students. The world they have come to know opens doors into an infinite land of opportunity. Extra curricular activities offered today often absorb all the free time of those who would become Odyssey of the Mind competitors. It is not unusual to have only three or four of the older teams compete at the district level in the world-wide event.

And Ed? He not only transports but loans tools and offers help in their use under the strict OM rules. Once on location he leaves our team for the day to become one of the judges at another event. Prior to the day Ed has attended how-to training sessions on the rules he would use in the process. Judging panels are much like those one sees at ice skating events where judges are seated at a sideline table with paper and pen. They are instructed to judge a number of categories including team work, originality, etcetera. The resultant decisions by each judge are tallied and become a team's final score.

Earlier, when our own four children were going through their school years Ed had been a football official. At six foot two and two hundred pounds he was formidable. He had a love for competition and of the rules that endeavored to keep it safe. Coupled with his love of kids refereeing was a natural. I remember so well the evening football game when a big linesman mistakenly tackled Ed and found himself on the ground on top of his referee. It was hard to tell who was the most surprised. Bound by the rules, Ed benched the poor kid while he brushed off his own black and white stripes to regain his dignity. When it happened I just sat there on the bleachers and held my breath. I watched until those on the field pulled the player off my husband and he stood up. Apparently he was none the worse for the well executed play.

Following the last OM event of the day all the contestants wearily find their way to the host school's gymnasium to learn who the winners of the daylong competitions are. Only the adrenalin which flows within every person in attendance keeps them from falling asleep. Everyone sits in team groups on the gym bleachers. A huge room, it is actually three basketball floors, which can be opened separately or used as one, dependent on the crowd size. It is opened full size and the drone of thousands of school children, their parents and coaches is overwhelming. Even the floor is set with folding chairs for the overflow audience. Disciplined to be attentive and orderly the crowd is as contained as the day's long pent up excitement allows.

My teams find a place about midway up the bleachers in the center on one side of the gym. Somehow they get a second breath as if the very energy within the room is flowing into their bloodstreams through undetected IV drips. Ed manages to locate the kids and me among the thousands of others in the crowd. Probably because the team shirts form a block of navy in a sea of rainbow colors.

We see others we've met from school districts across the northern half of Michigan' lower peninsula and call out greetings and wave. Throughout the day the kids have moved around, sat and waited, waited and waited. Of course, no matter whether a team performs first or last the day is just as long and full of time with nothing to do except wander about and watch other teams compete.

The room comes to a sudden and complete hush as the director of the event rises from her seat on the floor below us. After various recognitions of others who have contributed to the day I begin to more fully understand what an amazing bit of scheduling and planning has taken place. The director then recognizes the winners for all fourteen divisions of competition. She waits for each victorious team as they move out of the bleachers and onto the floor to receive its trophy. The applause is thunderous for every team, whether for first place or on down to honorable mention. It rumbles after them as they climb back up the bleachers and away from the podium.

Although Boyne's two teams aren't part of the winner's circle, they believe they will be the next year.

It is at the very end of the ceremony the director announces the year's OMER award is for a grandmother who not only coached one but two of the day's competing teams.

The kids catch on to what the director has said way ahead of me as they turn and say, "She means you, Grandma." I have become Grandma to the whole team.

I feel the mounting panic in herself. My eyes immediately seek an exit door. It is time to disappear. Before I can make my escape I find myself being propelled down toward the floor of the auditorium by my fourteen team members. When I turn for Ed's help I find his eyes on me. He knows my thoughts. Then a grin spreads across his face telling me once again I'm on my own. He remains beside his bleacher seat, as proud as the kids. People I will never know reach out their hands to help me climb down the bleachers. They voice their congratulations. I'm certain more than one coach in the huge room deserves the honor more than I do.

I know it should be wonderful to be honored when one has no idea there is such a possibility. Others would be. I had not heard of an OMER. In fact, I will have to research its existence and purpose after the event. Later I'm told, Zena, a teacher-colleague at Presbytery Point, a church summer-camp near Marquette in Michigan's Upper Peninsula is the one responsible for the submission of my name for the award.

The real thrill to me is the happiness and pride on the faces of my teams, grandchildren and husband. That is what it is all about. Through my recognition each of them leaves the competition as winners. I see it in their smiles and am immensely grateful.

Lunch, Mail Clerk and a Prom Date

Desperately needing to be unnoticed

For a woman to be five foot nine inches tall in Anne's generation was akin to being a lightening rod—sticking out for all to see. At least that was the feeling she had. Wanting to shrink she didn't have the chance, because Tracy never stopped reminding her to stand tall and sit straight with no hunching over. No sagging shoulders were allowed. All this was happening, when as a teenager she desperately wanted to be unnoticed; to be the short and the non-descriptive woman she wasn't. Anne believed her friends thought they envied her. She knew this was only because they didn't know what it was like to look down on the part in a guy's hair. Then there was her longing to wear high heels. Why is it that when women are young they are often dissatisfied with their appearance? With all the hair dyes around today my guess is that things haven't changed.

Just as our son, Dave set the pace through high school for our four children Laura runs interference for her brother and sister through their school years. When Laura takes her brown bag and climbs on the school bus to head out to the high school it suddenly hits me that time has somehow moved faster than I have realized. Our granddaughter is suddenly a high school freshman. She will walk through the same Boyne City High School doors as our son, Dave did in 1961, the year we moved to Boyne City and he began his upper classman days. Laura will even have some of the same teachers; although most have moved on. One way or another.

Wednesday is her first day. By Friday I'm aware the early excitement has completely vanished. Laura is no longer sharing the events of her days with me.

179

It is after four before the kids finish the hot climb from the bus drop at the foot of the hill and walk into the house. I have set out the lemonade and cookies but Laura shakes her head and turns to go down to her room. Something is definitely not right.

After Rachael and Pat have shared their latest news break with me, I search Laura out. She's stretched out on her bed, back turned toward the door. Crossing the room with its Raggedy Anne dolls and Teddy bear wallpaper I place my hand on my granddaughter's shoulder and gently roll her over to face me. There are tears in her eyes.

"What is it Laura? Can you tell me?"

"It's lunch hour. I don't have anyone to sit with. Everyone has a friend and I don't. I don't want to go back tomorrow. I can't Grandma. I can't walk into the cafeteria and sit all by myself one more day."

Oh, Lord, I think. She has my shyness. I know exactly how she feels. It is one thing to be part of a classroom, a passenger on an overly crowded school bus or even a member of a family, but to face another person alone is an ordeal I will run away from every time.

Even at seventy-two shyness still controls my life.

"What can I say or do to help" I silently ask, chiding myself for not being more alert. The family has watched Laura blush easily during her whole childhood and withdraw from attention and strangers. My only solace is to acknowledge that my own attention has been directed to the deaths of Pat and our son, Tom and then Mary. Then I dealt with the three grandchildren as a group so much that I haven't found the time to study each as individuals. No one should know better than me that children in families are all different, not clones of each other.

One thing is certain, I will not tell her to throw her shoulders back and walk right into the cafeteria, spot an empty seat at a table and join the group that is holding forth there. Or tell her she is smarter and lovelier than any other girl in the school or that she is old enough to grow up and not act like a baby.

At some time I've heard all these statements, some many times. None are possible to carry out. In fact, such suggestions or even demands only deepen the feeling of inadequacy shyness brings to the fore.

Instead, sitting on the bed, holding Laura in my arms I begin to tell her of my own life long battle with shyness.

"Laura, few people other than your grandfather know of my shyness as I have learned so well how to hide it. Shyness doesn't seem curable but everyone can find their way to live above it. Often those who suffer the phobia are among the more intelligent, empathetic and prophetic of people. Some stricken people can't face a crowd and become tongue-tied when asked to speak before a group. Others like myself, have no fear of groups. On the other hand I can't deal with individuals. A social life is impossible; I can't interact."

"The way I have found to leap over my shyness is to avoid at all costs any situations that leave me with someone I don't know, or know only slightly."

Laura stops crying and her eyes search my face.

I continue, "Shyness is not a phobia you ever learn to control, but rather you learn to circumvent it. I know this, Laura because I have been shy all my life."

"You are shy, Grandmother?"

"Terribly."

I begin to tell her of some of the things I've done in my life to cover up my shyness. Many had been really dumb and almost funny. We laugh together. Among the stories I tell Laura as we sit side by side on her bed is about my date to my high school prom. She seems to enjoy it the most. Although I was a class officer, had my fingers in every extra curricular pie and was even catcher on the girls' softball team, I had no date to my senior prom in 1941. The dean of women, Mrs. Watkins accosted me in the hall a couple of weeks before the event to ask me to bring my date in after school to practice the Grand March. As a class officer it was a must for me to participate. It never entered Dean Watkin's mind that a popular girl like me wouldn't have a date. On learning I had no plans to attend the dance; the Dean informed me, that, as class vice president, it was my responsibility to lead the march with an escort along with the class president and his date. I was to ask a boy to be my prom partner.

There was no way I was about to ask any of my classmates of the opposite gender to be my escort. I looked on them as friends, not boy friend material. Having a boy friend was not on my agenda back then. Not wanting to shirk my duty and because Dean Watkins was a favorite teacher I assured her I would show up with my dad and lead the Grand March.

"You asked your dad to be your date. Gram?"

"No, something better happened." I answer. Then I continue the story.

There must have been a phone call home because on my arrival after school Mother took exception to the idea of Dad as his daughter's escort. My back was to the wall. I remembered Timmy, a boy who had been my playmate in another school and town. He had lived across the street from me when we attended the fifth grade at Miami Elementary School in Maumee, Ohio.

I ended up inviting him much to Mother's complete bewilderment. He and his family had moved to Cleveland over one hundred miles to the east soon after my family had left Maumee. The moms had remained letter writing friends over the intervening years, so the date was actually arranged between the two of them. I never said a thing to Tim, nor did he to me. Word came back to me via Mother that Tim agreed to the invitation. He arrived on prom day, driving his dad's car from Cleveland and into our driveway to escort me to the prom. No high school student owned their own car back in the '40s.

That he was no longer a ten year old boy came as an abrupt surprise to me. In the panic of setting things up for the dean I hadn't stopped to think about our ages. Seven years had elapsed since the Maumee days when we had last seen each other. I suspect he was way ahead of me with his expectations. And another thing I didn't consider was the reaction my classmates would have when I showed up with a tall, handsome, dark-haired stranger. They were all agog. The two of us had a great evening despite the missing years. I was completely at ease, after all we had become great friends and playmates when we were neighbors in those earlier post-depression days. Tim was on my safe-to-be-with list.

Neither my mother nor the Dean Watkins understood the whole thing. Like everyone else they had no clue about my shyness. Thinking back to the time it is probable my dad might have suspected. If he did he never said a thing.

After hearing this story Laura realizes there is nothing she can ever do to match her grandmother's prom solution.

Telling the stories buys me time to find the right answer; the one, which will help Laura. Suddenly I know what it can be.

"I have a wonderful friend at the high school, Laura. Her name is Glenda and she's the secretary in the school's front office. We both worked at the electric cooperative back in the '70s.

"Oh, I know who you mean, Mrs. Graves. She knows everyone."

"I will call Glenda as soon as I get back upstairs to the phone and ask her if she has any idea that might help you. Does that sound OK?"

Laura, ready to grasp at any straw her grandmother might offer smiles and nods her head.

Glenda is still in the office. Her bubbly voice bounces into my ear. It is full of her love of life and people. I explain Laura's need.

Without hesitation my friend responds, "Tell your Laura to bring her lunch into my office tomorrow on her noon hour and we'll eat together. Then, if she'd like I will show her how to sort the staff mail. Golly, I have needed help with it all week. Would she like that? It's an answer to prayer for me."

"Yes."

The next morning before classes are to begin Laura and I go in to talk with Glenda. Laura watches as we exchange hugs and memories of the Coop days. Obviously Glenda is someone special. Glenda and Laura bond instantly. Childless herself, Glenda is everyone's mother at the school. She appreciates Laura's quiet abilities, her sense of responsibility and her smile. Laura is given the job of sorting mail each day and to help in whatever other manner she might be called upon.

The noon hour job continues for the four years Laura is a high school student. She graduates Valedictorian of her class. She is never aware of how much her fellow students hold her in high regard. Her memberships on the softball and the cross county track teams set the stage for strong friendships. One determined young man breaks through Laura's wall of shyness and convinces her to be his date at their prom. Her high school experience with Glenda will give her the ability to leave home to attend Alma College next fall. It is a one hundred and fifty mile drive to the south. She'll know how to handle her shyness.

Before Anne starts to write this story she finds a wonderful book on shyness, 'Living Fully with Shyness and Social Anxiety'. Written by Erika B. Hillard, it is full of surprises for her; the first being that shyness is now believed to be the third most prevalent mental disorder in the United States, affecting more than thirteen percent of the population. The affliction was not recognized as a social phobia until 1980 when it was listed in the Diagnostic and Statistical Manual of Mental Disorders. Secondly, that it comes in many forms and it includes beneficial aspects. That it molds a person throughout their lifetime and that each individual who endures the disease does so by learning to live beyond it is no surprise. She knows this is how her shyness has been put aside—a least for most of the time.

Patrick as a Christmas shepherd—1993

A Fat Tree, Bushel Baskets and Australia

An old saying is, 'Make the best of the situation'

An old adage that has found its way into the family says, "Make the best of the situation". Perhaps it was born during the Great Depression. It certainly was what everyone tried to do back then. Now, all these years later Anne learns a new twist to those old words.

This is the last year the Jordan River tree farm is opening its gates to cut-your-own-tree customers. The fattest of all trees found within the lot is a beautiful spruce with thick branches and close needles. It is the model for all Christmas cards ever drawn. It's next to impossible for us to drag it through the knee deep snow. We pull the tree down the rows and out into the back of the van. I admire Ed as he withholds his four letter vocabulary and accepts the suggestions of the earnest children. He truly has the patience of Job.

Once home it's my suggestion the tree be set back in the corner of the covered alcove, which forms the house's front entry. The tree will remain outside until it is time to bring it in to decorate.

I explain to the family, "This is on the east side of the house and the tree will be tucked back out of any wintry blasts from the north."

The logic of my words prevails. The spot becomes the waiting place for the tree for the next three weeks.

The Saturday before Christmas it's decided that the time has come to bring the tree inside to trim. Boxes of balls, tinsel and hand made decorations are wrestled down from the attic above Patrick's room. It is where I have stored all the things of Mary's the kids might treasure some day. There isn't much other than the holiday stuff. Most of the rest is small; a couple of lamps, a cabinet, knick-knacks, pictures and Halloween costumes. Over half of the boxes retrieved contain ornaments from the children's Christmases with their mom and dad.

It is hard for me to open the lids and see the reminders of those days not so long ago. Memories flood my mind and my heart seems to weigh in my chest. The children don't carry the same feeling of nostalgia. This concerns me. I believe the first five or six years of life often remain with a person not because he or she actually remembers their happenings, but rather because of what they hear others say about them. Conversations become what are believed to be memories.

I ask Ed, "Are we remembering enough with the kids about the Christmases they had with Mary and Pat?"

Ed thinks a second and says, "Probably not."

We admonish ourselves to do this more frequently.

In my logical decision to keep the tree fresh by hiding it in a corner of the front porch I forget to include the wind. Living on the very top of a hill as we do the wind is not a factor to be ignored. It's hard to believe, but I did. Ed didn't bring the subject up either. We both simply forgot. When snow storms sweep in from the northwest, southwest or even the northeast they are wind driven. Seldom does snow drop straight down from the heavens in its gentle intrusion upon Michigan's landscape. Snow flakes are far more likely to seek others, they are very social. They arrive in bunches.

How can anyone deny the presence of God when such a unique treasure brushes a cheek or lies in its unbelievable beauty on a jacket sleeve? I wonder.

Over the three weeks of waiting the tree has been the recipient of numerous blasts of snow as it was driven in great swirls around the corners of the house, its shrubbery and yes, even the porch roof supports. Now covered from top to bottom the spruce appears as if some baker has generously lathered it with globs of white frosting.

Dressed for the cold the family goes out to try to shake the tree clear of its snow. Its chubbiness and thick needles defy them, plus it is frozen stiff and so heavy not even Ed can move it. He can't even shake it hard enough to send the snow flying. Proceeding to brush the snow off with two brooms, one from the house and the beat-up one from the garage, we see no noticeable affect on the tree.

Then it is down to basics as the five of us begin to use mittened and gloved hands to not only brush the exterior layer of snow from the tree but to dig in between its closely grown branches. Unlike balsam the spruce is a very prickly tree, even with gloves on. It is a slow and cold process. Working in such close quarters its impossible not to get snow into each other's faces, careful as everyone tries to be. This generates a general warfare as handfuls of snow whiz through the air, numb fingers temporarily forgotten. Eventually the aching fingers demand a truce. Attention is focused once more on moving the tree into the house. The fun is over. The tree has not gone anywhere.

It is an hour later and every one is miserably cold and out of sorts; the tree still can't be shaken. It seems to weigh well over a ton. There is no end to the amount of snow that has been driven into its branches; seemingly lodged there until July's sun arrives. Since we can't remove the snow we decide to see if the tree can be dragged into the entry hall. It is tilted side-ways and headed in base first.

I think, Certainly any snow that might melt on the front entry's tile floor can easily be mopped up.

There is a point when it's believed the front door will be held open by the obese tree until the spring thaw. The beautifully plump spruce is wedged in as tight as a five hundred pound person would be in a revolving door. Ed and Pat are outside pushing while the girls and I are inside pulling with all our might. At least we three females have the warm side, although just the cold emanating from the tree is enough to chill us despite the house's interior temperature. The heat is hurrying out the front door while all outdoors is rushing in.

Eventually something gives and the tree is inside, leaning against the door of the lavatory. We three gals are sprawled across the flooding floor. All we have managed to do is to move the tree inside; its load of snow has not noticeably diminished. A summit conference is called. The kids bounce ideas off their heads. Ed and I listen as we have no clue what to do with this tree now that we have brought it through the door. Doing so is now viewed by both of us as one huge mistake rather than any kind of progress.

The suggestion that prevails is to cover the twenty feet of carpet the tree must be dragged across with old sheets and towels. We have planned that tree is to stand in the tiny library which is up a step from the living room, across from the front entry. The room is about eight by eight, the side facing the living room is open and only a railing and the step divide the two areas. It sounds like an impossible idea, but no one wants to voice their opinion. Tiredness forecasts possible short tempers.

The forces scatter to locate sheets and towels. They then diligently spread them out across the light grey-green carpet. All of them know pine trees must be moved trunk end first to prevent breaking off branches. In this instance the bottom of the tree is the heaviest and its roundness proves to be of no help. Patrick, Ed and Laura elect to do the tugging. Rachael and I are to keep the sheets from moving with the tree.

The tree is bounced down the one step from the entry hall into the living room. Rachael and I hold onto the sheets for dear life. Every inch of the jerky progress causes the packed snow in the interior of the tree to begin to fall out in hard chunks, which doesn't bothers us because we want the snow out of the tree. We had come to think it would never happen.

Hats and gloves are still on but coats begin to be un-zipped as the exertion of dragging the huge tree across the floor builds up body temperature. Eventually the hats are thrown out of the way. No one wants to remove their mittens; the needles are too sharp. It takes close to twenty five minutes to get the tree to the library step mainly thanks to Ed's and Pat's strength. If getting it down into the living room from the front entry was difficult, lifting it up into the little library is much worse. Laura, Rachael and I try to position ourselves in the cramped space to do what we can. Clumps of snow fall everywhere as all of us try to get a grasp on the tree and push it up onto the floor.

By the time it stands in the library, leaning against the window, it is dripping like Niagara Falls in the midst of a spring thaw. The water actually starts to cascade down over the lip of the step onto the living room rug. To say we have a real mess on their hands is an understatement.

Someone shouts, "Bring towels, quick."

It isn't me, but I know it's a great idea. Turning to get them and I come to a dead stop. For the first time I'm aware of the condition of the hall and living room. The floor is snow covered, not in a thin layer but in piles.

There is a silence behind me as the other four see the white, softening mess. Within seconds the order is out, "Get the snow shovels off the porch. Get boxes and bushel baskets from the garage. We have to get this stuff out of here before we have a flood."

As the snow removal and mopping gets under way the idiocy of the situation breaks on everyone and we dissolve into laughter. The snow is so wet and heavy the baskets become difficult to carry outside the door to dump. Gradually the carpet regains its original color but the supply of towels proves insufficient; we toss them in the drier to reuse them to soak the water from the floor. The equivalent of six bushel baskets full of wet, heavy snow is recovered from the living room floor by shovel. None of the workers will ever be able to erase the memory of this day and its Christmas tree from their minds.

Ed and I realize that such days as this one will become memories for the three grandchildren to cherish and share with their children someday. It will become a Christmas story to tell over and over again.

It is two years later in the evening soon after another Christmas tree is decorated that a disturbing noise is heard. The living room is quiet as all of us have our noses in books, just taking it easy after the job of hanging the tinsel on the decorated tree.

Rachael hears it first and asks, "Gram, what's that noise I hear coming from the tree?"

All of us turn toward the pretty tree with its lights glowing and reflecting in its shiny ornaments. There is a silence in the room as we strain to hear whatever it is Rachael has heard. Together the grandchildren call out, "There it is again. Did you hear it?"

Even though my hearing isn't very good, I hear a noise. I can tell Ed does also. It is hard to describe; a soft rustle of pine needles being moved as if something was crawling through them.

"A mouse," Pat states.

"Or a squirrel," someone else suggests.

"We could see a squirrel," Ed says. "Must be a mouse," he adds.

By this time the three kids are on their hands and knees to slowly approach the tree, yet not frighten whatever is in its branches away. Ed and I walk over to take a look, also. We all but walk on our toes.

The sound repeats itself a couple of more times, but in different sections of the tree. We don't see anything move. A feeling of eeriness fills the room.

It is then Pat says, "There's no mouse in there. That noise is just the cold branches of the tree relaxing; when they spring upward the sound of the movement is what we are hearing. I just saw one; watch and it will happen again."

All five of us stand like statues, eyes glued on the tree in fascination as we watch branch after branch relax. I wonder, Can it be this tree is as happy the trimming process is over as I am?

In addition to the family tree trimming each Christmas brings a different version of the Christmas story to the choir area behind the church's pulpit. The cast is the Sunday School. It is staged in the area normally inhabited by the choir on Sunday mornings. Their chairs along with the pulpit and other items are dutifully carried off to be temporarily stashed in the nursery. The microphones are set in place and tested. Some type of scenery is hung in place. Every season brings a different group of parents on hand to apply makeup, adjust costumes, wigs and beards. Crowns and staffs are brought down from the belfry along with the hand-me-down outfits. These are duly lengthened or shortened dependent on the current year's cast.

The year Patrick is ten I find myself working side by side with the parents of other cast members. I feel like everyone's grandmother. But my experience brings forth some mighty handsome crowns and costume upgrades. I have a ball helping get the play ready for its slated afternoon performance, the Sunday before Christmas.

Of the three boys selected as Wise Men, Patrick is the tallest. Because of this he is given the only speaking line allotted the trio. There is nothing to rehearse as it is short and to the point, "We three wise men bring gifts to the new born babe."

Unlike some of the cast, Pat shows no sign of nervousness or last minute jitters as I help him get on his striped bathrobe costume, beard and jewel-studded gold cardboard crown.

The shepherds usher in the entire pre-school class attired in cotton batting lamb outfits complete with pink lined ears. They advance to huddle around the manger, baby, Mary and Joseph. Avoiding the sound system, the Holy Family members mumble their lines. The little lambs steal the show trying to keep their head covers with ears from slipping down over their eyes. On cue the three Wise Men proceed down the aisle and step onto the stage.

Moving forward one pace and clutching his gift Patrick speaks his line in a loud, clear voice, "We three have traveled afar bringing gifts to the Baby."

Then he crosses the stage front with his two cohorts. They place their gifts before the infant and exit down the right aisle. It isn't what he says that surprises me, it is how he says his line; in a heavy Australian accent.

I turn to Ed and ask, "Did you hear what I just did?"

Shaking his head in disbelief he whispers, "I sure did."

After the program a fun time is held in the basement where the cast heads to change into their own clothes and enjoy Christmas candies, cookies and ice cream. By the time Ed and I reach the dining room, Patrick is already dressed and collecting his goodies.

When we reach his side I ask, "Pat, why the Australian accent?" I just had to know.

Grinning at us he answers, "Well, Gram. I figure when all you have is a one-liner you might as well make it as memorable as possible."

Patrick, Ed, Anne, Rachael and Laura in Nova Scotia—1997

Vinyl Siding, a Group of Ten and Honor

Where are the credentials?

In a small community the acceptance of a new idea is often determined by how it judges the person who presents it. The proposal's very value and benefits are measured by the initiators' validity. Are they well known? Were their parents pillars of the community? Are they? Do they give generously to community needs? Are they good citizens and have a wonderful family relationship? In other words, if the person has a track record of success and believes in the idea it certainly must be destined to be a winner. However, don't let an unknown try to garner support. Where are the credentials?

It is when Laura enters junior high school that I look ahead at my granddaughter's high school years and realize the Boyne City High School is overcrowded, computer void and sadly, far more conducive to successful sports programs than academic. Seven successive efforts to bring the structure up to date have not been accepted by the voters. The small town still struggles with its past which dates back to the dire affects of the depression days. The general feeling is that taxes must not be increased.

Ed refers to the small town of 3,000 some inhabitants as 'The Miracle of Vinyl Siding' because the old frame homes of the lumbering days are being renovated. A look of charm and grace emerges as home after home is reclaimed. The nationwide effort of the 1976 bicentennial celebration left a lasting result on the small downtown area. Sidewalks are wider and benches invite visitors to linger under beautiful red maples. New families and businesses have moved into the town, recognizing the pace of life is indeed slower. Boyne City is in the very

190

heart of some of the country's most beautiful lakes and hills. Its first settlers, John and Harriet Miller arrived from Ireland in the late nineteenth century. The appearance of the Boyne River as it flowed into Lake Charlevoix, then Pine Lake, brought memories of their homeland and its river, The Boyne, to Harriet. So the river was named.

As I think about the school system and all it lacks to produce the education the world demands in the twenty-first century only three years away, and then the past failures to approach its real problems, I ask myself, "What would Mary do?" Even as I ask my rhetorical question I know exactly what she would do. I know immediately.

Mary would get right in there and give it another try, expecting to win. It wasn't that long ago when my daughter saw the need of pre-school day care in the town. Mary wanted something better than the in-home small care centers. She felt a larger, carefully planned center where working mothers could leave their children not only for care but for learning was needed. Boyne City had three small factories at the time and their main source of employment was the women of the town.

With a like minded friend, Lisa, Mary set about making the center come into being. The generous owners of a local hardware store, Don and Shelly, helped with money to purchase the necessary land. The project was accomplished with no public funding. One of my favorite newspaper clippings is of Don and Mary, perched on the new structure's roof, hammers in hand nailing shingles in place.

Mary would roll up her sleeves and tackle the school facility problem, I say to myself in complete agreement with my own thinking.

I hunt Ed down in the garage and run my idea by him for his input

"You sure as heck can't loose anything by giving it a try, Hon. Let me know if I can help."

Before the day is over I insert an ad in the Citizen If flushes out nine interested people. As I hoped and expected, they are almost entirely newcomers to Boyne. Ed and I feel we are still considered transplants although we arrived back in '61. We are not part of the local clan and never will be because none of our four children have married into it. Maybe a grandchild will.

With the Group of Ten, I find myself surrounded by men and women of all ages and callings who have one important thing in common, they're college educated.

For them there is no excuse of, "Hey, I graduated from that school and look at me, I'm doing OK. I can read and write. What was good enough for me is good enough for the kids today."

As the group begins its research into the recent history of attempts to upgrade the Boyne school system it is hard not to become discouraged. In the past twelve years the issue had been taken to the voters seven times and defeated. None of us can believe anyone would challenge the expenditure of a few pennies a day to further the expansion of education.

The group bonds together. This is where we make our mistake. To the outsiders we are a bunch of newcomers who don't belong. How can we know what the town's kids need? The people who subscribe to this belief make up the majority of the voters. They will ultimately go to the polls and turn down the Group's effort; even though it is presented as a well thought out and developed proposal.

Heart sick, I once again think of the disappointment from Mary's point of view. I know my daughter would never let it die. The only thing I can think to do is to go to the home of a local business man, Jack. He is respected and beloved by the entire town. I think a lot of him, but at the same time suspect he has offered leadership in the defeat of the Group of Ten's school proposal. The very thought of knocking on his door and seeking time to talk with Jack terrifies me. This in turns infuriates me. Why in the world am I so afraid of visiting a man I know to be kind and generous? It doesn't make sense and at my age. I should be able to shove my fear behind me. Mary wouldn't think twice about doing it.

The more I think about it the angrier I become. Not about the failed proposal or Jack's possible leadership in its defeat but at myself and this thing I hold within me. The nameless fear of other people. It has nothing to do with the fearful monsters I read about as a child, or the scary movies every Halloween Eve. They have never frightened me as this thing within me manages to do. Good Lord, I'm seventy-nine and acting like a two-year old. At this point I think of asking Ed to go with me to visit Jack. He wouldn't hesitate. But this is my battle and not my husband's. Just go, Anne, just go. It will not kill you. What in the world are you afraid of?

I park right along the curb in front of his house. Keeping my mind blank of all thought I move as a robot across the grass the short distance to the walk that leads to the front door. I refuse to allow my eyes to check out the curtains at the windows that flank the door to see if there is movement. I won't allow my mind to tell me someone is watching my approach and wondering, Who is that old lady coming up to our front door? I am on the front stoop and knocking on the door without acknowledging to myself that I am where I am doing what I am doing. It must be someone else.

I'm welcomed into Jack and Marilyn's home. We have a great talk. My words I exchange with Jack and his wife are honest, yet being privy to my real purpose for this visit I feel as if I'm trying to soft-soap the man. In all honesty I am speaking from my heart. I remind him his own grandchildren deserve more than the current school has to offer them. Jack has been college educated and knows what the world is beyond the small town. He is a navy veteran of WWII, flies his own plane, and is an ardent skier and certainly a successful businessman. I do my best to convince him that he can gather together the local clan to produce a new school for the kids if anyone can.

By the time the conversation ends Jack knows I realize he has had a big hand in squashing the efforts of the Committee of Ten. At the same time the grandfather and businessman that he is knows his mistake has to be undone. He is the one who is going to have to do it. Jack succeeds. And I will pin a badge of valor on my chest that no one else can see. I have done what I believed I couldn't. I had managed a one-on-one conversation on my own.

The school which now stands on its campus at the southern entrance to Boyne City is incredible. Anne never stood with a shovel in hand when the ground was broken for its foundation work nor is her name engraved on its cornerstone. But she is as responsible for the new structure as her Mary would have been if she were living. Anne is satisfied.

By the time I complete my term as a school board member the school, well planned, is one of the finest schools in Michigan in every possible manner. Sidewalks and landscaped grounds connect it to the elementary and the old high school; now renovated into the twenty first century as the middle school. The High School boasts a six hundred and fifty seat auditorium featuring an orchestra pit and a stage with flown rigging, dressing rooms and set construction shop.

It is at the presentation of the annual drama production in which Patrick portrays Hook in *Peter Pan* in the spring of 2003 that Ed leans over to whisper in my ear, "Why am I watching him, Anne, instead of his parents?"

I know there are tears in his eyes because they are in mine, also.

Ed has said these same words to me before when one of the grandchildren has appeared for an honor or taken part in a public performance of one kind or another. All three have been in drama. Ed and I have painted sets for them for nine years; *Anastasia, Little Miss Sunshine, Oliver, Beauty* and *the Beast* and all the others. This year's *Peter Pan* has been the most demanding and exciting. Annually Mr. 'W' and his wife Jackie take the year's cast to New York City or Toronto, Canada for a three day siege of stage plays, sightseeing and fantastic food.

There was the afternoon Pat approached me to say, "What do you think, Gram? Will this work?"

I looked down at the sword Pat was brandishing in his hand. It was long, straight and the dull silver of duct tape. The handle was curved to fit his hand and from the grip I saw I knew the handcrafted weapon had been made to withstand some very earnest swordplay.

"Boy, Pat, I'm sure I wouldn't want you to be mad at me. I'd be as good as dead."

That's what he wanted to hear and left with a big smile on his face. The sword did go through a number of repairs and refinements but held together remarkably in the performances

We joke about our painting. Ed slaps on a good strong coat of black on the back of every set, from top to bottom. While he is working with his monochromatic theme on the backs of the scenery I work from a full color palette on the audience side of the flats. There I paint ornately framed pictures hanging on walls, furniture, china, hanging clothing, pianos, stairs, rocks, water, cars, animals and more. My biggest moment is when one of the cast members, upon entering the stage turns and sets his can of coke on the piano's top. Of course, as the piano is merely two dimensional the pop falls to the floor. At times there are as many as four retired art teachers working on the sets, the most important is Chuck, the visionary and designer.

The two or us, the grandparents, make quite a team. All about us the cast and support members busily go about their business and the coach bellows out instructions. The music of someone's radio fills in between lines and conversation. On break, over a cup of coffee and sweet roll Ed looks at me. Without a word each of us knows the other is wondering how we ever happen to find ourselves where we are; why we have paint all over ourselves. We are like an island in the midst of all the music, practice lines, seamstresses, sequins, feathers and wonderfully spontaneous and gifted kids. We have somehow broken loose from our life to float unguided into a place that would never have been on our travel itinerary if it hadn't been for the deaths of our daughter and her husband. Where is our sadness? Ed looks into my eyes and I into his. He grins his happiness and I mouth him a kiss.

The new high school offers a hospitality course with top-of-the-line instruction for those wishing to go directly into the vocation after high school graduation; or to continue further study in the field at college. Hospitality is a profession in desperate need of trained personnel. Particularly in the Boyne area where the main industry is tourism, all four seasons of the year. Dennis, the former chef of Boyne City's most prestigious restaurant chose to instruct the program.

As part of the school training, the class holds a special reception following stage performances. The students wearing starched white jackets and hats preside over a table of delicious sweets. All are of the class's own creativity. Nearby the cast forms a line to receive the accolades of their audience. Patrick, as Hook is so frightening that the small children who want to touch his horrible hook need intense reassurance from a parent that it is safe to do so. Next to him stands his best friend, Jeff as the hilarious Mr. Smeed. On Pat's other side is the gifted lead, Mallory, Peter Pan himself. The drama coach, Mr. 'W's ability to perceive a cast among his students is only the tip of the iceberg in his directing abilities.

Other vocations such as computer sciences, music, fine arts, metals and wood shop have equal facilities for career preparation. Every classroom is wired for computer access and the sports fanatics are thrilled with the new gym facilities. A large library invites the student to research and study. Mary would be so proud. Although the new high school is not completed in time for Laura's or Rachael's graduations it is there for Patrick and his class of 2003.

During the years the children are with us we applaud them in Boyne Meets Broadway, the annual dinner theater at the elegant restaurant, One Water Street. There are also recognition banquets for their academic achievements and athletic awards, including the National Honor Society induction. Ed and I listen to one motivational speaker after another at these events and find ourselves content in knowing what we are listening to has been part of our own words to the kids. But even more important we know we have demonstrated this through our own behavior; a tough essential in good parenting.

Back in grade school days there had been one certificate after another handed out in assemblies for citizenship, grades etc. And more recently Ed and I have had the fun of cheering Laura on at her softball games and the cross country finish line. Then came Rachael's tennis matches and Pat's soccer team tearing across the soccer field, maneuvering the ball from one end to the other. It is a game of great skill and non-stop movement which threatens great bodily harm. At least this seems so in my eyes.

She has yet to watch Pat play Lacrosse as a student at Alma College.

All I can ever find to say in answer to Ed's usual question of why he is watching the kids and not their parents is, "Honey, Mary and Pat are here. They are always with their children. It is why all three kids are so exceptional."

I believe this, without question.

Patrick, Ed, Laura, Anne and Rachael on Isle Royal—1998

Walking Sticks, Tang and Helicopter

The over all plan of life is kept in place

There is something about Isle Royal as it protrudes from the deep, clear and icy cold waters of Lake Superior, a tiny bit of Michigan's geological history, which visually recants the birth of this magnificent land. It reminds me we are really only humans in this world we call home. This isn't intimidating, but certainly makes me aware of my microscopic roll in it all. My vulnerability in the overall plan of things is kept in place because of the Presence felt around me. "There is no place I feel closer to my Creator," Anne says to me as we stand at the rail of 'The Isle Royal Queen III', the ferry which shuttles across Lake Superior between Houghton, Michigan and the island. We are engrossed at the large vessel's maneuvers which slide it into its birth at Rock Harbor. Standing shoulder to shoulder beside Anne the rest of the family have their eyes glued on the forest covered rock before them. A first time for the kids, it is only in Ed's and Anne's eyes that the look of joy for this return visit can be seen.

1999 finds all five of us disembarking from the Queen III outfitted with brand new good, light weight backpacks. Ed and I view them as investments for future travels by the three grandchildren who will roam about the world on their own down the road. The day's goal is to reach Daisy Farm, the first camp ground beyond the headquarters area, before dark. Ed and I have made this trek three times before so know what to expect along the trail. Ed is seventy eight and I'm seventy six, but we are feeling thirty nine, Jack Benny's lasting age, as we disembark and set out on the trail down island.

The three children elect to carry extra weight to lighten our loads. Even so the rocky path proves too much of a challenge for Ed's eyes. Since his Graves disease in his early sixties double vision has hounded him. The unusual illness affected not only his eyes but his heart and thyroid. Both of us know that only modern medicinal knowledge keeps him by my side. The constant need to watch his footing slows him way down as the trail climbs up and over the rocky terrain. Sometimes the path is adjacent to the waters of Moskey Bay and other times across the sloping hillside above.

Knowing the grandchildren are knowledgeable in their outdoor skills Ed and I send them on ahead to make camp We trust them to use their good judgment as they climb the wet rocks, slippery with moss, then in building and lighting a camp fire and pitching the tents. They have done it before up on the northern shore of Lake Superior in Canada's remote National Park, Pukaskwa. They understand the wilderness is not a place to be careless.

"Stay together. If we don't make it to camp by night don't worry. We will stop along the route and sleep. Wait for us in the morning. Understand?"

They nod their heads. I don't place one of the grandchildren in charge of the others. They are each in charge of themselves while at the same time are to be responsible for each other. The last thing Patrick does is to further lighten his grandfather's load. He is fourteen and strong and concerned.

It is dusk when Ed and I decide to quit for the night. Uncertain how much further it is we think it best to set up camp while there is enough daylight to see. Ed searches for a level spot trail-side and begins to spread out the sleeping bags. It is then we hear the approach of two men who appear out of the dusk from around a bend in the trail, headed in our direction. As they draw near Ed sees their questioning look and explains, 'My vision isn't good enough for me to continue on to Daisy Farm tonight. Anne and I are going to make camp here beside the trail and go on in the morning."

The two are in their late thirties or early forties. It seems strange to Ed they aren't carrying gear. Their reply explains why. "We are chaperones for a church group of teenagers and are on our way back to Daisy Farm to spend the night with the boys in our group. Why not join us; we can help you make it to camp. It isn't that much further."

They are determined to carry Ed's and my gear. With their flashlights and help Ed and I finish the trail. Camp is reached where tents are set up, a fire burning and dinner being kept warm. The kids are overjoyed to have us back. They excitedly tell of a fox they passed curled into a tight circle and asleep beside the trail. On their approach, it had merely opened its eyes and watched them as they quietly walked by.

The next day, Ed and I decide to walk back to Rock Harbor to rent a canoe. We feel there is no other choice. The alternative would be to shorten the trip and return home. To us that wasn't an option. We will paddle Moskey Bay to its southern end, meeting the children at designated spots along the way to eat and camp. The kids are delighted to be on their own and not have to be slowed down by their pokey grandparents. For Ed and me it is as if we are on yet another honeymoon, happily paddling off-shore with nothing but the beauty of the north-country and the waters of Lake Superior to fill our eyes and days. An occasional glimpsing of three small figures through a clearing in the pine or high on the Greenstone Ridge remind us our charges are actually on the trip; safe in each other's care.

When the canoe is brought ashore at meal time the kids take it over, endeavoring to learn to paddle as a team. One mistake brings a tipping and a ducking. Because they are all excellent swimmers thanks to their summers in the Boyne City's swim program Ed and I are relaxed, enjoying the expression on the faces. The calls of excitement and splashing bring an audience of fellow campers out of the woods and down along the shoreline. There is a sudden intake of breath when the canoe flips over and the occupants fall into the fifty four degree lake water. The gasp is echoed by those watching. It is a photograph I neglect to take and Ed is so engrossed in his shouts of what they have or have not done he never thinks of his camera, either.

It is at the end of Moskey Bay I have my accident. As hard as he searches Ed can't find a good landing spot for the canoe. The entire shore line is sloping granite rock, which disappears into the water. How far beneath the surface it slants is a mystery. Polished smooth by winter's ice and the merciless pounding of storm waves the shore is treacherous. Ed hunts diligently for a cleft in the rock that he feels will offer me a handhold. The one he finds is around the corner from the main bay where a small creek enters. He maneuvers the canoe lengthwise against the smooth rock allowing me to reach out and manage a firm finger hold in the fissure.

Knowing I can't push against the rock to help myself out of the canoe I crouch low to prepare to leap out onto the top of the rock's rounded surface. There's no way I want to tip Ed and especially our gear into the bay's icy water. All goes well until the tip of my toot boot, a name I picked up from the engineers of Michigan Tech, catches the rim of the gunwale of the park's aluminum canoe. Our beloved wood and canvass Old Towne we usually travel in has no such rim. To avoid falling back into the canoe and flipping it and to experience a fall directly into the cold water I opt to land on my hand; too hard. Despite the jabbing pain I manage to flop out on the shore much like a beached fish, with absolutely no grace. I do a remarkable catch with my left hand of the line Ed tosses me and secure the boat to the overhanging branch of a scrubby pine.

Laughing about my scramble onto shore I call out, "OK. Let's see you do it."

With a big grin he lands beside me, asking, "Are you OK, Snork? Did you hurt your hand." He reaches for it and admittedly it has turned the ugly red of bruised flesh.

"Go on up to the camp, Hon. I'll dig out the coffee pot and be up with some lake water you can soak that hand in. I don't like the look of it. I'll unload the gear later."

By the time he has this chore accomplished and everything carried up to the nearby Adirondack my hand looks lie a rubber glove someone has inflated.

Worried about broken bones Ed has me favor the hand during the evening and night keeping it in a cooking pot full of the ice cold lake water. The next day it remains badly swollen and stiff. But I declare my hand is no worse. The day is pure Isle Royale; cerulean sky reflected in the rippled surface of Moskey Bay and the air generously scented with spruce and damp earth. The decision is made to walk to the next lake and try some fly fishing. Fortunately I take the walking stick a friend, Al, from back home, made. The island's paths often are the bedrock of the island, complete with cracks and protrusions. But today's inland trail is flat and winds through trees and along sun drenched blueberry bogs. About halfway to the fishing lake a couple approach the five of us.

The man, muscular and trim for a fifty year old is limping; his lower leg and knee bound in bandaging. He supports himself with a length of dead branch he apparently has found along the way. The woman, probably his wife, also appears fit. She is strikingly lovely with black hair tied back by a red scarf. She smiles a greeting. The narrowness of the trails brings everyone to a halt. Scraggly thickets form six foot walls on each side, forcing a one way passage.

"What have you done to yourself?" Ed asks, concerned about the unavailability of medical assistance in the island's interior, completely forgetting the developments in communication since his first visit thirty some years before.

"Oh, I haven't injured myself. I have a chronic condition that has decided to flare up. As long as I take it easy and keep it bound I can make it back to camp," the man replies.

"Well, I don't think much of that dead piece of wood you are using for a walking stick. It's likely to snap any time. Here, use mine, I really don't need it," I offer.

"Oh, I can't do that. I would have no way of returning it."

"Just leave it for me in the Ranger's office at Rock Harbor. I'll pick it up on our way out."

At this point the man's companion speaks up, "Look at her hand, Jeff. She has injured it. Why don't you see what you can do?"

Glancing down at my hand the man, Jeff, reaches for it. Gently taking it in his he slowly explores it with careful touches.

"You're a doctor?" I ask in disbelief.

"Yes, I'm an obstetrician from the Houghton-Hancock Hospital. But I can do hands, too." He added to reassure.

By this time his wife has removed the pack from his back, opened it and handed her husband the dressings he needs to bandage my hand. The bandage will remain in tact throughout the entire trip and ease the soreness.

"I don't believe you have broken anything, just severely traumatized your hand. But I advise you to see your doctor when you return to your home; he may want to X-ray it."

As we turn to go our separate ways we both know we have met our Good Samaritan.

My walking stick is waiting for me at the main ranger's office when we return to leave the island.

It is the night of the trail meet I learn to make hot Tang. The rain starts in the late afternoon as a pelting downpour. By early evening, well before dark a group of four men walk into camp. There are no unoccupied shelters. One of the younger men appears at the door of our snug Adirondack. He asks if he can stack their gear on the lee side of our shelter in an effort to keep it dry. Of course, Ed invites the group in out of the rain.

Ed takes one look at the young man, rain water cruising off his face and replies, "Sure. And after that's done all of you come on in where it is dry. This stuff looks like it has set in for the night."

There are nine bodies, which keep dry this night at the end of Moskey Bay.

The leader of the group, a man in his forties, David, is from Grand Rapids, Michigan. He has brought three twenty-year youths with him to the island, driven by the mission of connecting them to a stronger Christian faith. He has brought them from the urban world to introduce them to God's world of nature.

In Ed and me, the grandparents, he finds the examples he believes he needs. Learning about the children and their parents and the grandparents place in their lives David reacts in the typical manner, that of elevating Ed and me to sainthood on the spot. Despite spending the evening endeavoring to explain to him that sainthood isn't the right word neither Ed nor I feel we succeed. Ed tries to tell him, "Love is the word that fits. First it was for our deceased daughter and son-in-law and now our grandchildren. In return more love fills our lives than most of our peers can dream of. While most our age are seeking fulfillment at the bridge table or on the golf course Anne and I are still living life. It's those, who in their retirement busily volunteer to care for something or someone else, who come the closest to the peace and contentment we know."

Somehow Ed isn't certain his message is understood. But the four visitors make the evening one to be remembered. The steady pounding of the wind driven rain on the roof and back of the Adirondack produces a rush of water in sheets that cascade off the edges and unto the granite at its base. This mixes with the sound of waves churned up on the bay which slash against the rocky shore to become a symphony for those inside. It seems so good to be bundled into sleeping bags and drink hot Tang from plastic cups.

David has broken out his small propane stove and heated water in which he stirs the orange flavored drink. A favorite trail beverage it is found to be even better hot, especially during a driving rain storm on a pitch black night so far from the world of people.

Gradually the conversationalists drift off, one by one until David, Ed and I are the only ones left awake. It has become a starlit night; a night that could only be found draped over Isle Royal. Its beauty can be seen out the screened, open side of the sturdy shelter. The seeming nearness of each brilliant star and its constellation is beyond belief let alone understanding. The freshness of the rain washed land and its growth saturate the air with a cleanliness the shelter occupants find unbelievable. Nature has renewed itself with a passion. The result hangs like a perfume over the island. To inhale deeply is to know that purity seldom found in the urban world.

"How can anyone doubt the presence of God when surrounded by His enormous infinity?" David whispers.

"I wouldn't know." Ed murmurs.

At daylight the cries of a raucous jay in a nearby spruce is the cock's crow of Isle Royale. Miraculously dry after the night's downpour the sleepy eyed hikers awake to a sun drenched, sopping wet world. It belongs to the Mergansers ducks who are pitching themselves in and out of the water of the bay, not far off shore and to the jay overhead in a spruce voicing his opinion of the day. One of the younger guests awakened early and the smell of wood smoke seeps into the shelter. Seasoned camper that Ed is, he had been certain wood was brought into the shelter for the night to be dry for a morning fire. Again hot Tang and coffee greet the occupants. Pancakes are enjoyed with my brown sugar syrup made in a camp skillet by mixing water, brown sugar and a dab of butter until the boiling mass thickens, its luscious odor making everyone ravenous.

It is while the utensils are being washed and stowed that the demanding sound of a helicopter suddenly breaks into the air about the camp.

Coming in from Thunder Bay, Wisconsin, the sound of the copter's low approach had been blanketed by the Greenstone Ridge until it broke over its edge. The throb of its rotors, thick in the air precedes the enormous body of the craft as it all but brushes the tree tops when it passes over our Adirondack. Without thought all nine of us rush for the trail to follow the monster hovering over our heads. Five hundred feet down the slippery rock and gushy mud trail we break through the trees to see the gigantic white air ship with a large red cross on its side descend onto a clear surface above the docking area Ed had missed spotting on our arrival.

The vast granite surface of the land slopes down into the bay. Hard and slick, it is unable to allow more than grasses and small wild flowers to toe-hold an existence. The rock isn't flat enough to permit the copter to more than roost on its back wheel as its expert crew evacuates a Boy Scout leader who has been stricken with a heart attack.

His two sons had run the trail along Moskey Bay back to Rock Harbor to find help for their father. Within minutes the Thunder Bay Hospital dispatched their copter to the island. Those of us from the camp silently watch the practiced efficiency of the flight crew as the man is stowed on board. The plane is airborne even as the door closes behind the litter. Those watching say silent prayers for their companion, unknown by name. The plane drops over the scoured granite tipped Greenstone to return to Thunder Bay, at the head of the Great Lakes.

We learn on our return to camp the following day that the rescue is successful; the father survived.

A Search, Death Threat and Diplomas

Group dynamics can be scary

Anne's shyness has always worked to keep her from becoming involved in one on one situations with one exception; her involvement with Ed. She's always felt relatively safe in a group, no matter its size. Age has brought wisdom, often the hard way, at least for her. It now seems to her group dynamics are far more fearful than that of any lone adult like she used to think. People in numbers terrify her. There's nothing for me to say that has or ever will help.

Because of my decision to run for the Boyne City School Board that I receive a death threat.

It doesn't make any sense. I'm a woman in my late seventies who goes out of her way to be law abiding, help others when she can, and tries to be a responsible member of her community. As a kid I didn't even try to take a cookie out of the cookie jar knowing Mother would catch me in the act. With Ed, I've been faithful at the polls, even taking a nine year turn as Evangeline Township's clerk. But being in the public eye can distort who one seems to be to others. That someone develops such a strong hatred of me that they would wish me dead just proves the point. Someone thinks Boyne City would be better off with me dead than alive.

I remember Mary's recognition of the need for a pre-school facility in Boyne City in the '80's and her participation in securing money for it. Mary sought my help in designing the building and then she actively helped with its construction. Because of this I now exactly what my daughter would do if she were living.

My decision to run for the school board leads me into one of the most disillusioning times of my life. I wish I could just erase it all from my mind. This can't be done. All I can do is learn and hopefully benefit from my four year tenure on the board. I discover it is possible to be in a situation where one has no control over what others set out to do. American's think they are protected from such situations. I learn that laws, such as Michigan's Open Meetings Act are only effective when enforced.

As I consider putting my name on the ballot as a candidate for school board I feel I've a number of pluses on my side. First, a college degree in the field of education will seem extremely important. Backing that up will be my time as an instructor in the classroom. I started out at Fresno College teaching ceramics during its 1945 summer session at the age of twenty-two. I still remember my opening day of classes when I discovered all my students were seasoned, middle aged teachers. They were seeking additional college credit during their summer vacations. Unnerved, my feeling of complete inadequacy spiked when I discovered one of my students was a woman who had a birth defect cause by Thalidomide. She lacked one arm; the second arm was partial and both had small malformed hands.

Why in the world would the registrar sign her into a pottery class? was all I could think.

Before I could carry that line of thinking any further I watched as others in the room burst out in happy greetings.

Almost in unison the members of my class called out, "Hi, Sunshine. Boy, am I glad you decided to come today."

The smile that spread across Sunshine's face reflected those of her classmates. Somehow the change in the room permeated me. My concern evaporated. During the following weeks Sunshine's work was outstanding. To watch her use the potter's wheel was inspirational; in fact, the woman has remained an inspiration to me my entire life. To me the word handicap took on an entirely different definition. Often it seems that those I perceive as handicapped are way ahead of me in their knowledge of life. Frequently what appears a hopeless situation is in reality used as an opportunity to grow.

In addition to my chance to teach at the college level I also taught elementary and high school classes. My year as a fifth grade teacher proved another surprise. I had no idea children at that level were so consumed with questions. There seemed to be no end to the areas in which their minds sought answers. Computers were on the horizon. The 'new' math dealt with twos as naturally as I had learned my time tables by rote thirty years before.

The opposite proved true in my high school art class. There I found at least half of my class included boys from the football team. They were seeking a no-work subject in which they could goof off in. Storm flags went up when I saw big discipline problems from a bored group of young men who individually out muscled and out weighed me. Then I had an inspiration! It must have come straight from above. I introduced them to a state-wide annual car design competition in which they could participate. At the time our two sons, David and Tom, were high schoolers and in the throws of working on their own cars so I had a ready advisory panel.

Although none of my students won an award they had a wonderful time. Probably completely unaware how much they learned about line, texture, color, form and design; all the elements of fine art were incorporated into the project. As a side bonus I had no discipline problems. The young women in the same class were fascinated with their interior design assignment. They also learned the same art principles as the football players. I don't know who had the better year, my students or me.

My eighth grade Michigan history class was the biggest challenge. Since I was a product of Ohio and had studied in California I knew nothing about Michigan other than it was the state our family drove through to go fishing in Canada. Every evening before turning in for the night I diligently read the test book in an effort to stay ahead of my class. Thank Heaven, it was an interesting study and has proven providential as I know more of Michigan now than the usual Ohioan.

In my innocence I believe all this experience will help me be a great school board member. I plunge into preparing to run for a position on the school board much as I had approached my marriage. I have absolutely no idea of what might lay ahead for me, but feels as prepared as anyone else.

The fact that I'm elected tends to cement this thinking. The night I attend my first board meeting the group is facing an unbelievably full agenda. I learn the superintendent is about to have his contract terminated, the high school principal is to be released after one year of service, there are staff problems as well as potential union trouble, a cash flow emergency and there is the new high school proposition to take to the voters. I believe as I sit in my allotted chair at the board table that this is going to be a wonderful and meaningful group and I am going to enjoy working with them.

Two years later it has become apparent to me I am one very naïve seventy-four year old. I should have turned in my resignation on that very first meeting back in 1998. It would have been prudent of me to have sent my letter of resignation by certified mail to its president.

In absolute amazement I watch it all happen. Despite board discussion pro and con; the administrator is gone. Before I know it we are doing a superintendent search and holding off the staff, union and fiscal problems until a new person can be hired to take over the helm. A man is found, but by this time the board is split on employing him. A simple majority wants to hire. It prevails. The man is so enamored with the system, its challenges and the little town that he accepts the board's offer to take hold of the slack reins despite the weak board support.

He is an experienced veteran in school administration and aware of the politics of school boards. He should have thanked the group for their invitation, bowed and left immediately. I shouldn't be talking, I was completely wet behind the ears and had on my rose colored glasses, envisioning great things in the future of the Boyne City school system. We did get off to a great start at that first meeting.

Quickly solving the cash flow problem with his own school finance history Blane then handled the public's rejection of the new high school principal. Next he worked hand-in-glove with the union rep on a new contract. This was followed with his negotiations to remove a long time instructor who verbally abuses girls in his math class. After that he helped bring about the approval of the bond issue and plunged into guiding the board into long range visioning for their schools.

Before my first year drew to a close I came to realize that all those experiences which I assumed would help me be an effective board member hardly seemed to matter. What did stand me in good stead were my years on the township board. Others all too often defend as the truth something they have only heard about and come to accept without verification. They do so without any knowledge of the facts involved. The sad thing is the believer will not change his or her mind. All I can do is remember this when I take a stand on an issue. I ask myself, is this first hand information or am I accepting someone else's point of view?" By the end of my third year I find myself standing alone on issue after issue. The normal loss of members to attrition and term endings finds those who think as I do leaving the board. After a particularly hard struggle over a policy issue I receive a phone call one evening from the board's president.

His voice is tuned to that of a dirge, "Anne, I can't tell you how disappointed I am. I have always had you up on a pedestal: this wonderful woman who cares for everyone. But now I have come to know you for what you really are. You don't give a shit for kids."

By the end of my four year term on the board I understands why all too often the people who have the most to contribute to the growth of local school education refuse to become involved. The possibility of their board action being misunderstood and therefore their standing in the community diminished is a price too dear to pay; especially if they are a business owner.

As for the poison pen letter, it's not signed. The writer chooses to remain anonymous. This destroys all possible menace as far as I'm concerned. Only a spineless wimp would lack the confidence in his own letter to not sign it. The letter is well composed, neat, hand written, in excellent form and features the vocabulary of an educated person. "You had better watch when you cross Water Street that a car doesn't tear around the corner and end your miserable life," the letter threatens me.

It is a simple matter for Blane to compare the writing with other samples available and the conclusion is no surprise. Who else but an adult male still living in the world of his glory days in the Marine Corps and now confined to the day in, day out sameness of a high school class room could come up with such a juvenile action?

The teacher assumes because I'm so frequently the maverick on the board that I'd been in on the administrator's decision to terminate his teaching days.

I can hear his mental wheels turning, "Someone has to be shown just who the boss around here is".

As I complete my last year on the school board I feel that I should be presented with a diploma that reads, "*In Appreciation of the Dedication and Devotion Displayed in the Study of Human Behavior We Present to Anne Thurston this Degree of Doctorate of Understanding and Survival at the Local School Board Level.*" And, a purple star should be affixed for courage under threat of death.

The up side of my four year term is the opportunity to hand both Laura and Rachael their diplomas at graduation. And to know the three grandchildren appreciate their grandmother for the work she has tried to accomplish on behalf of them and their classmates. After all, not everyone who serves on local school boards across the country receive death threats. I could consider it a compliment.

Patrick graduates the year after I leave the board. Although I'm not able to present him his diploma he is in the first class to graduate from the new high school facility, which I helped guide to completion. I can't help but wonder what Mary might have done differently if she still had been alive. Have I done what Mary would?

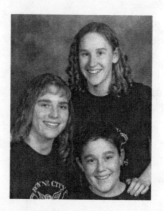

Laura, Rachael and Patrick—1999

Stones, Rabbit Ears and T-Shirts

The stones are just an illusion of reality

A Joan Kelly drawing of Lake Superior rocks hangs in Ed's and Anne's living room bay. Their hard, polished surfaces have been brought to life in soft pastels. Somehow the artist has manipulated the fragility of the chalks to wondrously reproduce the hardness, the solidarity of each unique stone. Anne's hand reaches out to touch and even hold what her eyes see, yet they're only an illusion of the reality of a shore far to the north. Anne is there even as she stands in her home.

I'm one of those people who really doesn't care to have their picture taken. Oh, family snap shots are great. Half the time, if they are group pictures at some family gathering there is always someone in the back row with two fingers sticking above the head in front of them as if suddenly there is a rabbit in their midst. Or there is the embarrassed teenager with a severe case of acne who solves it all by sticking out their tongue and looking cross eyed at the photographer no matter how a parent tells them to shape up or the photographer pleads for just one straight shot.

And if somehow the picture is snapped just at the instant when there is no face contortion or bunny ears, Great Auntie will choose that split second to turn her head to the side, looking back to ask her older brother, "Haven't you put on a few pounds, Joe?"

In the end it is the choice between the ears, the darn face or Auntie disregarding the photographer to needle her brother about a new pot belly he has developed over the last twelve months.

It is the posed stances one must assume before a professional photographer that turn me off even more. The tilt you head a little bit toward your husband, or let's try your hand resting lightly on his and now, let's think happy thoughts and let a smile show on the corner of your mouth. Worse are the cute commands to say money or cheese. They drive me to want nothing more than to say pickle relish or What's that smell?

Which is to say I'm no better than the teenager or the back row guy with the bunny ears; I just don't want to be part of the whole process.

This is behind my whole attitude about going into the church about every decade to go through the posed picture taking bit for a new church directory. The whole process is a highly polished bit of salesmanship, although the pictures are usually of a good quality. The publication of a small eight or twelve paged booklet with photos of all the members of the church has its merits. It is great for the newcomers to use to identify who is who in the church and the same is true for the older members as it helps us remember the names of the new members we meet as well as those we have known forever and whose names suddenly escape our memory.

Addresses and phone numbers are also included and a brief history of the church and pictures of the staff and pastor; all good information. And this all comes to the church for next to no cost as the photographers plan to reap their pot of gold by selling individual prints to each and every member and family that is involved. They are good at their picture taking and masterful with their salesmanship. It is all set up so even if a person isn't particularly fond of their shots they'll end up accepting at least one to go in the directory. From there on it is how many copies they decide to get for themselves, family and friends where the photographer's profit soars.

The grandkids make sure our family stands out among all the others in the church directory this time. Traditionally everyone dresses in their Sunday best clothes. The men all wear a tie with their shirt and jacket unless they don't own either, then it is their best sweater. The women add jewelry, get their hair done and otherwise try to look as great as their men. The kids are all spit and polish.

This time Laura is the one who determines what our family will wear. Her cross country team won the state division title a month or so ago. T-shirts were printed to commemorate the event as well as to raise funds for the team. All five in the family purchased their own navy blue shirt featuring the white team emblem and words of championship.

"Can we all wear our cross country T-shirts, Gram?" is Laura's request.

I hear her question and struggle to keep a straight face. Normally such an idea would be unthinkable, but when it comes to the three grandchildren, I know they are so dear to the church family they could chose to stand before the camera in almost anything and not be censured.

I laugh aloud and reply, "Honey, what a great idea. I would never have thought of it. Of course we will all wear our cross country shirts."

And so we are, the five, in the church directory in our navy and white short sleeved 'T's', smiling from the directory page. Ed is left front with his grin, I'm to his right with my nice for-the-photographer-expression, Laura with a big happy smile is behind her Gramp, Rachael and Pat are behind me, each proudly showing off their shirt; conspirators in the adventure of posing for the church publication. The only mistake made is easily spotted in the final photo. I forgot to wear blue jeans like everyone else in the family. Instead I have on bright red slacks. Laura will always remind me of my glitch.

Mary was a prolific photographer. I fail terribly in carrying on for her. This really bothers me. The guilt trips I lay on myself have nothing to do with the cost of film. Rather it has everything to do with my inability to remember to take a camera with me. But Ed fills in. He loves his camera and the world of photography. As the result I have boxes of snap shots waiting for that day somewhere in the future when I'll take the time to sort and identify them. Then I'll fill albums with all the wonderful capsules of the life the five of us have shared so intensely for these years. I have my favorites. It isn't so much the picture itself as it is the memory that is stuck to it. There's even a double exposure I can't heave out as the memories behind it are precious.

Some have been used for Christmas cards. One is of the five of us sitting high on an exposed glaciated rock on a ledge above Lake Superior. In another we are leaning over the top slat of a wooden fence along a narrow river somewhere out in Arkansas. The name hasn't stayed with me, but the day has. There's one Laura took of Major peering out of the Christmas tree's decorated branches the first year he came to live with them. All that can be seen are the two intensely green eyes between the spruce needles and tinsel. They stare as only a kitten can into the camera.

The memories each brings to me today?

The sound of waves breaking on the rocky shore of the Great Lake behind and below us in a Canadian photo. The spray is not high enough to show but we were are all aware of it. The ground we've climbed up and over is too worn to be called a mountain. The ancient glaciers scoured it like a camp skillet is ground clean by sand. Its smoothness is that of an infant's bottom. Granites displays an infinite variety of specks, striations and blends of colors ranging through the entire palette of earth tones; reds, ochre, rose, sienna, grey, white and black. Even the green of copper and the blue of cobalt can be found on lucky days. All these can be found in miniature replica on the beach below where their color intensity is heightened each time the lake's water coats their surface.

On the top of the cliff and as far back as it extends to disappear into the forest, every crevice is a miniature world of nature. The kids moved from one to another fascinated on what they find growing and living within the minuscule environment. Lichen and mushrooms are pointed out; often in all but garish colors that seem to shout out, look at me.

I don't remember who it was that found the salamander under a small rock. Once detected and its domicile defined more were discovered. Rachael learned she could braid the sea grasses, which cling to life in crevices close enough to the spray of the waves to flourish. She made bracelets for everyone. Patrick came across pieces of driftwood and fashioned himself a King Arthur dagger, Laura memorized the flora and fauna for distant days when she will return to this place in her mind. Ed stretched out flat on the rock in the sun, arms beneath his head while letting the occasional wisp of cloud plotting its way across the deep blue sky lull him into sleep.

I'm not a napper; I might miss something. I'll sleep when I'm old and there is nothing else to do. At least I think this will be so. That day I was content to be there in the land of quiet and solitude; the place in which there's never a doubt of the existence of a God. I watched the children and added a word of knowledge or appreciation knowing there was no place on earth I'd prefer being. I felt Mary and Pat there with us.

I noted the intenseness of the grandchildren's play and sensed their contentment. It was a day of perfection.

Looking at the photograph I desire the place and time to be theirs forever. That in their lifetime and with their children, and yes, their grandchildren they'll travel back to share its wonder. I know when they do Ed and I, like their mother and father will join them, although I have no idea exactly how.

Patrick and Rachael nailing rafters—1998

Nail Aprons, a Letter and Graduation

It is second nature to be critical

Anne has a calmness in the way she goes about living her life. Not me. Not at all. My style is to slam doors, throwing dishes on the floor, jumping up and down and then screaming in frustration. To Anne this would be a huge waste of her time. This has always been her way. She's aware there will never be enough time to do all the things she intends to do. She has told me more than once her list grows rather than diminishes as the years go by. She recognizes that, because as a person, each day brings her head-on with something, someone or someplace she hasn't known before.

Even her beloved reading has fallen victim to the same process. Once Anne's list included only the writing of Mother Goose and Frank Baum. Now the list is so extensive it'd take an entire book just to compile Anne's favorites. This calmness of Anne's is backed by a deep belief of being non-aggressive in most things. She seems to have developed a second sense about when something is worth getting bent out of shape over and what is best to let go. The letter's arrival could have been one of the oh-its-not-worth-my-time deals. As soon as the letter was read Anne knew it was something she would take on if it took the rest of her years. She never shares her concern with me. True to her saying, Don't criticize unless you have a solution to offer, Anne takes her time to find a solution for the horror of the letter,

The month of May of Laura's final year of high school arrives too soon for Ed and me. For us the years have evaporated before our very eyes. With the eighth anniversary of Mary's death on the horizon both of us find it difficult to believe that Laura is the young woman practicing her high school Valedictorian speech down in her bedroom. There she's surrounded with what now appears ridiculously childish Teddy Bear wallpaper. It was hung soon after she and her sister moved into our house and Ron had built the addition which became their rooms. This was all only eight years ago. Now plans are underway for her prom dress and graduation open house.

Laura will sew the dress because she knows exactly what she wants. It is to be a deep sapphire blue satin. With her beautiful blue eyes it will be perfect. Besides, Laura is gleeful with the amount of money that will be saved; well over one hundred dollars. And she knows the dress will be one of a kind.

Ed and I had decided to build a family room off the solar room last summer. It was needed. Instead of grandparents living in their retirement home with three small children we had become a family of five adults. Laura had reached her height at five foot ten inches. Rachael was running a close second. Pat was stretching skyward on a daily basis. I told Ed that I thought he was on a two hour feeding schedule. I heard the refrigerator door closing on a regular basis every couple of hours.

At seventy-nine Ed took on the new room. Once he had the footers poured and the blocks laid the kids and I joined him. Nail aprons tied around our middles and hammers in hand we built the stud walls. Then Pat and Ed straddled the top headers to nail the ceiling joists and roof rafters in place. Hearing of the project, church friends, Bob and Chris arrived to help. Pat tried to talk Ed into building a railing around the almost flat roof's edge and an access ladder so he could set up a deck recliner and enjoy the view out over the lake and hills. Somehow Ed couldn't be convinced.

With the added room the house has the floor space needed for all the grandchildren's friends. I'm glad we did it. Because of it I was able to invite the players and support workers of *Anastasia* out for its cast party. Every year some parent of a cast member steps forward to put this gathering together following the high school play's final performance. Always a late night event I decided to make that year's an all-nighter. I promised to cook the kids breakfast before they left the morning after.

The coach and his wife brought a huge ice-cream cake, a tradition for them; I furnished pop and the cast and crew carried in whatever struck their fancies in the way of snacks and good eats. Whacky gifts were exchanged and speeches made. The only way one could be heard was to yell above the din of over fifty teenagers and their music. If the decibel level was a measure of the night's success I should have given myself a ten. A few kids had to leave around two a.m. Ed hit the sack about the same time. One mother, an across the fields neighbor stuck it out with me. As the party participants found places on the floors and furniture to expire she and I kept each other alert by sitting at the old round oak table in the dinning room and talking. The top of the table was covered with partially eaten food, even the sideboard had its share of remnants. Nothing had maintained its original appeal and eventually Jean and I began to consolidate and cover all the leftovers, hoping whoever brought the stuff would do me the favor of taking what was left back home with them. Of course, I couldn't keep my fingers out of the chips. Never have been able to.

About seven in the morning Jean and I started the bacon, eggs, toast and pancakes. Because the rooms on the main floor of the house were open to each other it didn't take long for the smell of breakfast to bring the sleepers back to life. By eight thirty everyone was gone, including Jean. The grandkids crawled into their beds and I found myself in our bed next to Ed. No one thought to set an alarm.

Since that night, life here at the Thurston house has been as normal as it can get. During the week the three grandkids are out the door, headed down the hill for the bus by seven-forty. The rest of the day, until it is time to pick someone up after school is left empty for Ed and me. Don' t misunderstand, neither of us go back to bed, sit and watch daytime TV or lounge around with a good book. There is always outside work for Ed and inside jobs for me. Until March brings its thaws it is the snow and drive that keep Ed busy. After that the lawn and trees have their own demands. Plus he does all my hauling and odd jobs. He always has. For me the days plug themselves with washings, grocery shopping, cooking, cleaning and a jillion other things which just seem to appear. There are five heads to get to the barber's, after-school events almost every day, on going sporting events and various meets on the weekends. We both have catch up jobs that we set aside for the six weeks we work on the play sets out at the high school. Everyday is an all day event, complete with our brown bag lunches. After drama season passes Ed misses the box of sweet rolls and doughnuts that was brought in for our coffee breaks. He doesn't get that kind of special attention here at home.

Add church and Sunday school to these and it is Monday again. Ed and I never miss our once a month reading group and there's always finishing work to do on the new addition. I wouldn't call our life humdrum; I doubt if it ever reaches that state, but we do find it comfortable. I feel as if I have stabilized the financial side of raising the grandchildren. It is tight, but I believe that with their Social Security and what we have left in our retirement fund that we'll make it until the three kids can graduate from college. I guess what I am trying to say is that I have that great feeling that everything is under control. Somehow I have found a safe plateau on which we can all establish a path into our futures. My bank statements are free of overdrafts and the budget, refined to the most exact degree is holding on true north after all the twists and turns I have put it through these last years. We all have health insurance, the car has insurance, the house is insured and even the taxes are current and the credit cards are no more. You'd think that of all people I would have enough sense not to be so certain of life. March and April come and go.

Here in the third week of April my thoughts are all wound up with Laura's impending graduation from high school. The new room will come in handy for Laura's graduation open house scheduled for the end of May. I am really looking forward to the day. Both girls and I love to work with food and we have a list of goodies we plan to prepare to serve. We are expecting about a hundred since there'll be families driving in for the day and of course, our friends and those of the children. With any kind of luck the lilacs will be out and hopefully there will be late tulips and daffodils if the rabbits haven't eaten the bulbs over the winter.

All the flurry of preparation for Laura's graduation causes the days to pass even more rapidly. She and I drive over to Charlevoix to have her Senior pictures taken. Laura wants an informal pose on the sandy shore of Lake Michigan near Round Lake's outlet. She is truly an outdoor person. Ed and I plan to give her a kayak for her eighteenth birthday this coming July. She is an excellent swimmer and both her running and baseball have her in great shape. She'll handle the boat with ease. Much as Ed and I love our canoe we both admit a kayak is easier for one person to transport and paddle.

Next there is the decision to make about graduation announcements and all the other related things that seem to be part of the end of high school. I don't remember any of this when I left Sylvania High School, but Ed, whose memory is far more reliable than mine, says he recalls doing all these things at Maumee and suspects I did too. Of course, I do remember my prom fiasco.

In the middle my atypical life which is so typical of what has always been the American family I find myself once again in the roll of a mother. Thirty-five years ago I had been looking forward to our oldest son's, David's high school graduation. So little has changed. Today, as back then, everything needing to be done is being cared for. I have a wonderful feeling of life being as it should be. It is mid afternoon, the house is reasonably uncluttered and clean. I have decided what to have for supper and have the ground beef browning for spaghetti sauce. Mine is made from scratch, using my home grown and canned tomatoes. Even the basil and oregano are from my garden. Heck, the onions and garlic are also.

Taking a break I walk out the door and down our long drive to get the mail. It is in the mid-fifties, but sunny. Bucky tags along, his bushy black tail constantly wagging. It reminds me of the metronome Mrs. Letterman, my music teacher back in the thirties, sat on the piano where it ticked off the beat of my recital piece, 'Juanita'. The mail box is packed full. Three magazines, a bunch of junk mail and three or four other letters. As I riffle through it all I spot a government envelope. From the Office of Social Security, it's addressed to Laura. Its appearance doesn't fit the usual time-for-a monthly-disbursement-check. I eye the envelope suspiciously, having developed a type of caution with government mail much as one does with a distrusted adversary. I am well aware the generic appearing envelope may contain any unforeseen request, notice or information. As I stand with it in my hand thinking about all these possibilities it suddenly grows in weight, begging me to lay it down and think about something else, something more important.

Fighting an intimidating chill I decide to ignore the letter. After all it is addressed to Laura, which is the Social Service Office's practice. I leave it on the front hall table for my granddaughter to open when she returns from her cross-country practice. She's an avid runner. Her team practices on the trails and slopes of a nearby ski area. Laid out for downhill skiing the runs are real challenges for the runners. Laura has improved immensely this spring.

Being a spectator at a cross country event reminds me of the time Ed and I watched the bobsled runs at the Olympics in Calgary in 1988. We saw next to nothing except a blur as the sleds zoomed by our place along side the ramp. We couldn't even make out the colors of the country that crossed our line of sight. It is much better to watch such an event on TV. Of course, being on the spot is more exhilarating because excitement permeates the very air. So it is with cross country races. Occasionally we will catch a glimpse of color up on the hillside where the trail breaks out of a copse of trees, but the only actual race Ed or I can see is the last one hundred yards when the runners dash out into the open and head for the finish line.

Some time later, busy in the kitchen with dinner preparation I don't hear Laura come in the house. With my mind on other things I have forgotten the envelope when she calls, "Gram, read this letter. It sounds like bad news."

Turning the stove burner to simmer I reach for the paper Laura holds out to me. One white sheet, it has the appearance of a form letter. Its message is short and clear. Without taking my eyes off of the paper I reach with my other hand for a kitchen stool and sit down. Looking up at Laura who stands watching me, I say, "I can't believe this, Laura. Why didn't anyone tell us? Don't they understand we have to plan ahead?"

Laura is mute.

In the heavy silence I think, I hate to show this to Ed. Wow, talk about a knife in the back. I feel like I'm bleeding to death.

Then to Laura I say, "Please go find your Gramps. I think he's in the garage. Tell him that I'd appreciate his coming in to see a letter that has arrived. Thanks, Hon."

As Ed comes in the kitchen door, a concerned look on his face he asks, "What's wrong, Snork?"

"Isn't Social Security supposed to extend until college graduation?" I ask him.

Puzzled by the unexpected question he answers, "That has been my belief. Why?"

My answer is to hand him the letter. After reading the short message Ed looks up to say in an incredulous voice, "Apparently the law has been changed somewhere in the past without our being made aware of it."

The letter's intent is to notify Laura that as she turns eighteen this coming July 24th Social Security will no longer continue issuing her a monthly benefit check. At that time our eighteen year old granddaughter will be without any income unless she is able to find work.

When Laura's eighteenth birthday arrives on July 24ᵗʰ, the day before her grandparents fifty-sixth wedding anniversary she will have less than two months before entering college. The only money she will have is that which Ed and Anne have set aside for the children's college educations. This money became theirs as beneficiaries of their mother's insurance on her death. For some unexplained reason such benefits do not pass through the probate court system.

At that time Ed had placed the funds in secure investments. Despite the additional money it has earned in interest the amount has shrunk in value each passing year because during the same time period the cost of education has sky-rocketed. It will take studious management of the funds and many loans by the grandchildren to stretch their money to cover a four year college degree. That it would now have to supplement their daily needs is unbelievable. Anne shrivels inside as she thinks of the struggle that waits for each of the three.

At this point in time neither of us can think beyond our beloved grandchildren. But the day will come when, as her load of parenting responsibilities diminishes, Anne will begin to talk to me about others who are hit in the same manner. At first the numbers she throws at me are unbelievable. But her anger and near panic tell me in no uncertain terms that she is speaking facts. Every parentless youth receiving Social Security benefits in the country receives the same letter as their eighteenth birthday approaches.

The more I study the contents of the letter I have to admit that even though Laura will be loaded with more scholarships and grants than any of her classmates, she'll be destined to head forth to college with not a cent in her pocket. At least this is what the powers to be who shape the rules of the Social Security program contend. My mind frantically wonders, "How about her everyday needs? What about Band-Aids, tooth paste and gosh, lipstick? What about those once a month necessities? Isn't she to even have a Coke or a piece of gum once in a while?"

Stunned I stop before adding clothing, transportation, medical and dental care; or a jillion other things taken for granted daily by Americans. Even if Laura works all summer here in Boyne where she can share the Areostar with the rest of us it will be for some minimum wage job. Her income could never stretch to include a place to live, food to eat, medial care, and a car and its insurance, even if it were an old jalopy.

Ed calls and the information is confirmed. Just a few years before during the Reagan presidency the Social Security Administration decided it could forget about all parentless and foster children once they turn eighteen. Though they are barely old enough to be considered eligible to vote, the belief prevailed that young people certainly should get out there and find some kind of work, which would support them and eventually a family.

Obviously Anne and Ed are shocked. We all have to wonder what governmental drones got together on their coffee breaks and came up with this grandiose proposition. Certainly, many adults, once they are comfortably set in homes with families raised and retirement goodies in the offing might forget their beginning years. Now with items such as boats, golf club memberships, travel homes and investment incomes these people have a tendency to deny their pasts. Those times in their early twenties when they ate baked beans five days out of seven and accepted money under the kitchen table from one sympathetic parent or another have been blanked out.

No, their vision impaired, it must have been just such a group that decided, "Let those eighteen year old parentless kids find their own way. We need the money to grant the wealthy a larger tax break, or to fight another war, take a deeper look in space or build a bigger airport in some Timbuktu place such as Wellston, Michigan. Let those interested pray that if the young genius destined to discover the cure for cancer will also be successful in finding a way to finance its research on his or her own." Admittedly these snide remarks lurk in my mind. Whether or not they are also Anne's thoughts is not for me to say.

The day Laura graduates high school; after we had all left the hot auditorium to stand on the grass in the school's front yard to enjoy the cooling breeze coming in off Lake Charlevoix she turns to Ed and me and says, "You know Gram and Gramp, while my friends were busy working at the Dairy Queen for low wages to pay for their college I studied and earned over $80,000 in scholarships and grants for mine."

Our pride for our granddaughter notches itself upward; her maturity amazing us. But being all too human I know we'll worry and constantly seek ways we can lighten her way in the years ahead.

Ed and Anne will scratch the bottom of their finances. Monthly Social Security checks will become the grandparent's sole income. Too old to be eligible for part-time work employment it will no longer remain a solution. There is no job market for those who are in their eighties. The equity in their home will become their only rainy day source of monetary help. It'll help them keep their home as one to which the kids could come back to for summer work or holidays. After all, Anne and Ed, unlike the government are committed to being both parents and grandparents as long as they live. They come to realize that money is not for possessing. Rather it is the means to help those who wrestle daily with life's basic needs to survive.

There are so many.

Rachael and Laura model the dresses they have made—1989

Mrs. Cassidy, Mrs. Thomson and $45,000

The Pledge of Allegiance brings tears

Anne is so patriotic she gets tears in her eyes when she says the pledge of Allegiance. She stood and cried when she read about the founders of our country at the famous mountain side carvings on Mt. Rushmore. Anne tells me she honors the office of President although she may find it impossible to honor the man. She's certain our beliefs are worth preserving and that it is the duty of each of us to do so. All this said, Anne does find it difficult at times to excuse the lack of foresight her government all too often displays. And for me, this ranking of Republicans versus Democrats belongs in the same silly game of Ohio State versus Michigan, each an avenue of escape from the real issues at hand; a smoke screen to hide behind.

The girls and I are seated at the dining table. It is the same round oak table of Ed's childhood that was moved in on that snowy pre-Christmas afternoon so long ago. How time has flown. Here the three of us sit, both girls well into their college years. In fact, Rachael will begin her sophomore year in a couple of weeks. The strange, absolutely unexplainable thing about all this is that I am still me. I can't find any change in me. It must be that once one reaches a certain place in life that we just put on the hand brake and sit there. The problem with this thesis is that I can't put my finger on a date that this happened. This is not the first time I have felt that I am in a time warp. The thought is not a stranger to my mind. I have considered it at various points along the passage of the weeks and months. So far I have not come even close to an answer. I suppose I should just give it up, but I can't.

Why do I recognize all the growth and maturing in the girls and Pat while I am parked somewhere in time. Ed fits into all this. Like me, somewhere along the way he has set his hand brake. I laugh somewhere inside myself as I play around with the idea that he has been bald and older than I am all along, our whole life together. He must have set his brake a bit later than I did. Oh, I have a few gray hairs showing up, but not enough to change my dark brown mop noticeably. I'm not a candidate for wrinkle cream and my chin still hangs where it should.

Admittedly my body is beginning to cave in; in the area of the knees, and I'm due for cataract surgery and would love to peel off thirty pounds. But none of these surface problems have a thing to do with where I am in my age. Mentally I must have quit aging somewhere back around my forties.

It is mid morning. The day is one in late August that promises an afternoon thunder storm. It's hot and muggy. Pat is off at soccer practice and Ed's outside staining the deck. The conversation around the table is serious. This is a gathering Rachael has called. She has arrived with two papers in her hand and a pen in the other.

I become concerned as I notice Rachael's expression. There's no smile or twinkle in her eyes.

"Grandma, I can't afford to go back to Alma for my second year. It's too expensive. I can attend Michigan State University for half as much. I wouldn't have as many student loans to repay after I graduate and get a job."

She spreads two sheets of paper in front of me on the table. I see neat columns of figures. One list is headed Alma and the other MSU

"Are you telling me you would rather go to MSU?

"No, I really like Alma. But it's the money. All I have is what Dad and Mother left me and it just won't last if I go to Alma."

Rachael is seated across from me, the carefully prepared tables of expenses for the two learning institutions is spread out between us. She has come to the conversation ready to change my thinking.

Laura speaks up, "Rachael, at least go one more year. The smaller college makes it easier to get through the year. You get a lot of personal help you won't see on a big campus. Look how well I've done."

Rachael's mind is set. I can see it. There's probably nothing anyone else can say to get Rachael to choose Alma, even if for just one more year. Laura's pleas too, have fallen on deaf ears. I dread the idea of Rachael changing to a large, impersonal campus. All she knows of life is what she's rubbed elbows with in Boyne City. A small town of about 3,000 people plus those who live on its perimeters and its summer people is all she's familiar with. Oh, there have been brief visits to the malls of greater Detroit. And the jam packed days of travel in the United States with our family. But none of this is like actually living on a large campus such as Michigan State's.

The phone rings, slashing through my thoughts. There are times I feel as if I could gladly throw the darn thing out a window. It has a way of ringing at the most inappropriate times; when I least want to be interrupted.

I push back my chair and go into the next room to answer its summon.

"Mrs. Thurston?"

"Yes."

"This is Gregg Saltsman, manager of the Petoskey Social Security office. Are you the guardian of Patrick and Mary Anne Cassidy's three children?"

"Yes, my husband and I are. How can I help you?"

"Did your daughter remarry after the death of her husband, Patrick? And if so did her name become Mary Anne Thomson?"

"That's correct, Mr. Saltsman."

"I find myself in a most embarrassing situation, Mrs. Thurston. It seems the Social Security Insurance program failed to recognize Mary Anne Thomson as Mary Anne Cassidy and therefore didn't share her Social Security Insurance benefits with her children. It would be helpful if I could schedule an appointment with Laura and Rachael in the near future. The amounts due them should be discussed. I will also need to meet with you about those due Patrick."

I can't believe I say my next words. But somewhere in my mind I apparently do some very complicated math in a matter of less than ten seconds.

"Are we discussing a large sum of money, Mr. Saltsman?"

"Yes, Mrs. Thurston. And it is my concern it be dispensed to the beneficiaries as soon as possible."

Anne deserves a lot of credit here. She immediately sees a possible reprieve on Rachael's request to move her education onto a large campus. Perhaps there will be enough available in Mr. Saltsman's office to do the trick. She doesn't want to wait a minute longer than necessary to find out all she can about the error. She needs to know on the spot whether there will be the money needed to help her granddaughter. She is certain it will take weeks and maybe months to recover any forgotten money. She has no confidence in her government's ability to move fast when it is moving for someone or something other than its own interests.

"The two girls are due to return to college within the next ten days. They will be over one hundred miles away. Is it possible that we might come up to meet with you today, let's say after lunch?" I ask.

My answer is exactly what Mr. Saltsman wants to hear.

"I am at your disposal, Mrs. Thurston. Would one-thirty be good for you?"

"That sounds perfect. The four of us will be in your office at that time."

"Don't take a number, just tell the receptionist your name and she will bring you back to my office."

I think, Wow, this guy is really in a panic. We're getting preferential treatment. This is certainly a departure from the normal procedure. He's rolling out the red carpet.

After a quick lunch, my standard quickie of tuna salad sandwiches, milk and apples the four of us are on our way. Ed elects to stick to his painting job. We are so excited we find nothing of any consequence to talk about as I head for Petoskey and the Social Security offices. Our minds are ahead of us, already inside the doors of the building.

I find Mr. Saltsman a man in his fifties, the typical administrator. He's a few pounds over weight with glasses, graying hair and a business like manner. His excitement in his position has long before given over to the satisfaction of doing his job well. I'm certain he knows all the rules of the Social Security System, is a fair but firm boss and runs the Petoskey branch office in an exemplary manner. These observations help explain the shock he is ill equipped to handle in learning of the error. It has been discovered in the Chicago regional office. Until today, Mr. Saltsman has believed the system infallible. A small error here or there along the way could be expected and accepted. But this one doesn't fit in that category.

The amount of money which should have been paid to the children since their mother's death twelve years before proves to be $45,000. Rachael's share will allow her to attend Alma College until she transfers to the Michigan State's College of Architectural Interior Design a year from now.

As a result of my nudging Anne she asks if interest is being paid on the amount due. She is assured that Social Security doesn't recognize the accrual of interest on underpayments, just on amounts owed it by a subscriber. This doesn't surprise me, but why not ask? Just watching the expression on Mr. Saltsman's face when he gave Anne his answer was worth asking. He carried it off very well. His face showed no change. In thinking it over the answer truly reflected Mr. Saltsman's beliefs, he had completely fallen for the whole procedure. He saw no disparity in the government's rule.

I more clearly understand why, no matter how hard I've tried to raise the children on their Social Security, it hasn't been able to stretch far enough. Ed and I have been shorted from the beginning. Suddenly, I feel better about the money I've used from Ed's and my retirement investments. No wonder they are as low as they have become. But I don't plan to reimburse the account. The children will need the money more for their education. Their entire future lies ahead of them. I feel Ed's and my lives have been without comparison. So wonderful that neither of us would change any of it. We're doing OK. The miraculous windfall has arrived at a most appropriate time.

Ed and I find the whole debacle less a terrible mistake than a miracle, which arrives as a gift at exactly the right moment. We look at each other and then up toward the heavens and think, Thanks.

As for Mr. Saltsman I suspect he is able to let go of his shock of having to disclose such a lack of vigilance by his employer. He appears absorbed in the delight of the three wonderful young people and their grandmother. Standing in his office doorway as we leave, Mr. Saltsman experiences a feeling of joy his position has never put in his path before. This must be a shining moment for a man who does not have too many in his work life.

I see it on his face as he says to himself, Well, that certainly worked itself out far better than I could have ever thought. I was certain I was in for a terrible time, but there was no blame, just thankfulness. It is great to know none of those kids is going to rush out and buy a new car with their windfall—somehow I have the feeling they'll use it wisely. As for the grandmother, I have never seen a happier woman.

Honors, a Job and a Blue Jay

Being a woman requires special skills

Anne's mother grew up the youngest in a family of six. Helen was a complete surprise to her mother and father, arriving when Grandmother Eisele was half way through her forties. She was adored not only by her parents but by three older sisters and two older brothers. Of all the children she was the only one who received a college degree. She was fortunate enough to be still at home when her father bought one of Columbus's first automobiles. To top this off Frederic Christian, her father permitted her to drive it back and forth to the Ohio State Campus. Helen's twenties embraced the Charleston, prohibition, bound busts, dropped waistlines, WWI and the bobbing of women's long tresses. All this left an indelible mark on Anne as she learned that being a woman requires special skills. She believes there is absolutely nothing inferior about being female and at the same time she accepts the fact that men and women are born to be different. She thinks that difference is the spark that ignites the joy of being a woman. It isn't something that can be legislated.

I love standing at my kitchen sink and looking out into our copse of aspen trees. This place is a haven for the red headed wood pecker, the raucous blue jay and the tiny chickadee who with numerous cousins carry on endless conversations with themselves. When I step out on the back deck and 'dee, dee, de' back to them they will answer although there has never be a formal introduction.

Today I see them flitting in and out of the upper branches. There are five. They are hardly larger than the aspen leaves dancing about in the summer breeze.

The trees were mere youngsters when Ed bought the old cherry orchard back in the sixties. Today they stretch skyward, their slim trunks reaching seventy feet above the bracken covered hillside. There is a definite lean toward the south east, a result of their lifetime of being pushed by our prevailing winds from the northwest.

Three of the older trees have broken off during storms when the wind worked itself into a frenzy of over fifty miles an hour. But even they serve a purpose; their dead lengths are riddled with woodpecker holes. It was just last summer I heard, and then spotted the Disney-like Palliated Woodpecker clinging to the side of one of the fallen trees which had been caught half way on its descent to the ground by a neighboring upright aspen. There it hung, suspended in mid fall with the huge bird busily gathering a noon meal of some delicious insect.

The house is quiet as I stand here by the sink, cleaning up the breakfast things. Ed is content in his chair around the corner from me in the living room. As it is mid-summer both Pat and Rachael are down town at their summer-break jobs. Pat is making fudge at Kilwins and scooping ice cream for cones. Across Water Street, Boyne City's main drag, Rachael is selling beads and tea at Bali and Beyond.

Laura, our Alma graduate, is down state in Ann Arbor on her first job since she left the campus. Ultimately she wants to go on towards a masters in language but at this point lacks the self-confidence to think she will be admitted into a master program at any university despite her prestigious highest honors in a foreign language from such a well known college as Alma. Nothing I can do nor say helps her think otherwise. Somewhere she has read that the best way to access a masters program is with some work experience on your resume.

With the promise of a room in the apartment of the daughter of her former youth leader at church, Laura left after a few days at home earlier this summer to live in Ann Arbor and search for work. Ed and I are helping her out in this transition from student to employee by selling her our '89 Taurus. The old Aerostar, which we bought soon after the children moved in is still faithfully getting the rest of us to and from wherever we might have to go. It has well over 100,000 miles on it. I am certain both Ed and Pat could name exact figures. Laura will make a small monthly payment for the car and take care of its maintenance while we carry the insurance until she reaches the point where her income will permit her to pay it. Ed and I know how little she has available in her diminished savings.

The job search went painfully slow and Laura ended up with a placement firm which connected her with a small computer company about five miles from her rented room. A third of her monthly earnings go out as a finder's fee. She was employed as the company's bookkeeper only but discovers that she is also the receptionist and Girl Friday.

"I don't mind it, Gram. Actually I enjoy it all. The math part is really easy for me, even though I have never had any business courses. It doesn't get anymore complex than simple addition, subtraction, division and multiplication. And I do everything on the computer. Mainly I work with time sheets and job tickets. The computer automatically keeps the stock inventory up to date. If I see something getting low I place a re-order. In the end I issue pay checks, prepare and mail out a statements. In turn I process the incoming payments, record them and complete the deposits."

When I asked about her co-workers she said, "Besides Mr. Flatt, my boss, there are about twenty guys about my age who are in and out during the day. They sell and service computers. There is one girl who does the same. Sometimes in the middle of the day only my boss and I are in the building. There are even times when he goes out, though not very often. They all carry cell phones so they stay in touch with the office."

A few weeks into the job she calls to report, "My boss has me brewing the coffee for those in the office, keeping the front entry mopped dry during rainy days and running out for lunch pickups. I guess I am a real Girl Friday."

All this bothers me far more than it does Laura. I do a slow steam, but keep my opinion to myself. I have been this route. I hadn't been on the job a week as cartographer at the rural electric cooperative back in my forties when my boss suggested that I become the coffee maker. Older and wiser than Laura I had purposefully made such lousy coffee that no one could drink it. The job went to someone else.

What bothered my granddaughter was the level of her entry pay and the one third the placement bureau was keeping. Her contract with them is for one year. The light at the end of the tunnel is that at the three month point she will have a promised review with her boss and a raise that will make life somewhat easier. In the meantime she is stretching her meager work wardrobe over a five day work week, packing her lunches and relegating her gas money for to work and back home driving only.

Her landlady, the youth leader's daughter proved to be some ten years older than Laura, set in her life as a single and very rigid. Laura who had been experiencing a rather loose and spontaneous life with her brother and sister and grandparents finds it easiest to retreat to her room; just stay out of her landlady's way. This certainly can't be the life she had looked forward to after graduation.

I've lost track of time. Something I seem to do a lot of these days. What is it about summer that blows all my normal routines out of the window. When I think about it nothing has been a normal around here for twelve years. All the time those beautiful aspen out on our hillside have been adding inches to their height Ed and I have been adding years to our ages. As I stand here today on July 16th, 2003 I have to acknowledge I am now eighty years old. Of course this is according to the method man has generated to measure time as it relates to human beings. It has nothing to do with the time clock each of us maintains somewhere within our beings and which we alone hold the key to wind each day. I know in my heart that I am no more eighty years old than my husband is eighty two going on eighty three.

My mind flips back to Laura. Seems to me that her three month trial period should be ending about now. I wonder if she has heard from her boss about more money in her pay check.

As if by some long distance act of mind reading my phone rings. I answer to hear Laura's voice. Between sobs I catch fractions of sentences but not a clue as to what she is so upset about.

"Laura, Laura, Honey. Take a breath. Slow down. You aren't making any sense to me. What's the trouble? Are you OK?"

I immediately realize I have asked a dumb question. Obviously something has to be wrong or why would my granddaughter be in such a state. And why a phone call in the middle of the morning?

There's a long pause and then I hear Laura. In a voice held under tight control she says, "Gram, I didn't get my raise. When I went in to ask Mr. Flatt about it his answer had nothing to do with how well I was doing the work here."

This doesn't make sense to me. I ask, "I don't understand, Laura. What is the problem."

I could hear the tears trying to come back into the conversation as Laura answers, "He just looked at me, Gram, with this funny grin on his face and told me that I am too unfriendly and if I wanted to get my raise I was going to have to pay more attention to him and be a whole lot more friendly."

Gram, I couldn't believe what he was saying. It made me so mad. I just turned around and walked out of his office, cleaned up my work area, packed up what stuff is mine and left the place. I'm back at the apartment and I don't know what to do. I have to have that job. I need to work. What am I going to do?"

I am on the spot furious. It's a good thing I'm over a hundred and fifty miles away from Ann Arbor and Mr. Flatt. Almost any woman who has had to be out in the work field knows this gut wrenching feeling of debasement. Although there are those who have fought and will continue to struggle for women's rights, and laws have been passed and offenders occasionally brought to their knees most of us understand we will never be treated by some males with respect. And being who we are we will continue to use our natural wiles to bypass their traps, leaving them completely unaware of how it all transpired. Some things simply can't be legislated.

I have learned which battles to engage in and which to step around. I know this one that Laura is involved in is not worth putting on armor for. The job is not one that will enrich Laura's life or further her career. Mr. Flatt and his petty world are not of any value to the overall plan of things.

The blue jay lets out one of his demanding calls as I try to bring my world into focus. That loud call helps me. Mr. Flatt is nothing but a pompous egomaniac like the jay. He has been intrigued by a young woman way out of his league. Her mental capabilities and young beauty have no place in his world. There is no way such a man could understand his inferiority. Let him look for another victim. In the meantime he can take part of his noon hour to go out and pick up his own lunch, answer the phone and work the adding machine.

I turn my attention back to my granddaughter. "Laura?"

"Yes, Gram?"

"I couldn't have done what you have just done any better. Everything you did is perfect. You did not argue with Mr. Flatt. This is excellent as he would never understand what you would say. It is beyond his abilities. Secondly, you did not show your anger to him. If you had it would have made him feel good. It would have caused him to believe what he asked of you was Ok; something a lot of men take for granted as their dues in their position of authority."

"Third, you left quietly. You left your work in order and made certain by taking everything that is yours with you that you would not have to return. I am so proud of you."

"But, Gram, I am sitting here with no job and an apartment I can't afford to pay for. If I leave and go back home I will be a quitter; a looser. I can't do that."

"No, Laura. You are wrong. There is nothing about being a quitter or a looser in what you just did. Anything but. It took enormous guts to walk out of that office. One of the hardest things to do in this world is to admit you have made a mistake and decide to start over. Often times the mistakes we make have little to do with us and everything to do with the outside world. You had no way of pre-determining what kind of employer Mr. Flatt would be. I assure you this is not the first time he has pulled this on a young woman. And probably won't be the last. Just be glad you got out when you did."

"But what about my room here. I just paid my rent a week ago. I'll loose three weeks of it if I leave."

"That, unfortunately is the way things workout sometimes, Hon. I suspect that your landlady will send you your overpayment, especially if she re-rents the room right away. Come on home. Take the rest of the summer to get things lined up better. You are always welcome here, Honey. But I am going to make three conditions on your spending the summer with us. First I want you to promise me to complete the thesis you haven't finished for Alma. Secondly that you write a really good resume and third, that you apply and obtain an invitation to work toward your masters at some university or college for next fall. Think you can get this all done?"

"Yes. And thank you, Gram. I will be leaving here in under an hour. Love you."

"And I love you. I can hardly wait to get my arms around you. How are the tears?"

"Gone."

"And that Irish anger of yours"

"Gone, Gram. I'm find. See you soon."

I continue to stand looking out the kitchen window, however my eyes are not attentive. My mind is racing. I'm still angry about the treatment Laura's boss handed out. Why is it that once you have children and then grandchildren and great grandchildren that it is harder to watch them be mistreated than it was to have gone through the same problems yourself? I would love to be able to walk into Mr. Flatt's office and tell him exactly where he fits on this planet. I believe I could treat the lecherous man to a memorable few minutes. This thought taken care of I smile and revert to my normal way of thinking in which I accept that the man is probably too heavy, balding and overburdened with a business which is developing and hard to keep on track. My next thought is one of sadness because so often our world manages to work itself into situations which could be avoided. All Mr.Flatt needed to do was to keep his word and treat Laura as he would want to be treated.

I think; bet he knows the Golden Rule, but has yet to understand it is meant to apply to him and those he knows, not just everyone else in the world.

Diagnosis, a Sale and Electrical Tape

*Finances can bring to marriage thoughts of
murder and divorce*

*Anne has read stories of women being widowed and left with no understanding
of the world of money because their husbands had always taken care of such matters.
This is hard for her to understand as she and Ed have always shared the whole gamut
of the financial side of marriage. They have both been its earners and spenders. In
fact she remembers all too well the times when the discussion of money matters became
much too heated. It was the only time when thoughts of murder or divorce hung been
the two. Fortunately the other facets of her marriage to Ed were too precious for her
to ever consider giving up married life. Somewhere in the very beginning Helen, her
mother, had told her daughter, "Don't ever end the day angry with each other. That
is what the double bed is for." Helen claimed the advice was not original but came
from the writings of Benjamin Franklin. From all reports it's likely he did what he
preached. The Bible mentions this advice, also.*

During a routine check up in 2001, the fall of Rachael's last year in high school
Ed is diagnosed as being in the early stage of Alzheimer's. Ed and Anne roll with
the punch. With Ed in his eighties and Anne just around the corner they both
are aware their clocks are running down. They both are relieved the diagnosis is
not one of cancer. For Anne to watch another one of her family, especially her
beloved Ed die of the slow and painful disease would be almost more than she
could handle. It has always been her wish that she'd outlive Ed. Statistics indicate
the scale is loaded in her favor. Anne accepts the fact that of the two she is the

caretaker in the everyday plan of things. Without her she believes Ed would live on peanut butter sandwiches and ice cream.

For their children, Dave and Nancy, the news is not entirely unexpected as they both had become aware their father was having memory problems. The thing Anne finds is that both she and Ed suddenly realize they are indeed aging. The passing days and years had not made it very clear until now. They have been much too busy.

Anne considers attending Alzheimer's counseling sessions and support groups. She decides not to. The last thing she needs is to spend time listening to others discuss their problems in coping. Somehow Anne understands she and Ed have earned their masters degree in the subject.

With Ed she talks about things they might do to help slow the progress of the disease. Together they come up with ideas and begin a regimen of playing cards ever day after breakfast and lunch, or working on crossword puzzles or SuKoDu together. They play Mexican Train, a domino game and Scrabble. Neither has taken the time to learn chess. Cribbage has been relegated to their backpacking days.

Anne subscribes to magazines that are Ed's favorites and brings home books which he can read in bits and pieces. They have no plots or plans that must be followed. Anne accepts the fact Ed's 'now memory' is an off and on thing. Fortunately Ed is a history buff and never has been able to consume enough information. Unfortunately his eye problem, the same one he struggled with on Isle Royal, gets in the way of his reading. Fifteen minutes at a time becomes his top ability. Books on tape are tried but fail to hold his attention. The reader's voice lulls him to sleep.

To Anne, Ed's problem is manifested in his inability to create new memories. The more he exercises his great mind the longer he will stretch its competency. She conversationally reviews the happenings of the previous day's activities to help her husband fix its transient facts in his mind. Anne, unbelieving, watches Ed's abilities at card games slowly improve. Cards have never been of much interest to him, taking a low priority in the realm of things to do. She finds it almost impossible to win at Scrabble. Dominos tend to be more her success than his. As time goes by it will seem more and more to Anne that her husband has been misdiagnosed. Anne believes he is simply developing an old age loss of memory. Probably, a close cousin to Alzheimer's.

At the time of the diagnosis Anne turns to me. There is a limit to how much 'talking over' Ed can effectually do with Anne in making long range plans. His here-today-gone-tomorrow memory doesn't help at all. It natural for me to always be hanging around and know her well. We've been through so much together down through the years. Hopefully my help has made a difference.

Hounded by money matters she considers her options for the future; the immediate and the distant. It circles itself around Ed and the grandchildren. It always comes back to how their remaining money can be stretched to last. In a year and a half, the last Social security check will arrive when Pat turns eighteen on May 1, 2003. Anne can't help but feel the anger bubbling up inside of herself. She knows once Ed and she are gone their three grandchildren must live their entire lives without the support of a close family and its love. She can't believe the government feels the wealthy need a tax break more than parentless youth need assistance through their college years. Those that had formulated the insurance program hadn't anticipated the greed of politics.

Once again she shelves her anger and turns to the matter at hand. How is she to manage their money in a better manner? If it had been me the answer probably wouldn't have been the solution she finds. She looks at their only major asset, the house and the property it sits on. It is Ed's love, the farm. To even think of putting the house on the market hits her as being as radical as major surgery. Anne sees no alternative. But she knows she must do it in a way to keep Ed's farm and the grandchildren's place that has become their home.

She formulates her plan. It will fulfill all the restrictions she has placed on her idea to sell the house. Their house sits on the seventeen acre remnant of the farm's original 130. Down in the southwest corner of their acreage four are missing. They were sold with the original farm house. A gentle slope covered with the old apple orchard crosses the property between the original farm house and their present home. Anne decides to keep the front half of their property and build another house there.

Gathering together information I visit the bank and the realtor, another Irishman named Pat. Then I walk through the old apple orchard and down the hill to the place where the terraced fields are the only visual reminder of the glorious cherry orchard that had once grown there. It was the orchard which had triggered Ed's purchase of the land. At the bottom of the hillside just beyond a copse of aspen I find a fallen tree. I sit on it's dry trunk in the chill of the late fall day and remember.

Years long gone flood back over me and I watch vignettes from the past. Mary and Nancy's horses, Babe and Punch stand by the far fence line. The pinging of hammers float down over the ridge of land from the barn where Dave and Tom work on their cars. Ed drives up the road in the International Blazer, spattering gravel into its ditches. A light goes on in the kitchen bay of the farm house. I see myself in the open doorway, waiting for Ed's hug and kiss.

I'm certain that as long as we stay on the farm it won't seem as if we are moving away when the house on the hill behind me, sells. I smile with the thought that Ed and I once built it as our retirement home. We sold the wonderful farm house with its five bedrooms and left it behind. Little could we in our wildest imagining have thought we would need more than one bedroom ever again. And now I'm about to go through the same process once more. I'll sell the expanded retirement home and build a smaller one down the hill beyond the apple orchard. I'll almost return to where Ed and I started.

"This is crazy," I say to myself. "But then our whole life is border-line lunacy."

My mind, back in the present begins to visualize the new home. Turning to climb through the trees back up to the big house the ideas start and I know I must get them onto paper. I'm aware the need for new house plans is some ways down the road; first our house has to be placed on the market and sold. But I'm confident it will all happen.

After working my plan out I ask Ed to walk with me down through the orchard to the fields below. The day is sunny and crisp. The trees have blossomed, burst into full leaf and born their fruit, most of which now lies on the ground. We see tracks of deer who have already begun their fall harvesting. For them this is a time of plenty. A time to fatten for the winter months ahead when they retreat to the swamps to eat the cedar has high as they can reach. Ed often calls my attention to the precise line left on the cedars along the road. It is as straight as any hedge man could trim.

The birds have returned to winter homes in the south. Their nests remain tucked into the branches of the fruit trees. Many will be reused next year. It is quiet with the birds absent. Ed and I carefully skirt a couple of dead limbs that have broken off during fall's wind storms.

I turn to Ed and say, "Nature goes about pruning the old fruit trees even when man gives it up."

"Its sad I never had the time to care for these trees. Some of them have wonderful fruit even yet. There is an old fashioned snow apple over there by the top of the hill." Ed points off to the southwest and I nod my head, I've seen them. Rosy red on the outside, yet their middles are snow white and so sweet.

When the two of us break out of the orchard and work our way through a small copse of aspen, I stop and turn to Ed.

"The big house is going to be too large for us once Pat follows his sisters off to college. And even more importantly, it is becoming too expensive for us to maintain. What would you think if we offered it for sale and built a smaller home here by the aspen?"

Never thrown off base by my ideas Ed looks out across the pasture and up the hill to the old farm house and barn. He smiles and turns to gaze on me. He doesn't hesitate. "If you think it would be best then it's OK with me. Have you any idea what you'd like to build?"

"I've been keeping my eyes open. In this months *Home and Hearth* I found an idea. When we get back up to the house I will show it to you. Its lower level could fit into the hillside where we are standing. That area could be for the kids. With a separate heating zone we could cut it off when they aren't home. I think they would enjoy having a part of the house to call their own, like they have had before."

Ed grins and says, "This time we won't need to install a two-way listening device. Better yet, why don't you do some drawings and let me go over them with you. Who are you thinking of doing the building?"

"There's a custom pre-fab builder near Merritt, Michigan about fifteen miles from Nancy and Paul that I think we should talk to. They actually pre-build the walls and roof in their large shops. I think we probably will do the interior. It would be financially feasible that way."

When the grandchildren are told they have little to say. Ed and I think it is because a move of seven hundred feet to the south is of small consequences compared to what has already transpired in their lives. Remaining on the farm softens the blow for all of us. Together we respond to the realtor's suggestions on readying the home we are in now for the market. He explains that the money we spend to do so will be recouped in amount the house will sell for. Within six months he nods his head in approval of our work and hammers the 'For Sale' sign into the ground down by the road.

I begin the process of cutting through the red tape necessary to building in 2002. Things have become far more complicated than ten years before. Now there is zoning and hearings have to be held. Ed had been the township zoning administrator a few years so neither he nor I anticipate any problems. We should have known better. The small town grapevine kicks in. Next door neighbors, down the hill neighbors and across the field neighbors get on their telephones and convince each other Ed and Anne are going to haul in a house trailer to call their new home. Not one bothers to call and ask what is planned. They join forces to prevent the land split we request.

After a series of hearings and appeals in the township hall to the tune of over $700 in fees, we finally receive the permission needed to divide our property. The lower seven acres will be the site of the new home. Fortunately our friend, Doug is the township supervisor. In the 80's Doug had been the fine printer who had helped me launch my P's and Q's quilting business. Every Sunday he stands shoulder to shoulder with Ed in the church choir. He alone on the township board knows us as the people we are. I win our struggle by reminding those who sit in opposition that our grandchildren have not only lost their parents but their first home. There is absolutely no way Ed and I will stand by and allow the township board to deny our grandchildren the right to stay on the property they now call home. With Doug's leadership the board is shown how to say yes to Ed and me.

The sale of our home allows me to successfully pay off the mortgage on the hill-top house as well as all the credit card debt accrued over the recent years. Their use had become necessary after the children's Social Security bowed out of the picture. I find myself debt free. There is enough money in the bank for Ed and me to complete the new house. I am euphoric. Once again I am starting over. This time it will be the interior of our new home. Unfortunately we must move into it before it's ready, but we've done that before.

The house, my design is built by the company in Merritt. On site assemblage is delayed until late June because of the late ground thaw and mud. By August 2002 it sits as if it has always been on the land. The catch is that only the exterior is completed. Inside the house is a world of see-through 2X4 studding interrupted only by the sub-flooring and the roof above. The stair well connecting the three floors resembles an open elevator shaft. Ladders are used until steps can be built. In my mind I sees the interior the way it will eventually look, completed with wallpaper, curtains and furniture, not as others see it. I can even smell the cookies baking in the oven.

Craig, the husband of Mary's close friend, Corinne arrives to do the heating and plumbing. Ed plans to do the wiring and painting. They are two of his favorite things. He discovers his eyesight will not permit him to paint and his memory problems make it unwise for him to tackle the wiring. Then the family steps in to help. I arm myself with Home Depot's *How to Wire a Home* and plunge into the world of wire, snips, boxes, switches, strippers, plugs, electrical tape, reciprocals and needle-nosed pliers. During the next few months Rachael, Laura, Pat, Rut, Doc, Dave, Paul, Jeff and Nancy arrive at various times to complete the house's interior. Ed, once again is the officer in charge. Eventually there are enough light and appliances that operate to enjoy an almost normal life.

There is a funny side to this handyman story. I have thought of leaving it out as it has made me the brunt of too many jokes. But I might as well share the goofy thing I did. I've tried basically to ignore all the barbed remarks and laughter about my wiring, but I have to admit here that through my ignorance, the house is wired with outdoor grade wire. A more heavily insulated wire than the common interior type it made the entire job more difficult. I had to feed the wires into electrical boxes and secure them to their proper terminals. This was all but impossible because there wasn't room needed to manipulate everything. At the very end, six years after we moved in I call in an electrician to tidy up after me. He laughs his way through the work, assuring me he had never been involved in such a job.

Room by room the drywall is nailed in place. Then it is taped, sanded, undercoated and wallpapered. The trim is cut, nailed, puttied and painted. I consider the venture done when I hang my pictures and move our collection of books onto the shelves on the stair landings. The grandchildren move into their lower-level domain.

Their rooms have walk-out doors, reflecting their independent adulthood. I hand them their own toilet brush and clothes hampers. In the end it is eighteen year old Pat who says it all. After taking part in all phases of the construction of the new house he announces, "When I get to the point where I need a place of my own I will have someone else build it."

Ed walks Laura down the aisle—2004

Eighteen, Flex-line and Survival

Life always has another lesson to be learned

Life always has another lesson to be learned. Although Ed and Anne have every reason to believe the experience of raising their three grandchildren will climax their lives they are forgetting what both should have learned by now; that life is not of their planning. What may or may not transpire within their life times may be a far reach from what they think. It isn't another death that will redirect their lives but an editorial Anne reads in the April 2006 issue of the Petoskey News Review. It's apparent she's ready for the course of action it ignites.

As each grandchild packs and leaves for college neither Ed nor I are aware of a tug of loneliness or separation. Alma College is close enough for occasional visits to attend a concert or cheer at a football or Lacrosse game. There is the fun of 'moving in' day and meeting roommates. The parking lots hugging the dormitories of the small campus are plugged with cars. They are being rotated as they double park to discharge their occupants and contents. New students and parents of all ages stretch themselves as they climb out of cars which seem on the verge of explosion with boxes, trunks, hanger suspended clothing, bags of food and shoes. Upper classmen appear with their offers of assistance in locating assigned rooms hidden down labyrinths of hallways. Then they help muscle TV's, overstuffed recliners, refrigerators, fans and amplifiers up and down stairs to their new headquarters.

Alma's football team is well represented among the muscular young men who do most of the heavy work. Ed suspects that there's an ulterior motive to check

236

out the incoming freshmen girls. Between treks in and out of Clarkston hall I barely have time to look around the shaded grounds with their carefully tended flower gardens. Although the campus is not the same one Ed and I attended, we recognize the same excitement and expectation hanging in the air. After lunch in the cafeteria and a well planned afternoon program in the packed auditorium it's time for goodbyes as we head home in a strangely empty car. We repeat this feat when each of the grandchildren at eighteen move up onto the next rung of life's ladder.

It is Laura, the first to leave, who has the most difficult time saying goodbye to us. She knows that I understand how hard it is for her to embrace all the unknown places and people around her. In the emptied car Laura and I push back her departure with talk. The conversation goes on and on. Occasionally Laura tries to climb out of the van to head to the dorm. The tears well up in her eyes and she gives the try up, crawling back into the car. There is more talk as the two of us try to find the words which will allow Laura to leave. I know she'is determined to do so. It is just a matter of the timing. Thank Heaven for Ed's patience and empathy.

Two hours pass and the parking lot has slowly emptied. Ed breaks the gridlock by suggesting we go get something to eat. The lights along the campus walks and over the entries to the dormitories have come on. Most of the windows are lit and movement can be seen in the rooms. By this time there is no longer any one entering or leaving the cafeteria. It has closed. Laura and I latch on to the idea of eating and we head for the campus pizza hangout Laura had learned of during her summer orientation visit. Once we order Ed is the only one who really has an appetite.

But the time in the restaurant becomes the key for Laura to take charge of her feelings. When Ed once again drives into the parking lot in front of the dormitory Laura quickly climbs out, gives both of us a hug and kiss. With a huge smile and tears streaming down her face she turns her back and walks to the dorm's entry. Ed and I watch her disappear into its hallway, never turning around. There is no last wave. I will always have the picture of Laura's goodbye smile in my mental photo gallery.

Unknown to us is how Laura's journey through her education will unfold. The close friendships, great experiences, travel and awards are all in her future. Today's only a blend of apprehension and excitement.

The flip side of all this is when classes end each year. Everything is packed to come back with the kids for the summer. In between friends are brought home on breaks to ski or snow board. Holidays are celebrated as if no one had ever been away. Even summer times are easy as the kids find local jobs just two miles down the hill in Boyne City. Pat makes and sells fudge to the tourists and Rachael clerks across the street in a gift shop. Laura seldom makes if home for the summer months. Her choice is be elsewhere studying German.

A certain routine develops. E-mails become central to communications. As I sit at my computer and send off a short note to the grandkids I smile. My mind has traveled back to the days when I faithfully wrote home to Mom and Dad once a week. I remember it was always on Friday because I knew if I got it in to the post office that day my folks would have my letter on Monday. I would have Mother's reply by Friday. Dad was never the writer. Today we 'instant message'.

By late 2004 the new house is all but completed, everyone is doing great in college and Ed is holding his own remarkably well. I'm the one who finds myself on the verge of being where I had been in 2001; simply about to run out of money. The jobs the grandchildren find at their colleges help them meet their expenses. They are managing their college costs with grants and loans. My problem is maintaining a house large enough to be home for five on an income meant for two, our Social Security.

When it is suggested that Ed and I once again consider down sizing as so many folk our ages do and move into a smaller place, just large enough for two; I can't consider the idea. I know that until each of the grandchildren has their own home they must have the one they share with us. If the children's parents had lived the kids would have had a home with them. I recognize that an eighteen or even a twenty two year old needs to have a place to call home. It allows them to have the freedom to grow into the adult they are meant to be.

Ed's and my parents had barely recovered from the Great Depression and WWII was on the horizon, when we went off to college. Our rooms were kept for us to come back to whenever the need might arise.

So I begin going through my litany of possible cures for our money problem. Hardest of all is not being able to toss around ideas with Ed. But his inability to string things together chronologically makes his involvement ineffectual. I'm not ready to disturb Nancy and David with my problems since I know they have their own. It is then I turn to my friend, Grace. Over the years she and I have remained close in our long-distance friendship. Through letters and occasional visits plus rare phone conversations we have listened to each other's family crises and money issues. When Grace decided to add a miniscule screened-in porch on her home of many years, she called me. She needed support to carry out the dream. Like most people she had to have the stamp of approval she was unable to give to herself. Later, at eighty, Grace decided to down-size her home. Shocked, her family saw the idea as extremely radical and spontaneous. Not only did she sell the family home but threw out the accumulation of years. She packed to move to Michigan's land of winter snows.

For five weeks Ed and I drove her around the counties surrounding Boyne City in search of a log cabin in the woods. With me, Ed was concerned that such winter isolation for a single woman in her eighties might not be wise. Both of us were immensely relieved when our friend found a condo in the center of Boyne City, which answered all her desires. A brisk walker in all kinds of weather, Grace found she could walk to the bank, grocery store, drug store and other services she might need. Topping all this was the walk along the shores of Lake Charlevoix and the climb to the top of Barn Mountain, both right in town. In the winter she fastened on her cross-country skis to head out on the trails around the area.

Recently, as the owner of the condo Grace became enmeshed in various fees and payments that had not been on the horizon at the time of its purchase. She has no desire to burden her children with her own needs. A long time single mom, yet not unlike me, she finds herself still in the position of caring for a son and daughter who are unable to lead fully independent lives. It is then she reads about home equity loans. Grace investigates the various types available and chooses one. In the decision making process she brings me up to date on her thinking. When I find myself once again faced with the how-to-cope-with-the-increased-cost-of-living-on-a-minimum-income I visit the bank and make my own inquiries on flex-lines.

It was only fourteen years ago when Ed entered the same bank to float a loan to build the addition to our retirement house to accommodate the grandchildren. Now I'm doing the banking. My memory goes back even further to the times Ed increased the mortgage on the old farm house four times as our own children headed off to college. I'm certain he would approve my decision to do the same now. I find myself amazed at the change these years have brought. Each day I find new inner reserves of strength. To me there is an inexplicable feeling of being loved and cared for that permeates my very being. I truly know I am being watched over.

Normal day by day occurrences, which would have been impossible to deal with are taken care of. When Laura needs a car to access a job after graduation I'm able to purchase a 'new' used one. I don't hesitate to drive Ed to his 92nd Motor Squadron reunion in Green Bay, Wisconsin over the 911 weekend. I'm able to have my aging, overworked appliances repaired. I enlarge the office to use as a bedroom once Ed and I find it difficult to climb the stairs. When Melissa, Nancy and Paul's daughter is dismissed from active duty in the army just two weeks before her benefits were to kick in I convert our vacated upstairs into an apartment for her. Job opportunities are better here than in the area where her parents live. The military's reason for her dismissal? She was diagnosed with Desert Asthma. Then it is a hearing aid for Ed and a lower partial.

When Laura's first employer demands more than her job description includes I'm able to welcome her home until she can gain admittance to grad school. Remember the ridiculous Mr. Flatt? But of all these expensive unplanned happenings the most exciting is Laura's wedding and reception. I am so grateful for the beautiful ceremony and gathering afterwards. In my heart I believe Mary and Pat would have done it exactly as we did if they had lived to see the day.

In fact when Ed leans over to ask me with tears in his eyes, "Why did I walk Laura down the aisle and not her father?"

I can answer, "Honey, you may not have been aware of it but her dad walked all the way with the two of you and Mary was standing by my side. There were many others here this evening who were aware of them both."

Josué, Laura's love, is such a remarkable young man. He is Brazilian. How right Ed and I were when we set the goal of teaching the grandchildren how global our world has become. Laura sees nothing strange about accepting in marriage a husband from a non-English speaking country outside the United States. The fact her husband speaks seven languages. His grandfather, as a young man, traveled to the U.S. to study at Princeton Seminary; not an usual thing to do. To Ed and myself it is amazing for anyone of our generation. We would not have thought of it. And the fact that Josué parents have sent all three of their children to the United States for their high school and college educations makes us understand how fortunate he and I have been not to have had to make such a sacrifice.

After their New Year's Even wedding in our beautiful church on the corner of Pine and State streets the newlyweds flew to Brazil where they once again exchanged vows in the presence of Josué's family and friends. Grandmother Araujo treated the two to a honeymoon on a historical island off the coast of Salvador. Now Laura is adding Portuguese to her list of spoken languages.

A year and a half latter I am standing by to help Rachael and Pat as they graduate from college. Rachael will move into the world of employment and Pat will seek avenues to enable him to continue his studies in medicine.

The flex-line allows us to live, not just exist.

It's my prayer that my ability to support the flex-line will prevail as long as the grandchildren need a home. With this I pray Ed and I will be here with them. I'm determined the government's *Out the Door* policy will never wrap its tentacles around Laura, Rachael and Pat. That it won't tear their education, emotions and futures apart as it does thousands every year.

Patrick in his prom zoot suit—2003

Ferraris, Wrong Train and a Tsunami

Peace begins at home with each family

Back in the forties when Ed and Anne became parents they believed that if they raised their children to be of service to mankind and the Lord in their adult years, they would attain the goal of parenthood. And if every other parent around the globe would do the same the world would indeed become a place of peace and love. They felt it all began at home for each family. This belief remains even stronger as they raise their grandchildren.

I wasn't surprised by Rachael's request to visit her sister in Europe. Laura had studied for six months in Germany the year before. She had returned home with her wonderful stories of places she had been and people she had met. The initial trip to the country and now her current one are under Alma College's overseas learning opportunities. Colleges and universities offer overseas travel experiences in their recognition that it is the youth within their class rooms who will eventually bind the world's wounds. Through the exchange of education and friendships understanding and empathy will evolve. Alma College arranges their overseas study opportunities in a tidy one month bundle during May of each year. Two are suggested for graduation. The longer sessions such as Laura's fall in place as a result of the shorter, one month sojourns as often the mini session opens the doors to more extended study.

I believe Laura's involvement in the college's United Nations debate course whetted her appetite to become a citizen of the world. A semester course, it prepares teams of students to travel to the U. N. Headquarters annually to debate an issue with students from all over the world. The students sit in the same seats in the same room where the U.N. delegates meet to discuss world issues. It is a heady time. Alma College returns with two top honors both years Laura participates.

The exposure to different cultures and homes leads her into obtaining a major in the German language. To do so she left the US to study at the Europa Kolleg, a language institute in Kassel, Germany. As Christmas vacation looms ahead in 2000 the two girls get their heads together and envision a trip for Rachael to join Laura in Germany for a week.

So Rachael asks, "Laura has invited me over to visit her during my first week of Christmas break. Do you think I can go?"

My answer is immediate.

"Of course, you can go, but on one condition, you must take Patrick with you."

As Anne's alter-ego what she says or does doesn't usually surprise me. At least most of the time. But this time her answer does for two reasons. First, that she says 'yes'. But more so by the condition she affixes. Pat's just a senior in high school and other than the trip to Nova Scotia and to New York and Toronto with the drama group to see plays his overseas traveling supposedly looms ahead of him. It seems Anne is rushing things somewhat. But she has her reason.

Patrick is now a six foot four hunk of manhood. Although still seventeen he has the manner of a much more adult teenager. All the grandkids do. They have had life experiences many adults don't face until they are middle aged. Ed and I believe it is the direct result of living through their parents' deaths and then being raised by a couple of ancients like ourselves. I know I'm going to feel much easier about the two girls roaming about whatever towns they decide to visit in Europe with their younger, yet big brother as their escort. I don't share this reason with anyone but Ed. I need his understanding to win his approval of my idea. My husband is way ahead of me. He acknowledges Patrick has to be there with his sisters. It is our hope he always will be.

I'm thrilled when Rachael excitedly agrees that Patrick will be invited. Passports, luggage and money are all gathered. Ed and I allow the kids to withdraw what they will need for the trip from their college funds. We view travel as a form of education that can't be duplicated by text books or classroom discussion. Our only wish is selfish. We would love to go along. But we know if the trip is to be successful the kids must do it on their own. Isn't this why we have traveled with them? It has all been about observing others and developing self confidence and the ability to care for themselves.

The postcards the kids mail back home are after the fact, arriving days following the grandchildren's return. So Ed and I wait and pray and control our longing to be with them. An occasional phone call or e-mail from a café confirms their presence on earth. It is only after they are home that we learn about the nitty-gritty of their adventure. Patrick tells of buying hot bananas from a street vender in Frankenmuth to keep his freezing hands warm. His story of sitting with his sisters in beer gardens while they flirted with German guys makes me glance at Ed and think, "When did our three get this old?"

And Rachael and Laura tell of the night they all boarded a train and ended up in the wrong city after midnight with no place to stay and no return train to catch until morning. Of course, none of them was willing to part with any of their limited resources to pay for a room or even food. The three huddled together in the December cold on a bench outside of the closed station house to wait for morning. When a night janitor arrived to clean the building he invited them into his tiny cubicle of an office to keep warm. The kind man brought additional chairs from the station's waiting room to sit by a small oil heater. He placed them in his miniscule domain like the last three pieces of a complicated jig saw puzzle. Then, as they recount their adventure our grandchildren break into hilarious laughter describing the girlie posters on the man's walls and Pat's refusal to look in their direction.

In yet another city the girls succumbed to their desire to have their hair streaked European style while Patrick waited outside. With only one vote out of three he had little choice. Their whole trip as a trio worked out perfectly as Pat's height and weight belied the fact he was a seventeen year old. However his sisters didn't let him forget it.

Once enrolled in Alma, Pat is tapped to be a member of the college's prestigious choir. It is not usual for a freshman to become a member, his voice is one the director can't turn away. The group travels widely in the states and during alternate years goes overseas to perform. His freshman year Pat journeys with the group to the Netherlands and Germany. There he stays with host families many nights. In a small German city he is taken in by a doctor and his wife. Fascinated by their city home, Pat describes its glassed atrium entry and fabulous interiors. On the side his host is a brewer and Pat is treated to the results. The college, in recognition of the culture and the prevalence of alcohol at the European family table, sets a ground rule for their traveling students of one drink. Pat adheres to the rule I understand, my mother was the daughter of a German born father. In their home no family gathering or celebration was complete without the presence of alcohol, yet there was never any abuse of it.

It was the following day, the day Pat was to leave with the choir for their next stop that he discovered his host father had three Ferraris parked in his garage. The host was so taken with Pat's awe and appreciation of the cars that he couldn't stop apologizing to Pat for not having taken him our for a drive.

In 2006 Pat travels to Scotland, the land of another of my ancestors, my great, great grandmother. Ed and I were in the breathtaking, rugged British Isles in '87 when we visited my only living Irish relative, Jamie Cooke. He was still on the family farm near Donegal. Somehow his grandfather had reached into Scotland to find his wife.

In 2003, Pat went to the British Isles during Laura's year of study at Westminster University in London, England. This time he went alone as Rachael was saving her money to make the long trip to Thailand to visit the family of her friend, Rut. The friendship had begun Rachael's first year at Alma College and has continued although he has graduated and now lives in Bethesda, Maryland. He is a bio-chemist who works for the United States Health Department in research.

Pat flew over to meet Laura at her apartment and from there the two toured London, the famous city of kings and queens before catching a short flight into Dublin. The brother and sister must have been received as locals as they both have the Irish looks and ways. Laura is the fair skinned, blue eyed lassie one sees in every market place. Patrick is darker skinned and has deep brown eyes, the by-product of the ancient days when the Spanish Armada left some of their crew on the land. More than one found himself with an Irish gal. Pat is the descendant of the Black Irish. My favorite photo he brought back is the one Laura shot of him standing in front of a Dublin pub's sign, 'Cassidy's'. Another is one of Laura standing next to a bright red phone booth in the middle of a busy round-about.

Rachael went to Thailand over Christmas break that winter. The flight was almost as long as the one Laura had taken to London the year before. She had first flown to South Korea on her way to visit an Alma roommate for two weeks. From there she flew over Russia and on to England.

During the grandchildren's high school years in the mid 90's Ed and I rented a condo at Nubs Nob Ski Area during Easter breaks. A slow time for the ski hill because the snow condition in the Midwest is always questionable if the holiday falls late in the season. The accommodations were available at a discounted rate. It was during these sojourns that Ed and I would ask our wonderful friend, Grace to come up from East Lansing and join us. Each year she brought with her the college student who was renting a room from her. One year it was Hortense, a young woman from the French family where Grace had been a nanny in '87. The next year it was Yuko from Okinawa. Being able to spend a week with such special girls the three grandchildren first began to understand the universal family. Special dishes for each other were prepared and their laughter filled the pre-spring air as they descended the ski trails.

Rachael's trip to Thailand with her friend Rut was an adventure, complete with the opportunity to ride an elephant and swim in the Pacific Ocean. Rut's sister is a competitive swimmer so Rachael saw much of the country as she accompanied the family to meets. The architecture of the land fascinated her as well as their sense of design. She observed it all through the eyes of an artist.

The night the TV brings the news of the tsunami that devastated the shores of Indonesia and Thailand Ed and I were consumed with concern for Rachael. Our horror and disbelief was for everyone involved, but zeroed in on our granddaughter. When word arrived that Rachael and Rut were swimming off the eastern coast of the country rather than the south-western beaches we thanked the Lord for her safety and prayed many others would receive the same good news. Rut's father, a transmission helicopter pilot was called into service to survey the damages incurred by the power company and assess the reconstruction needs. Safe in the more northern regions of the land the rest of the family was out of danger from the sea's rampage.

Ed and Anne don't berate themselves for allowing Rachael to travel. They are far too aware of the dangers right at home. Every day we put our lives in jeopardy by living the lives we do. Man always has. But God has given each of us the will to live and the means to do so. He has left the responsibility with us to use His gifts in a way that will keep ourselves and those about us out of harm's way. It is Ed's and Anne's hope they have taught the children this.

A family wedding picture with Laura and Josue

Eighty-five, Sparklers and Roses

Everything is possible with love, faith and hard work

Anne's father once told her that she could do anything in her life if she was willing to work hard enough to make it happen. His words lodged in her mind and are still stuck there. She has found it true, if simplistic. Experience has shown her it takes much more than hard work. It requires the help of others, health and a mountain of Faith. And, for Anne it has taken Ed. Together they, in Faith, have made their life what it has become.

When Ed's eighty-fifth birthday arrives it seems as impossible as an ice storm on the hottest July day. Such an occurrence would defy belief.

If Ed indeed has ticked off eight and one half decades of living, anyone with simple grade school math, given the birth years, can proceed to figure out I'm eighty-two pushing three. Laura will be twenty-four. Rachael, twenty-two and Patrick, twenty. When did this happen? Where have the last fourteen years gone since Ed was almost 71, I was 68 and the kids, 6, 8 and 10?

As if this isn't enough Patrick will leave Alma with his pre-med degree in the spring of 2007 and Rachael will be working part time on an interior design internship prior to her graduation from MSU the same year. Laura will earn her masters at Asbury Seminary next spring but as Mrs. Josué Araugo.

Yes, she and Josué will be married New Year's Eve in the family's church in Boyne City. The candlelit early evening ceremony will be in the same church in which Mary celebrated both her marriages. Also it will be the one where the gorgeous honorary pallbearers carried her body down the steep front steps.

246

It is the building in which the family worships. The church members have supported all of us down through the years we have been a family. It is where Ed's and my children attended Sunday school and where we've taken our grandchildren. In its basement rooms both of have taught Sunday school. We've have taken our turns as Elders and Ed has been our Presbytery's delegate to the General Assembly. Laura was once the Mary in a Christmas pageant, Rachael a blond angel, wings aglitter and Patrick spoke his memorable words as a wise man in an Australian accent. Within its walls they have experienced more love and care than they have known pain in the world outside.

Weddings are fun to plan. I don't see how anyone can consider them work. Yet I hear that expression all too often. Josué is Brazilian and the man Laura thought she'd never find. From an amazing family, who have been of service to their country in many ways Josué plans to become a pastor in the United States. His grandfather is a Presbyterian pastor in Brazil. Josué and Laura understand the wedding budget will be minimal, but are appreciative of even the little there is to do with. She and I plan to make her gown, but Laura find's one she loves and which will cost less than if we make it. Though disappointed not to be able to sew Laura's wedding dress I have to admit the readymade is breathtaking on Laura. Instead, I opt to do the wedding cake.

I realize everyone in the family is suffering extreme anxiety at the very thought. Laura's twenty-first birthday cake will be the one they'll call to mind. I had my problems with it as I took it out of the pan and endeavored to stack its three layers to frost before it cooled off sufficiently. The more I worked the more if fell apart. In the end I secured it to itself with ice cream and numerous tooth picks, carried it into the dining room as everyone sang happy birthday while staring in disbelief. It's mounded sides had dribbled chocolate frosting cascading over a layer of white frosting. Fourth of July sparklers—twenty-one to be exact, their long shanks part of the cakes inner structure were lit and sent their sparks off in all direction. I thought it beautiful. Apparently it was destined to be a one-of-a-kind cake to be remembered as the most ridiculous sight imaginable.

But that was a once in a lifetime creation. I refuse to believe the wedding cake will be a disaster. It will be tall, elegant and breathtaking.

This isn't because I've an overgrown ego, it is based on the knowledge I gained when teaching ceramics, including pots on the wheel, at Fresno State College in central California. Then, some years later my mother for kicks, twisted my arm into going with her to a class in cake decoration at the University of Toledo. It was back during my Hasty Road days when I had broken into my thirties. The two episodes relate because it was there I discovered cake decorators use revolving disks when decorating their cakes. They were much the same as those I used when glazing my pots at the college. Plus Mr. Murdock, the night class instructor at the university, was Toledo's most sought after caterer one could engage in that metropolitan area.

There was something about Mother that never grew beyond her teen years. She was always up for a good time and could become convulsed in laughter more easily than anyone else I've ever known. So much so that I would find myself weak kneed, tears streaming down my face, doubled up with uncontainable glee just because Mother was doing the same. The two of us would stand, feeding off each other's merriment to the point of having to pray we didn't pee our panties. And that did happen, more than once. Fortunately my kidneys were stronger in those days than now, but not Mother's.

I don't remember which of us read the class announcement in the Toledo Blade, but neither of us hesitated signing on for the class. Actually the course was a short series of evening classes. We found it part lecture, part demonstration and also hands on. All eleven of the class's students, of course, knew the hands-on-time is what we all were waiting for with the greatest anticipation.

The last evening of the class Mom and I sat next to each other as usual. Mother had selected a front table from the very beginning. On the first night she had introduced herself to Mr. Murdock by mentioning some functions he had catered that she had attended. My mother was extremely impressed by society's upper crust. Part of this is because her two older sisters were married to very wealthy men and she knew first hand what all that money meant.

This side of Mother made me cringe since such familiarity with a stranger is something I couldn't even think of doing. From that night the two of us became Mrs. Cook and her daughter. I remained nameless throughout the entire session despite the fact I felt very mature at thirty, the mother of two.

The last class session Mr. Murdock arrived with a baked, three-tier wedding cake. Not a huge one, it was still quite large. The students held their breath in expectation at the thought of what it was to become by the close of class at nine thirty. His worktable was right in front of Mother and me. In his white starched version of the Tin Man, complete with his high baker's hat Mr. Murdock appeared unapproachable at over six feet and weighing in around two fifty. He was one huge hunk of self assurance as he proceeded to set the cake upon a revolving standard. He then iced it. His assistant shared the frosting recipe with chalk on the class room black board as Mr. Murdock worked.

The students copied the words as they watched this man of magic apply the smooth final layer of frosting.

Moving the cake to one side and he sought each of the students' eyes saying, "Now, watch carefully. I will demonstrate making a rose bud, a full blown rose and a leaf. These will be set aside to harden as I pipe the cake with swags and a fluted edge."

Then, eyes gleaming he leaned forward to share a secret, which his listeners were led to believe should not go beyond the walls of the university.

"I gently infuse a drop of coloring on the center of each flower and bud. Tonight's choice will be yours. Do you prefer a soft shell pink or the golden glow of a faint yellow?"

What a terrible choice we were asked to make.

The awful thing is Anne no longer remembers what was decided, only that it was done and became the obvious reason a Murdock cake was to die for.

It is likely the class chose pink, but then again, it might well have been yellow. Of course, pale yellow would be my preference. It isn't unusual for me to be out of step, though.

Deftly, on top of a tiny hand held disk mounted on a stick, the teacher fashioned one rose after another. He layered the frosting petals around a miniature Hershey Kiss like center with its hint of color. A variety of blossoms grew before our eyes. Their sizes depended on where in the process he stopped. The leaves were simply shaped petals that remain unattached like those that fall one by one from an autumn tree. Down the center of each he carefully etched its veins with a tooth pick.

Pausing he asked for questions. Then he opened a cake box he had brought into the class room. It disclosed roses and petals his helpers had made in advance. There were enough to decorate the cake that evening. Handling the box as if it were about to explode, our classmates passed it around the room to better see the beautiful flowers. It was like peering into a bit of fairyland to see such extravagance.

The class's attention was recalled as he approached the cake on the revolving cake standard set center front on his table. The device was about twelve inches high, making the cake much easier to work on. Instructing the class he filled parchment bags with decorating frosting and selected a metal tip to produce the desired fluting design around the cake's edges—no plastics back in that time. Rather than moving his hand held decorator Mr. Murdock gently and slowly twirled the cake pedestal. As it circled the magic tip placed a lovely fluted edge on each of the cake tiers.

Looking out upon the class much as the successful gladiator of old must have as he stood, foot on the chest of his dead adversary, the decorating artist smiled at his students and asked, "Who would like to come up front and try their hand at fluting?"

Every single one was dying to go give the thing a spin and try their hand with the decorating tube. However, certainly none wanted to try in front of each other and mostly, not in front of intimidating Mr. Murdock.

It was then I heard Mother say, "Oh, Anne, you can do that. Go give it a try."

There are times; much as she loves her mother Anne really could strangle her. Doesn't she after all these years understand Anne's shyness? There was no way her daughter could stand up in front of all those women to decorate the cake. She has known them less than a month. Even though it appeared very similar to working on the potter's wheel Anne just couldn't do it.

Mr. Murdock was quick to jump in for the kill. This was what he had been waiting for. Someone to stand up in front of his class and through their pitiful failure demonstrate how great and adept he was. His eyes gleamed.

They scared me.

Mother was not going to let it go. Speaking to the instructor she began to elaborate on all my skills, assuring him her daughter could do a beautiful job.

"She's a Fine Arts graduate from Fresno State University and does beautiful work. She even taught ceramics there the summer she graduated."

That did it. Mr. Murdock was by my side, firmly pulling me up out of my seat and leading me around to the work side of his domain.

All of me felt numb. I silently prayed the fire alarm would sound or a sudden unexplainable power failure would darken the room. How welcome they would be. Neither happened.

So much for prayer, I thought. God is leaving me alone on this one. There is no sympathy anywhere.

Putting the room and its occupants aside as I had taught myself to do when I was caught in an impossible situation I stood up, refusing to look at Mother, who I knew would be smirking with pride and went around to Mr. Murdock's side of the demonstration table. There the cake stood, waiting. I reached for a parchment bag and filled it with perfectly made icing. Then I selected a point for its narrow end. With a tentative squeeze I loosened some of its contents onto a piece of parchment on the table. A tiny shell appeared as if by magic. Turning to the cake I gave it's pedestal a light twirl with my left hand to start it turning. With the tube in my other hand I began to add the tiny shells next to the fluted edging Mr. Murdock had executed.

I have to admit that I was enthralled. Oblivious to my presence and to those watching all the skills I learned during the time I studied and taught ceramics in Fresno returned to my finger tips. It thrilled me to move back into that long gone world. I proceeded to complete the addition of tiny shells and then add swags of icing on the cake's sides.

Suddenly the present rushed back beside me. I knew the roses had to be added next. I looked up at the instructor for the first time and was appalled by the look in his eyes. It was immediately apparent he was very unhappy with me. I had done too much too well. And to top it off I obviously had a wonderful time and way too much fun. I knew I should feel terrible. But none of it bothered me a bit. I thought the pompous show-off deserved the whole thing.

I quickly asked, "Mr. Murdock, are you going to show us how you add the roses on the cake once this basic decoration is done?" I left the table quickly, hating the applause that only forced Mr. Murdock to have to add his congratulations. This had not been in his mind when he asked someone to come forward and try their luck at decorating.

Mother was beaming with pride. I instantly forgave her. I was aware Mother had no idea how she had spoiled Mr. Murdock's evening.

The cake was a bit of fairyland when he placed the last leaf in place. There was no doubt in any of the students' minds but that their instructor's secret he had shared about the hint of color was what set his cake above all others. Mr. Murdock regained his sense of well being as he absorbed the veneration of his students. It was then he reached the finalé of his cake decorating class.

"I have the tin here in which each of you placed your name when you arrived at the first session. I am going to ask Mrs. Cook to draw a name out and that person will be given tonight's cake to take home with them."

This announcement was a complete surprise to everyone. Silence entered the room as all eyes turned to watch Anne's mother. Helen was flattered to be the person to draw the name. She was all a-twitter as Mr. Murdock beamed down on her and held the tin forth. How a petite five foot four inch woman ever brought a five foot nine inch daughter into the world was a wonder to me. Mother looked like a small child as Mr. Murdock invited her to draw a card. Although he might never realize it, Mrs. Cook had wrapped him around her little finger that night.

A name was drawn and handed to the instructor as everyone held their breath.

Mr. Murdock looked at the name and hesitated. At the time the hesitation was taken as a bit of theatrics, but after the name was announced I was not so certain.

"Mrs. Cook has drawn the name of her daughter as the winner." Again, I was simply just Mrs. Cook's daughter. He turned to me and shook my hand in congratulations. Indicating a large white cake box I was to use to carry the cake away. He turned to his helper.

I was surrounded with envious classmates as Mother became the brunt of good natured comments about drawing her own daughter's name. While this went on Mr. Murdock and his helper busily cleaned up their work space, packing and carrying everything out to their van.

A hurried call thrown over his shoulder reached the class, "Sorry to rush off, but I must get back to the bakery. Good luck with your cake decorating," and he was gone.

Mother and I were the last to leave. We actually turned off the lights. Mother volunteered to carry the purses and notebooks if I would carry the cake. She opened doors and guided me back to the large front entry of University Hall. It was a dark night at almost ten o'clock but the circular steps down from the front door were well lit.

I was part if its happening, but have no recall how it happened. Somewhere between the top and the next step down I lost my hold on the stiff, shiny cake box. In my endeavor to regain command of the darn thing Mother offered her help. Encumbered with purses and notebooks her assistance only produced more chaos and I watched as the cake box launched off into space on a trajectory aimed at the grass lawn five steps below and off to the right.

In horror we watched the night's trophy sail in a high arc through the air. Changing course as it parted company from its box the gorgeous three-tiered wedding creation turned to the left and crashed on the bottom step. Unprotected, the cake exploded, smashing into a mass of mashed debris. Smeared icing and beautiful roses were strewn over an area of ten square feet. The box, pouting, lay off to one side. One lone, gently tinted, full blown rose and its bud hid in a corner of the mutilated cardboard, orphans of the evening's tragedy. I wish I could describe the whole thing better, but words fail me.

Commercial icing is loaded with fat of one kind or another. Fat is very slippery when it is under foot. Mother and I found our way down the steps aware of the dire possibility of having our feet slip out from underneath us, flying off into space. I could just picture a repeat flight of the cake.

After trying to negotiate the first two steps we decided the only thing to do was to sit down and scooch our way down to safety. By this time we are both deep in the clutch of all but hysterical laughter. We sat side by side in the beautiful goop and fragile roses with slightly tinted yellow centers and laughed until the tears flowed. We weren't able to get out a complete sentence without going into convulsions of giggles and whoops of laughter. Effective communications were at a stand still.

Apparently all the other night course students had left for home and the two of us were left to solve our problems by ourselves. Actually Mother and I were thankful no one else was privy to the mess we had made of the beautiful wedding cake. Mother was determined no one was to ever know, most of all Mr. Murdock. Getting a grip on ourselves we worked our way down to the grass through the mess by scotching on our backsides until a safe foothold could be had. Looking back up the steps we were appalled at the mess. Obviously it would have to be cleaned up before anyone came along. But how?

A gardener above all other things, Mother decided there had to be a water spigot somewhere on the outside perimeter of the huge building. After all there were thriving shrubbery and flower borders. Worming herself behind the picky juniper and dogwood planting Mother not only found the faucet but discovered it had a hose attached.

Dragging it out of its seclusion she turned the water on full blast. Starting with the top step we began the job of removing all the evidence from the crime scene. What we thought would be a cinch proved not to be so. The ice cold hose water had little effect on the fats of the frostings. Both of us knew we couldn't leave such a treacherous situation as slick steps leading up to the front entrance of the university. We could picture a young college fellow rushing to class, hitting the first step and sliding off into space. His books and papers would fly on their own travel itineraries. Again Mother and I succumbed to gales of laughter as we embellished the imagined scene with his comments and efforts to regain his dignity and class work. Our sides literally ached.

It was getting late and the mess wasn't going to clean itself off the steps and grass yet Mother and I found it all but impossible to settle ourselves down and re-approach the job in front of us.

In the 40's there were no stores open in the evenings so purchasing a solvent wasn't an option. It was way before women would consider wearing jeans or slacks. So, we ended up using our slips as mop rags. Down on our knees Mom and I rubbed the steps clean of all signs of the cake. Pieces of bark and broken sticks became handy crud removal tools. The fact that the white residue of the icing and crumbs would linger in the grass and under the shrubs had to be overlooked. We hoped for an early rain to further disintegrate the sugar and water.

As long as Mr. Murdock would never know and no one would slip on the entry steps, we headed home looking as if we had fallen in the Maumee River and barely managed to climb ashore.

With memories like these why should I worry about my ability to create a beautiful wedding cake for Laura and Josué? It will be my gift to someone I love beyond words as will Ed's act of walking his granddaughter down the aisle. Rachael will stand beside her sister as a bridesmaid and Pat will join Josué's sister, Anna, in singing the wedding song.

Important to all is the knowledge the Cassidy clan, the Thurston family and their wonderful friends will be there to wrap them together in the tissue and ribbon of love.

In the late fall of 2005 the day arrives for Ed and me to celebrate his eighty-fifth birthday. The day finds us having a MacDonald's Thick 'n Juicy with my senior coke and Ed's chocolate malt down by the lake front. There we watch the white caps rush toward us from Charlevoix, twelve miles to the north.

Ed says, "Let's drive up to see the waves coming in on Lake Michigan. They should really be hammering the pier right now. I love to see the big lake on a stormy day."

The seventeen mile drive is glorious with the trees in their vibrant fall gold. I feel as if I need to stop and grab a breath as they all but take mine away. On the lake front we find the deep blue of the distant waters a vibrant sea green near the shore. Not far from the sandy beach an abrupt drop-off, once the shore, causes the color demarcation. Contentment washes over us as the whitest of white water caps each incoming breaker.

"It's looks like new snow has fallen on the crest of each wave," Ed comments.

No one is in the water. The air has turned too cold, although the water temperature probably won't drop fast. Only three weeks before two young men in wet suits rode the breakers on surfboards.

Out of no where I get an idea. "Honey, since we are only a couple of blocks from the doctor's what if we go get our flu shots?"

Fifteen minutes later we have our shots and head home. Sneaking my eyes away from the road and my driving, I take a second to look across at my handsome husband and think, "How can he be eighty-five and I still get goose bumps when I see him?"

What I say to Ed doesn't reflect my romantic thoughts at all, "Hey, you need a hair cut if you are going out to dinner with me tonight. Let's stop at the barber's on the way to the house."

So it will be that the two of us spend the entire day together climaxing it with a wonderful steak dinner complete with a toast to 'many more happy ones, dear."

Times like these Anne completely forgets me. This happens more than can be counted. When Anne is with Ed she doesn't need me. It has always been that way.

On the way home after dinner Ed and I find ourselves talking about the future. Not just ours but that of the grandchildren.

"Anne, I am not only planning to be on hand for Pat's graduation from pre-med at Alma, but I am going to be there four years later when he gets his doctorate."

I put my hand across on his thigh and rub it. His hand is on mine right away.

"Oh, I'm not going to start anything, Honey," I assure him.

"Yeh, I know you." he laughingly replies.

"Honestly, It's just that I love you so much that I have to reach over and be sure you are real. I'm afraid I'm dreaming. It's people like you who set next to impossible goals and always reach them. I remember Mary's goal of staying with Patrick and his sisters until he entered the first grade. I always felt she had your genes; you had so many similar ways. I can't explain it, but I believe you'll be in the audience when all three of the kids graduate from college."

"I wish I could be here another forty years to watch their lives unfold." Ed adds.

"I know Honey, those are the years I have been concerned about since we started on this adventure with the three. The years after we're gone. But in my heart I know they will be wonderful years for each of them. They will be full of love, friends and the demands of leaving the world a better place. Mary and Pat started their children's journey and we have added our bit. What a trio they are. The wonderful thing about love is that it never dies. It's so transient, moving from one to another, but in the process it doesn't really leave, it only spreads."

"Like ours," Ed says and squeeze's my hand.

"What a gift to receive and give," I answer.

Love; the timeless Gift.

PART II

And To Live Happily Ever After

Anger, Numbers and Mistakes

Waste, greed and hatred are without excuse

Anne recognizes her feelings of anger can become intense given the situation at hand. That anger comes to the top whenever she becomes aware an injustice is being committed. In her thinking there is never any reason for violent, thoughtless actions against another unless saving ones own life is the more important outcome. Waste, greed and hatred are without excuse. Her long life has allowed her to understand where such attitudes begin. Developing compassion for those inflicting them has helped her harness her anger. Better yet, Anne has developed a code of behavior. It reminds her to keep her mouth shut unless she has a remedy to offer for the problem she sees or hears. It is this, which allows her to walk away from those things she can not resolve.

My mind is at rest on money matters, at least for the time being. The flex-line is there if I get a call from a campus or if a non-budget emergency such as a tooth extraction rears its head. Here in the late winter of 2005 my thoughts pick up where they were after reading Laura's *Eighteen and Out* letter from the Social Security office in 1999. Hard for me to believe, but that infamous day was over five years ago, yet I can see that envelope as clearly as if it had just been put in my hand. The hurt, disappointment and anger it fostered have never really faded. Somewhere inside of me, beneath all my day by day thoughts, they flare as hot as back then. In fact, they have been on a slow simmer waiting for something to fan their flame. I haven't been consciously aware of all this. Too much else has been in the forefront. Guiding the three grandchildren through their high school days and now on into college and beyond in Laura's case. Then Ed's horrible diagnosis in 2001; Alzheimer's.

When Rachael's and then Pat's notices arrived it wasn't the same as the day Laura put hers in my hand. Admittedly it did rekindle the flame for a few moments each time. But those correspondences lacked the surprise, disbelief and shock that Laura's notice generated. I have never let myself take the whole termination letter by the neck and hold it in front of my face. Why is it continuing to upset me so much that it stirs up this anger deep inside me? At my age and being a woman, how can I even think about taking on the US government? After all, suing for what might have been is not the issue; it is the hateful, thoughtless dismissal of young adults at their most vulnerable age that nags at me. I'd have to be downright stupid not to understand the terrible consequences such a law must inflict on those orphaned and parentless youth in our country who haven't been as fortunate as our grandchildren. It isn't the material things they must live without but rather someone to love them and help them to prepare to live their lives.

Instead of embracing the problem I allowed it to remain in one of those back-in-the-mind files people maintain; to which other happenings can be added from time to time. The biggie, of course, that joins the *Eighteen and Out* letters, is the incident over the $45,000. Although at the time it had all the appearance to me of being a gift out of the blue, as some would say. And I have to include, a God Send.

It stumps me why it takes Anne so long to re-open the Eighteen and Out file. One thing that must be said on her behalf is she does it intentionally and seriously. This isn't just a revisiting to moan and groan over what should not have happened. Anne doesn't deal with past events that way. She understands it is self-destructive. No, this time Anne intends to re-evaluate the whole process she and Ed had to work within parenting their grandchildren. She has come to accept the fact that even though she is a woman and is in her eighties that there very well may be no one else as qualified as she is to search for an answer to what she believes to be a horrible mistake. In other words, she's mad enough to try her best to do whatever she can to find a just answer and then search for a way to work for its acceptance. She asks herself, "What else is there I can do with the rest of my life that could be more important?"

My little Queen Anne desk with its cubby holes is in our granddaughter, Melissa's apartment now. She, Nancy and Paul's only daughter, moved into the upstairs bedroom in our house after it became too difficult for Ed and me to climb the steps last fall. The climbing up and down had become too painful for Ed. His old college football knee has come back to haunt him. Besides, Mel is at a time in her life when she needs a little boost and we happen to be the ones who can do that for her. Just five months younger than Rachael she is like another sister to Laura, Rachael and Pat. I dearly love her and it is fun having her with us. She fills in the emptiness the kids have left behind as they go off to college.

I have converted my mother's small walnut drop-leaf table to a desk. It sets in the bay off the living room and is an ideal place to work. Where I sit at the table it's a good ten feet down to the lawn. The five windows of the bay look over the farm from the south to the north; a view I never tire of. I watch the seasons bring their own weather, birds, skies and progression of trees and plants. Behind me, in the living room Ed spends most of his day contentedly snoozing. He has his favorite high backed, wing chair with its chintz covered pillow. Unless she is outside checking the perimeters of the fields our Tipper will be at his feet, willing to sleep as long as her master might. Beginning to grey around her muzzle she is a remarkably gentle dog despite her size, long wavy, jet black hair and deep bark.

A type of stock dog her big brown eyes have their own vocabulary. Often in the evening the two of us carry on lengthy conversations as to whether she wants food, water, to go outside, play tug-o-war or just needs a bit of love. Somehow she has never felt it necessary to teach anyone else in the family her silent words. I am her sole contact with the world of man.

Yet despite this deep love we share she remains Ed's dog. Tipper is really bi-lingual. In addition to the language the two of us share, she has also added many human words. There are times when I communicate with Ed that I have to spell certain words. If I forget and say cookie she's immediately in the kitchen, nose on the counter pointing to the cookie jar. And so it is with out, in, car, ride, walk, eat, drink, where's Ed? and on and on.

On the drop-leaf I keep the reference books I frequently uses when writing. The files of current work, household accounts and personal ones of friends and places are nearby. Underneath the table is a fishing tackle box of art supplies if the urge hits me to paint. Next to the table, under a second window in the bay is Mary's sewing table, which Patrick finished for her before his death. Within its drawers and doors all my sewing paraphernalia is stashed for easy access.

Lifting the table's drop leaf and sliding its support into place I reach for my old files with the annual Social Security reports and those sent to Probate Court. Both came to a halt in 2003 when Pat turned eighteen. With pencil and paper for notes I start to search for figures within the reports, seeking what will become the true final report of those twelve years we parented and loved our grandchildren as our own; fulfilling the promise I so spontaneously gave our Mary the year before her death. It all seems so long, long ago. And yet, perhaps it was only yesterday, why else do I feel tears within myself?

Anne's relaxed schedule during the months the three grandkids are in college releases the time she needs to do her research. Her quest is for an answer to what she can no longer deny has been and remains a major problem. We bat ideas back and forth as she finds the facts she needs and works with them. It does me good to realize she has returned to the $45,000. The Social Security Administrator in Petoskey, Mr. Satlsman's answer to her question about a possible interest payment on the government's mistake was totally unacceptable to Anne.

My admiration for Anne escalates on the spot. Excited about her project, it is obvious to me that what Anne has in mind is a determined effort to right a wrong, not against herself, but against millions of children. We have some good talks about the ways to accomplish what we both agree has to be done by someone, sometime and someplace. It is just a matter of who, when and where. Why not a couple of oldies like us? We both have our own entry points when we set out to do something. Anne's isn't mine, but that's OK. It's no news to me that the two of us are as different as night and day in many ways. Yet there is an almost twin-like manner about us.

I decide to start with the $45,000, not that it will have that much to do with the end results of my research. I think I do it mainly to satisfy my curiosity about what might have been. I have no intention of going anywhere with the information. But I am really surprised at the answer I find, it's a sizable amount.

Because I have learned to deal with first hand information rather than what I think or someone else might come up with I stop by the bank and ask Nan, the branch manager for her help. I know she works with figures, zeros, percentages and decimal points routinely.

I understand others might simply sit down with a calculator and poke buttons. If I did I would be hounded with the thought I might have used a wrong mathematical path. Starting with the $45,000 Nan, through the use of her investment tables, figures out what the interest payments might have been over a period of twelve years on the lost sum at the investment world's mean rate of 10%. The base is determined and the answer comes in slightly over $29,000. This represents the interest the government never paid on the under payments in the grandkids' Social Security. To me the whole governmental booboo is an example of sloppiness, not just that of a lowly clerk but all the way up the ladder to the manager in charge of disbursement. I can't let myself think about what might have been all those years for the grandkids, Ed and me.

But it gets worse.

The next step is to add the $29,000 to Ed's and my retirement account. After all, our investments had been used as a source of money to bridge the loss in Social Security payments. I recognize also, that if we hadn't had to dip into our retirement money, the amount we used would have accrued interest at 10% or more. The total loss to Ed and me has been approximately $156,000.

I look at the over one hundred and fifty thousand dollars that has trickled off my ledger sheets over the past dozen years and am flooded with a feeling of release. I understand why, no matter how I struggled I was never able to balance the budget. After all my guilt feelings it hasn't been my mismanagement that beat us down into the dust. I have managed our family income as well as anyone else might have. There is an elation over knowing I had done as well as I could.

As I sit at Mom's drop-leaf table I wonder how a human being can be filled with so much anger and pain yet at the same time rejoice that none of it has been her fault? Is it my deep anger, deeper pain or sense of joyous relief that explains the tears pouring down my cheeks. Outside it is a beautiful day, inside Ed and Tipper contentedly sleep. I cry, completely out of control. My emotions are so tangled I can't explain any of it to myself. I don't try.

I have no idea how long I have been sitting here in the bay. The tears have stopped. I suspect my mind has been in a stupor; a type of no-man's land where the emotions go to sort themselves out. My mind is clear. I dry my eyes. I am back to being me and knowing that when the government makes an error its citizens live with it. With this issue resolved I move ahead knowing full well crying over spilled milk won't do a bit of good. No, what I want to do with what is left of me is to work toward repairing our nation's *Eighteen and Out* fiasco. After all, I have already survived one death threat. What can be worse?

Six Million Beyond Foster Care

One in twelve of our country's children are without birth parents.

With the matter of the finances cleared up Anne turns to discover what is known by others about parentless children and youth in our country. For two years she keeps a file of clippings from magazines, newspapers and web sites that contain stories of parentless children. Most of it centers on Foster Care. Of that the largest percentage falls in the range of horror stories. She also researches all the books that have been written on the subject. This is pretty much a blind alley as most are clinical in nature; one Foster Care case study after another. Of the well over one hundred editions many are out of print. Only David Pelzer's 'A Child Called It' has caught the public's attention enough to make the Ophra show and the New York Times best seller list. But again it is a horror story, although written by a successful survivor. It troubles me that she'll become discouraged, but the day arrives when she finds the number the US census has failed to disclose.

As my research is going forward I contact my various senators and congressmen for supportive statistics. But it isn't until I visit the web site of Senator Hillary Clinton that I find a number I have suspected existed but which has alluded me. It is the number of parentless children being raised by family or grandparents; those that are hidden outside of the national statistics for Foster Care children. Unless adopted or assigned conservators and guardians they have escaped the government's detectors.

The Senator writes' *"Nationwide, more than six million children—1 in 12—are living in households headed by grandparents or other relatives . . . . as caregivers who often become parents unexpectedly, these generous family members face unique challenges to successfully raising children. These challenges are physical, emotional and of course, financial."*

I process the number in disbelief. It is so much larger than I have imagined. This is where Ed and I fit. Our three grandchildren fall within this number. My immediate question is, Where in the world are the other 5,999,997? Then a second thought surges into my mind. Not all these children are parentless because they are orphaned. Many have reached the designation because their parents have simply walked off and left them, are physically or emotionally ill, or are even incarcerated. If the child is not an orphan because of death there can be no support from their deceased parents' Social Security as there has been for our three.

I shudder at the thought of having to cloth and feed these unexpected family members without financial help. Especially if retired, beyond the age of employability. How could the substitute parent manage the day to day necessities and even hope to enrich the child's life with travel and education? Adding a needed room on a home, obtaining a larger car or buying new shoes when the toes begin to be pinched, let alone taking off to go tubing down a remote river on a summer day or skiing down a mountain side on second hand equipment; all fall under the impossible. All would be out of reach. How could a councilor's help be sought or a soccer uniform be purchased, let alone a college education planned? Guilt floods me that I have allowed myself to even once feel that it had been hard to manage our finances over the past few years. After all, we had our retirement nest egg and in the end I did receive the $45,000 shortfall in the grandchildren's benefit payments.

Early on I had learned the number of Foster Care parentless children was somewhere around 500,000 on any given day in the US. In addition to this I discovered that 25,000 Foster Care youth are released annually onto the streets of this country on their eighteenth birthday. This happens because their Social Security support is terminated. With few exceptions the Foster Care parent can not continue to furnish the youth shelter, food or clothing. This sad situation is experienced by many of the children left with grandparents or family because from the very first day there is no financial aid for them. The only hope is that the care giving family knows of available financial aid through Home Services. I admit to myself that there must be many, who like Ed and me, are without this knowledge.

I take time out to read Senator Clinton's book, *It takes a Family* and find it hard to believe there are countries doing a better job of caring for their hurting children than we are. I have always thought that Americans are the most caring of all people. The truth hurts.

My discouragement is assuaged a bit when I discover the Jim Casey Family Foundation through an article in my daily newspaper, the Petoskey News Review. A visit to its editor, Ken Stanley, cements my interest in the foundation's work among those in Foster Care. He had interviewed a member of a local Casey youth group. The foundation was founded by Jim Casey, the man who established United Parcel Services. The business had grown out of a childhood effort to help his mother with the household expenses by running errands for others on his bike. Today the program addresses the problems of youth about to emerge from the government's Foster Care program. Although Foster Care is an entirely different facet of the parentless youth problem than that of youth being raised by family it is part of the puzzle. And that part although small, approximated at 500,000, has generated more media interest than the other 6,000,000 parentless children and youth thought to be in the United States. I wonder if that is because Foster Care is a government program while the realm of parenting by grandparents or other family members remains out of view of the bureaucrats. I do find statements by those involved with the needs of the parentless that indicate the level of care is much higher for those living with family than those in Foster Care.

I meet the regional director of the Jim Casey Kids, Norvilla Bennet and start attending their weekly meetings in Petoskey's new public library. The title 'Casey Kids' belongs to those youth who chose to attend the foundation's area meetings and participate in the dollar-for-dollar matching-money savings program that helps the attendees become financially responsible. The five young people I meet, all high school students, hold down part time jobs while attending school. The work they do is in the low pay area of the fast food industry. Currently a full time position within the industry nets no more than approximately $550 a month. As part-time employees they are receiving far less and without benefits.

During the six meetings I attend I watch Casey people in a one-on-one manner coach three of the students for college entry. Marta is headed for a degree in social work, Ryan's interest is in communications and Neta's goal is to become a secondary teacher. Under the stimulation of the Casey staff all have bumped their senior year grades up to a four point.

I also become privy to the students voting to assist another Foster Care student with a gift of $100 for college clothes. He has none that will permit him to attend class. This amount comes from a discretionary fund that the Casey Foundation sets aside for the core leadership youth of the group to tap as they see a need. The three youth leaders exercised great responsibility with the money they were giving to their peer.

Through Norvilla I gather the names of some of the Casey staff at the national level. By an exchange of e-mail I am able to toss my long range goals by Dr. Peter Peccora, head of research for the foundation. He greatly encourages me when he remarks that my ideas are 'on target'.

Discovery of the Foster Care Continuing Opportunities Act that Senator Barbara Boxer of California has written and which is supported by Senator Thad Cochran of Mississippi and Senator Sheldon Whitehouse of Rhode Island helps me feel a little better about the government. I realize just because the bill exists is no guarantee it will ever be voted into law. Basically it is an effort to patch the existing eighteen-and-out version of Social Security that was chopped to end on the eighteenth birthday during the Regan years. Sadly it will only be on the behalf of those youth receiving Social Security benefits. The Boxer bill would have the national government partner with the individual state in funding the extension of benefits to parentless youth in Foster Care to the twenty first or twenty second year. These were the original termination dates of the law.

No one believes the law can simply be returned to its original and very effective form which continued Social Security benefits through ages 21/22. Politics get in the way. After all, the almost 7,000,000 parentless children in our land do not have political clout or the means to lobby. Even a $2,000,000,000 endowed group such as the Jim Casey Family Foundation can't waste its energy in tangling with such a dead issue. They can experience better results in using their money more directly with the youth that desperately need it.

Not a day goes by that I don't garner more facts and figures. What good is there in this? How will it help me help the parentless? Here I sit, miles from any metropolis, outside a small town of less than 3500 residents. To top that I am pushing 85 and my knees are caving in to all the roller skating and skiing I enjoyed for years. On the plus side I have my computer and I love to write. I believe in the power of the written word. Some notable person once said '. . . the pen is mightier than the sword.' (Hard to believe, this was not Ben Franklin or any other American, but a Frenchman, a Cardinal and statesman, Armand Jean du Plessis Richelieu, back in 1839. And it was a sideways slap to the great of his day).

Even today, I believe this is absolutely true. It only takes one person to tell a story, to write a book. I decide to tell my story as I have lived it. I will let the country know that there are almost 7,000,000 parentless children within its boundaries and of those only 500,000 are in Foster Care. The others are silently being parented by grandparents, family members or someone who simply cares. They all need help. They need it desperately. Many have absolutely no additional income to facilitate this commitment.

Children are gifts of God. They are given to us to nourish, love and cherish. When the mother and father die, become dysfunctional or disappear the child is the responsibility of the society into which it entered. Let us look among ourselves and reach out in a meaningful way to those who best can fulfill this responsibility. The government must help, but only its people can meet the challenge. I believe our country is learning to care for its elders as they enter their final years. We can do as well for our parentless youth who are part of this country's tomorrows. America has the passion to care and the entrepreneurship to solve its problem.

The Home Town Center

A tapestry of answers

At times a person and their alter-ego can come close to driving each other insane. There's no particular occasion in my mind, but it must have happened back in our late twenties or thirties, when we probably really went at it The years have taught both of us we aren't as right about things as we once thought; guess others would say we have 'mellowed'.

My intentions have always been to be helpful. There have been times when my efforts were really blown. Our conversations are much more civil now then they were back a few years. Anne has always been far more careful about her choice of words. This is because she is aware she might be overheard. For me, that's not a worry. My words have always been for Anne alone. Much as there was the desire to butt in between Anne and Ed, it hasn't happened. The ability to do so was just never mine. Guess he has his own A-E to contend with. Besides, Anne let me know right from the 'get go' that he was her exclusive property. It is hard for me to explain, but there was something about it all that led me to understand there would never be any exception. So, whenever the two of them are together doing their man and wife thing; you won't find me around

The hardest times for me are when Anne gets all tangled up in her shyness. It is so difficult for me to hang on to my patience when she's into one of her struggles. It used to be awful. In Ed's business there were the occasional times when he found it necessary to attend a social function. Of course, he wanted Anne with him. He thought she was the most beautiful woman in the world. As a typical man full of male ego he wanted everyone to know she was his. Ed knew from their first evening together at Hennicks, a campus hang-out just a block off the OSU campus, that she was shy. At the same *time he recognized Anne had the ability to over-ride her affliction. He always gave her the space she needed to pull herself together.*

It was me who had to watch her drag the few clothes she owned out of her closet. With tears streaming down her checks she'd climb in and out of them muttering, "Why do I have to do this? What should I wear? Why do I have to have a husband who loves people?"

My mouth was glued shut until her sobs would get to me. Then, it was, "Wear the outfit you like. What the hell do you care whether someone you don't know from Adam-knows-where, likes it or not?"

Over the years, she has accepted my advice. Today she dresses in whatever darn well pleases her. If she likes something she wears it until it falls apart. She still has clothes in her closet she can't even get into because of her after-menopause-weight-gain. But she tells herself (and none of this is my doing) that the day will come when she will loose thirty pounds and wear them again.

Anne was talking to me just the other day about our conversations with each other. She thinks there are some people who believe their inner voice is the Holy Spirit speaking to them. This shocked me. Me, the Holy Spirit? No way. And please, not the Devil's Advocate either. Both of us believe that if God speaks to us through the Holy Spirit it is on a direct line. There's no middle man like me in the process. Both of us have experienced miracles too frequently not to be absolutely positive about this. When God has stepped into Anne's life it has been such a profound experience it has left us both on our knees. This whole business of raising her grandchildren and stumbling into the tragic world of parentless children is one of these times. At least we believe it so.

There's no sense in my arguing with Anne beyond a certain point. It's right on the money to me; her idea of creating the American way of living for those who turn eighteen. The recognition that many of the youths have scars all but too deep to be healed can be accepted. A friend's adopted son, Eddie, is living proof of this. So severely traumatized by the time he was adopted at two years of age, he has never been able to accept the love of another. Eddie had learned as a toddler that such love could disappear overnight.

From infancy he had been shuttled from person to person. At two, when he was adopted one after another, his care-givers had vanished from his world. This trauma stayed with him until three weeks before his high school graduation as a top student, Eddie packed a few of his things in a backpack. Then, opening a bedroom window he crawled out into the night leaving his mother and father of sixteen years. He left the security of their world, his home, his school, a planned college education, church and friends. He left their love. Eddie's fear of losing them was so great it seemed best for him to be the one who left. That way he wouldn't hurt as much.

His adoptive parents still remain in contact with him. Along the way Eddie has fathered a child, but again he had to leave those he loved. Eddie's adoptive mother, has established a bond with the young mother and her child. She now has a granddaughter to love.

Even though tragedies like Eddie's are re-enacted every day the opposite also happens. An early maturity in many parentless kids is not unusual. By being denied childhood they are fast-forwarded into adulthood. In many ways they are ready for a helping hand. In other ways they are in need of a push.

Anne believes all these children, whether accounted for or not, must experience life as a family if they are to be effective adults. A few have been fortunate to have done this. Far more have not. They must, after-the-fact, be given the things of childhood to augment their premature adulthood. To accomplish this she would make available an opportunity for them to move through five years of monitored adulthood. To me this makes sense. Every American homespun tradition should be pushed their way, even candles on birthday cakes and holiday celebrations which the majority have never had. Pumpkin pie, roast turkey and Christmas trees; the whole nine yards should be theirs. These young kids need to reclaim those childhood things which were all too often withheld. We don't believe it is just about becoming adults, it is becoming part of a family and a community that is needed so desperately. It is about being responsible and loving and being loved and cared for.

Anne's goal is the creation of a jumping off place for parentless youth; ages eighteen through twenty-three. She feels they should have a better option than fast food employment and a too rapid plunge into marriage and parenthood. Plus, they should not need to resort to the illegal to live. She'd give them the option of a place to call home for up to five years as they leave childhood. She would set in place active recruiting teams to insure all those eligible understand their option. After their five years it would be a place they can return to as alumnae, whether to work, volunteer or just reunite with friends and staff. To insure a real family experience we believe the location should resemble a small town with businesses, community activities, government services and a surrounding residential area.

Basic to her vision is the inclusion of the Casey matching fund plan for all the residents. The concept matches a dollar for every dollar the individual puts into their savings. Unlike the Casey program the youth will not be making money from private businesses such as the fast food industry, but through job training positions within their own town. This could be in automotive repair, hospitality or assisting at the primary health care center. Other examples include public services, electronic repair or clerking in the small branch bank or post office to list a few. In addition, each resident would be expected to do volunteer work within their range of interest.

Community activities in theater, band, orchestra and vocal music along with sports and physical training will augment a GED program and a two year vocational education or college program. A library and performance center will be located on the town's main street. Mentors from area communities as well as visiting professionals will broaden the community's diversity.

At the core of the health center will be mental health counselors, marriage and parenting counseling. Eye and dental care will be available. An ecumenical worship center will be another feature of the town. Grocery, clothing, drug and hardware stores will be part of the downtown.

The residential area will wrap the town. Its assorted housing will accommodate single and married youth. House parents will be incorporated, not to be enforcers but to be parents. Green space will be emphasized in recognition of the environment. Transportation to nearby communities will be town operated.

Anne recognizes the enormity of her suggestion. It is not an exact replica of today's retirement centers or villages; but then eighteen year old youths are a far cry from octogenarians.

She doesn't think a skateboard park would be a high priority for the aged, but suspects an ice cream parlor would fit either place. And although an eighteen year old might consider a game of shuffle board, it would be more likely they would head to the volley ball court or ball field. And as far as serving a meal, fixing a computer or car, the retiree in all likelihood would say, "Find me somebody to do it, will you?" The youth would die for the opportunity to do one or any of them. No, there are basic differences from one end to the other, in creating the right living situations for the elderly or the youth.

In addition, Anne recognizes a wealth of professional and skilled workers is available. They are now in Human Services and related areas. College degrees are offered in many aspects of community care. As well as pro-bono work, there are volunteers and retirees who would welcome the opportunity to routinely give of their time; whether to coach a team, direct a jazz band or teach art, sewing or drama. All these learning opportunities should be available for the young adults.

Then Anne says, "When I play with the numbers research has developed, it appears that from one to four Home Town Centers would be required in each of the fifty states. This would depend on size and population. The country has already watched thousands of elder-care centers spring up across the land. Anne believes the comparatively limited numbers of youth centers needed would represent no more in cost. She believes the money the government spends today on the social problems created by these lost youth could be used as loans for entrepreneurs to initiate the construction and operation of such Home Town Centers. Another cost reduction factor would be the possibility of a basic design which could be adjusted to fit climate and location.

In the same vein, Anne is aware there are groups who would do feasibility studies, seek legal avenues and work in marketing fields. With vivid memories of her learning experience as a school board member, Anne is all too aware many will want to apply Band-Aids to the existing system. They will say, "What was good enough for my generation when I was eighteen is good enough today. Let those kids get out there and find a job and grow up."

It is Anne's further suggestion that with the acceptance of a change in the parentless child benefits law such as in the Boxer Bill that each eighteen year old will be eligible for continued benefits for an additional five year period. And with that income can have the option of moving onto one of the Town Center Campuses. Ninety percent of their extended benefit payments would be paid as tuition, board and room for their time of residency. The remaining ten percent would become part of the youth's own savings program and 'spending money'.

What scares me is that Anne is ahead of her time. And she isn't good at politics. Not at all. Remember that death threat? My fear is that as effective as her conception would be, there are too many who won't be willing to leave their comfort zones and accept change. They believe children should be tucked away; out of sight, out of mind. Anne's answer to me is to say, "That is exactly why I am writing about the situation. So people across our nation can respond to this need. They do so for every disaster called to their attention. Remember what they did after 911 and then Katrina and are still doing? So much of that happened while the government fumbled to respond. The American people were there immediately. Their response to this crisis of nearly 7,000,000 children could be awesome."

Then she gives me that blue-eyed look of hers and adds, "No child asks to be born. They are gifts from God. When their birth parents die or are unable to raise them, they become the responsibility of every person in our country. Parents believe they will be with their children for years. They don't consider the fact that a long life is not guaranteed. Even if a parent dies and leaves a large sum of money for their children, there is no certainty the money will be used wisely or the right people will raise the children. There is no existing, nurturing way in place in our country to care for a mother's or father's most prized possession, their child. What is in place through foster care ends too abruptly. For the outcast youth there is no opportunity to return or to carry its care and love with them if indeed one or both have been part of their experience.

It is recognized today the very best answer for the care of parentless children is for blood relatives, such as grandparents like Ed and Anne, to become the guardians or adoptive parents of the child. But even this can play itself down to the poverty level when at age eighteen, Social Security money stops. It becomes a desperate and heartbreaking scenario when the loving grandparent or aunt or uncle can no longer afford health insurance for their ward or assist them in their day to day needs; let alone in obtaining a college education. It's happened for Ed and Anne.

Anne still gives me the hard blue-eyed look, saying, "I don't know where I'd be today if I hadn't stumbled across the article about the Jim Casey Foundation. As long as there are institutions like it everything is possible. I believe America can give a real life back to its parentless children. This may not happen in my lifetime, but it must in the lifetime of the over seven million parentless youth in the US. This is my prayer. In Faith I know it will happen." Amen

After Word

This week has been very traumatic for Anne. She had her favorite realtor out to start the process of selling the house for a last down sizing. The market is so low here that he told her he could not get her money out of it. She would have to sell for less than they have invested. What a blow!

She spent the next two days doing research and discovered he was absolutely on the money. She was stunned. As she could not brainstorm with Ed as to the wisest move, she talked to Nancy and Paul—also Dave and Cathy—something she had carefully refrained from doing down through the years, figuring they had their own finances to deal with. Dave solved the problem Wednesday evening, when he and Cathy drove down from Pickford to tell her that they had agreed to offer to buy the house, giving Ed and Anne lifetime residency. He would take over the burden of the mortgage, taxes and insurance. It has been a long, long time since Anne has been free of money worries. She is so at odds with this freedom that she turned to me to help understand it all. My help is in the form of listening. There are long silences between us. Neither of us can find any words to say. We simply bask in the peace of it all. Anne finds herself accomplishing nothing; strangely it bothers neither of us.

She knows that Dave and Cathy are getting a great deal. Nancy is thrilled to see them finally invest in a home. She and Paul as well as Sue Ellen have their own. And of all the kids, Dave is the one who is tied to the farm—it is home to him. He will love what is left of the original farm and set about making it his. He is restoring a couple of Tom's old MGs. Because the original barn burned three years ago he plans to build a pole barn for his hobby. Cathy is an ardent flower and veggie gardener so Anne's gardens will have lots of loving nurture. Maybe the small orchard she and Ed have dreamed about planting will happen. Cathy and Dave love the woods, wildlife and birds that we have here. She grew up in the UP so they are both accustomed to our winters.

273

God continues to work powerfully in our lives. He far outdistances the dreams Ed and Anne have shared for so many years. In perfect contentment Anne told Ed today, "Honey, do you realize your beloved farm is now a four generation home to our family?" He grinned his happiness and said, "And that family became bigger than we ever dreamed".

The End

Ed and Anne 2001

Printed in the United States
117613LV00009B/112-141/P